AN EXPLANATION OF MARTIN LUTHER'S SMALL CATECHISM

FIELD TEST EDITION—JULY 2016

An Explanation of Martin Luther's Small Catechism, Field Test Edition, July 2016

Copyright © 2016 Concordia Publishing House
3558 S. Jefferson Ave., St. Louis, MO 63118-3968
1-800-325-3040 • www.cph.org

Manufactured in the Unites States of America

ABBREVIATIONS

AC	Augsburg Confession
Ap	Apology of the Augsburg Confession
Ep	Epitome of the Formula of Concord
FC	Formula of Concord
LC	Large Catechism
LSB	*Lutheran Service Book*
SA	Smalcald Articles
SC	Small Catechism
SD	Solid Declaration of the Formula of Concord
Tr	Treatise on the Power and Primacy of the Pope

July, 2016

Dear Friends in Christ,

The 2013 Convention of The Lutheran Church—Missouri Synod directed the Commission on Theology and Church Relations (CTCR), in concurrence with the Office of the President, to update the 1991 edition of *Luther's Small Catechism with Explanation* (Res. 3-13A).

Much has changed in the twenty-five years since the Synod last published an edition of the *Explanation*. We have entered an age of computers, smart phones, and virtual reality—a world in which bullying involves text messages as often as physical confrontations, where Islam is in the news on a daily basis, and the word "marriage" has taken on a radically new, unscriptural, court-mandated meaning.

Along the way, the United States has become increasingly secular and religiously diverse. Christianity has not only lost its privileged position, but its teachings are often casually scorned and Christians themselves are sometimes treated with hostility. Those who are catechized today are faced with an old question that holds a new sobriety: "Do you intend to continue steadfast in this confession and Church and to suffer all, even death, rather than fall away from it?" (*LSB* Rite of Confirmation).

A first draft of the revised *Explanation* is now complete and ready for field-testing. Several aspects of this revision are noteworthy:

- It is rich in Scripture, with several hundred more biblical references and narratives than its immediate predecessor volume.
- It is rich in confessional Lutheran theology, with numerous references to other writings in the *Book of Concord,* most especially the *Large Catechism.*
- It is rich in contemporary application, seeking to address questions and topics that have emerged in recent years.
- It serves as an "apologetic" tool, providing both a scriptural and, where appropriate, reason-focused and natural law-based foundation for moral and social teachings.
- Finally, it is rich in adaptability. Potential uses include
  - as a missionary tool to introduce individuals or groups to the Christian faith;
  - as an instructional tool for youth confirmation;
  - as a guide for thematic Bible classes;
  - as a tool for individual or family devotional use and study;
  - as a quick reference for sermon preparation.

Catechism is about teaching the faith. Luther saw the absolute need for that in his day. Five hundred years later, our need is no less than his. Please give this proposed revision a careful look. Share your reactions and suggestions with us at www.surveygizmo.com/s3/2855978/2017-Catechism-Explanation-Revision. You will have until October 31, 2016 (Reformation Day) to share your thoughts.

In Christ, the Center of the faith we teach, believe and confess,

Joel D. Lehenbauer
Executive Director, CTCR and Chairman, Catechism Drafting Committee

An Explanation of Martin Luther's Small Catechism
Field Test Edition

Preface

The coming year, 2017, will mark the 500th anniversary of the Reformation. Our Synod will encourage this observance in many ways, and not for nostalgic or merely historical purposes, but because we are convinced the Reformation's emphases continue to be central for the health of Christianity and the well-being of the church and its mission. When Luther posted a call for discussion on how one is saved, the "Ninety-Five Theses," to the Castle Church in Wittenberg in 1517, his theses began a movement that continues to change the world. Luther helped believers in that little town, in Germany, in Europe, and, eventually, on every continent, to remember and to be confident in the Gospel's promise of forgiveness, life, and salvation graciously given through faith in the Lord Jesus Christ. His subsequent teachings gave men, women, and children assurance that the Holy Scriptures preserve and communicate these saving promises. Such truths—such words—stood stronger than hostile human authorities, the fallen world's threats, and Satan's wiles and rage.

It is worth asking how this Reformation message reached the world that it came to shape in so many ways. Such a question has led to answers in countless volumes running into millions of words. But it is no exaggeration to suggest that the single *most* important reason Luther's message prospered is the *Small Catechism*. First published in 1529, Luther's *Der Kleine Katechismus* (*Small Catechism*) numbers less than 3000 words (in German). It condenses the biblical story and message and provides succinct meanings for the Ten Commandments, the Apostles' Creed, the Lord's Prayer, passages about Baptism and the Lord's Supper (with Confession).

This little document, the *Small Catechism,* has been a powerful tool for a task the church has engaged since Pentecost—teaching the Christian faith to new believers and children. Luther composed it because he discovered an appalling ignorance about Christian faith and life in Germany—baptized Christians "with no knowledge whatever of Christian doctrine." It served the purpose of providing basic, crucial knowledge of the Christian faith for those first users. It has continued ever since as a tool that teaches what God forbids and what He commands (the Ten Commandments); who He is and what He has done for the world (the Creed); how we may and *should* seek His richest blessings for our lives (the Lord's Prayer); how He has made us His own (Baptism); and how He sustains and nurtures us in repentant faith and in the confidence of His forgiving presence in Christ (Confession and the Sacrament of the Altar).

In the years and centuries that followed, the *Small Catechism* has been wonderfully adaptable, serving as a foundation and starting point for learning and growing in the faith. Already in Luther's lifetime countless versions were produced—versions that included not only Luther's text, but also additional explanatory material. With the expansion of Christianity beyond Europe into the Americas, Africa, and Asia, the *Small Catechism* has been been translated into numerous languages and became perhaps the single most important Lutheran missionary tool for bringing the Gospel to people who knew nothing of it. Already in the 1600s the *Small Catechism* was the first book translated into a Native American language in the Americas. In other parts of the world, many Lutheran churches were established with the *Small Catechism* as the first (and often the only) confessional document—understandably so, as it provided an eminently practical tool for new believers as well as a confessional framework for thinking as a Lutheran Christian.

Here in the United States, the *Small Catechism* was part of the layman's library for Lutheran immigrants alongside the Bible and a hymnbook. In LCMS history, a German edition of Luther's catechism with explanatory material by Johann Konrad Dietrich (1575-1639) was of great significance. C. F. W. Walther (1811-1887) modified Dietrich's work. Heinrich Christian Schwan (1819-1905) then built on that same heritage. In 1943 the Synod revised the material in response to the needs of its day. In 1991 the Synod revised the explanation section yet again.

The 2013 Convention of The Lutheran Church—Missouri Synod recognized that once again it was time to address new questions and circumstances. The assembly adopted Resolution 3-13A "To Update Synod's Catechetical Materials." The resolution tasked the Commission on Theology and Church Relations (CTCR), in concurrence with the Office of the President, to update the explanation portion of *Luther's Small Catechism with Explanation*, last revised in 1991. Only the *Explanation* was to be revised, not the actual *Small Catechism* from Luther himself. (The translation of Luther's texts has not changed from the 1991 edition.) A key reason for the revision was the "many changes in the understanding of morals, civil law and natural law in church and society" since the Explanation's last revision.

The CTCR appointed a planning and drafting committee which worked throughout the 2013-2016 triennium. During the first phase of work, a series of electronic surveys were conducted with the assistance of Concordia Publishing House, inviting input on the 1991 *Explanation* and suggestions for improvement. The committee also developed a four-part structural template for the project. After each section of the catechism (for example, the First Commandment) the proposed revision would include (1) The Central Thought (summarizing the key point for Christian identity and faith, with an illustrative biblical narrative and questions for reflection and application); (2) A Closer Reading of the *Small Catechism* (giving specific attention to the pattern and wording in Luther's text with key supporting Bible passages or *sedes doctrinae*); (3) Connections and Applications (providing wider application and addressing additional relevant matters, together with further biblical and confessional support); and (4) a suggested hymn verse and brief prayer inviting devotional use of that portion of the Catechism.

A further electronic survey provided sample sections of the revised *Explanation* that enabled respondents to assess the value of the proposed structural template. The responses to the suggested template were overwhelmingly positive and provided helpful insights to the drafting committee.

This revision is guided by several goals. The draft seeks to be

1. Basic: focused on the actual wording of Luther's *Small Catechism* and its powerful biblical insights

2. Biblical, providing both:
   a. key verses for treasuring in the heart through memorization and
   b. memorable narratives for thematic illustrations and further reference

3. Stimulating: inviting the user to learn the basic truths, and then to explore ways the *Small Catechism* encourages further study and growth in faith and life

4. Flexible: a text usable by adults and children (for example, the pastor could simply use the central thought portion in an adult catechetical class)

5. Devotional: encouraging the use of the central truths of Christian faith for prayer, praise, and further contemplation

6. Responsive: especially to the questions and concerns raised in the catechism surveys.

The committee's work has incorporated not only worthy suggestions and ideas from the surveys noted earlier, but also recommendations from the CTCR after its extensive examination of the material, having worked through it section by section. Throughout the entire process the President's office has also considered and concurred with the drafting committee's work.

Now it is time for the Synod as a whole to consider this revision of the *Explanation*. This book is a "proposed draft," not a finished product. It is here made available for the congregations, pastors, teachers, missionaries, professors, deaconesses, and other church workers and lay people of the LCMS to explore and "test." Just as Paul encouraged the Thessalonians to test what was being taught, so we invite you to "test everything" that is in this book and to "hold fast what is good" (1 Thess. 5:21). As you examine this humble effort, we pray that you will help us, as a Synod, to identify strengths and weaknesses with regard to the questions, answers, supportive passages, explanatory notes and so forth.

Some things to consider as you review this draft include:
- The relevance and clarity of questions and answers
- Applicability and value of supporting Scripture references and narratives
- Communicability of the language used—its simplicity and clarity
- Adequacy regarding contemporary issues and concerns

This manuscript does not include certain things—most notably the entire text of the *Small Catechism* itself prior to the *Explanation*. In order to save space and costs for the field-test, we have not included that, or such things as the Table of Duties, Christian Questions with Their Answers, Luther's Preface, indices, and so forth which will be included in the final publication edition. In addition, this field-test document did not go through extensive copy editing or the kind of professional formatting that will be necessary prior to final publication.

The goal of field-testing is improvement. You will have the opportunity to share comments and suggestions. You can provide your reactions at www.surveygizmo.com/s3/2855978/2017-Catechism-Explanation-Revision anytime before October 31 2016. Responses to the draft that are posted through this online tool will be evaluated and considered in the final editing of the project. After final revisions, the *Explanation* will go through doctrinal review. It is our prayer that the completed revision will then be published in the 500th anniversary year of 2017.

Your servant in Christ our Lord,

Joel D. Lehenbauer

Executive Director, Commission on Theology and Church Relations
Chairman, Catechism Revision Committee

(On behalf of the Catechism Revision Committee: Dr. Charles Arand, Rev. Wally Arp, Professor Thomas Egger, Dr. Joel Lehenbauer, Dr. Jan Lohmeyer, Professor John Pless, Rev. Larry Vogel)

An Explanation of Martin Luther's *Small Catechism*

Introduction

1. What is the Christian faith?

   It is the faith of all those who confess that there is only one God, the creator of all things, who is known in three persons—the Father; His only Son, Jesus Christ, the world's savior and redeemer; and the Holy Spirit.

2. What has this one God and creator done?

   God made all things and loves His creation, especially His human creatures. Tragically, they rebelled against Him and fell into darkness, death, and rebellion. But God the Father sent His only Son into the world, to become human like us and to redeem and save humanity by His death and resurrection. God sent His Spirit so that people might once again be His own, trusting through faith in His Son, who is the world's only hope, life, light, and salvation.

   1. **John 3:16** For God so loved the world, that he gave his only Son, that whoever believes in him should not perish but have eternal life.

   2. **Luke 2:11** For unto you is born this day in the city of David a Savior, who is Christ the Lord.

   3. **Galatians 4:4-5** But when the fullness of time had come, God sent forth his Son, born of woman, born under the law, to redeem those who were under the law, so that we might receive adoption as sons.

3. What is a Christian?

   A Christian is someone who trusts in and confesses Jesus as Savior and Lord and, through Baptism in the name of the Father, the Son, and the Holy Spirit, is adopted into the Father's family, the Church.

   4. **Romans 8:15** For you did not receive the spirit of slavery to fall back into fear, but you have received the Spirit of adoption as sons, by whom we cry, "Abba! Father!"

   5. **1 Corinthians 6:11** And such were some of you. But you were washed, you were sanctified, you were justified in the name of the Lord Jesus Christ and by the Spirit of our God.

4. What does it mean when I confess Jesus Christ as Lord?

   Confessing Jesus as my Lord means that I trust Him in life and in death as my Savior, for He is one with the Father who made me and the Spirit who works faith in me. His death and resurrection have atoned for all sins, including my own, and assured me and all believers of our resurrection to eternal life. It means that I am His and I want to live as His own.

   6. **Romans 6:23** For the wages of sin is death, but the free gift of God is eternal life in Christ Jesus our Lord.

   7. **Romans 10:9** If you confess with your mouth that Jesus is Lord and believe in your heart that God raised him from the dead, you will be saved.

   8. **1 Corinthians 8:6** Yet for us there is one God, the Father, from whom are all things and for whom we exist, and one Lord, Jesus Christ, through whom are all things and through whom we exist.

   9. **Matthew 7:21** Not everyone who says to me, "Lord, Lord," will enter the kingdom of heaven, but the one who does the will of my Father who is in heaven.

5. Where is God's truth about our Savior Jesus Christ made known?

   This truth is made known in the Bible (the Holy Scriptures of the Old and New Testament).

6.   What is the Bible?

The Bible is the written Word of God. It is a collection of writings by God's chosen prophets and apostles over a period of more than a thousand years, which testify to God's saving work from creation until Christ's future return and renewal of creation.

> **10. Hebrews 1:1-2** Long ago, at many times and in many ways, God spoke to our fathers by the prophets, but in these last days he has spoken to us by his Son, whom he appointed the heir of all things, through whom also he created the world.

> **11. Ephesians 2:19-20** So then you are no longer strangers and aliens, but you are fellow citizens with the saints and members of the household of God, built on the foundation of the apostles and prophets, Christ Jesus himself being the cornerstone.

7.   How do Christians regard and use the Bible?

Christians regard these writings as the authoritative Word of God, which brings the Gospel of Christ to them and guides their lives of faith.

> **12. John 20:31** But these are written so that you may believe that Jesus is the Christ, the Son of God, and that by believing you may have life in his name.

8.   Why do Christians view the Bible as different from other books and as the authoritative and inerrant Word of God?

The Bible's entire message is focused on Jesus Christ and His saving work. He is the heart and center of Scripture and the key to its true meaning. We trust the Bible because it has led us to trust in Jesus as our Savior and Lord. The prophets who wrote the Old Testament and apostles who wrote the New Testament were inspired by the Holy Spirit and their writings are trustworthy and truthful in every way, as our Lord Himself assures us.

> **13. John 5:39** You search the Scriptures because you think that in them you have eternal life; and it is they that bear witness about me.

> **14. John 10:35** Scripture cannot be broken.

> **15. John 14:26** But the Helper, the Holy Spirit, whom the Father will send in my name, he will teach you all things and bring to your remembrance all that I have said to you.

> **16. 2 Timothy 3:16-17** All Scripture is breathed out by God and profitable for teaching, for reproof, for correction, and for training in righteousness, that the man of God may be competent, equipped for every good work.

> **17. 2 Peter 1:21** For no prophecy was ever produced by the will of man, but men spoke from God as they were carried along by the Holy Spirit.

9.   What is the Small Catechism?

*For centuries Christians have used a collection of important texts as a basic summary for teaching the Christian faith and life. The texts, often referred to as a catechism, include the Ten Commandments, Creed, Lord's Prayer, and often certain biblical passages on Baptism, Confession, and the Lord's Supper. The **Small Catechism**, written by Martin Luther, includes these texts along with brief explanations.*

10.   What are the central or chief parts of Christian teaching and life?

We may speak of the six parts of the catechism as the central parts of Christian teaching (doctrine):

*(1) Christians believe that God has made known His will through the **Ten Commandments**, which summarize how God wants us to love Him and love our neighbor.*

(2) The **Creed** summarizes who God is and what He has done out of love for the world: creating and preserving all things out of fatherly love, redeeming the world in the death and resurrection of Jesus Christ, the Son of God, and calling and gathering believers into the Church by the Holy Spirit.

(3) In the **Lord's Prayer** (or, the Our Father), God the Son teaches Christians how to pray as God's own dear children, confident that what we are praying pleases Him and is for our good.

(4) Scripture teaches us that in **Holy Baptism** we are cleansed from our sins and belong to the one true God, Father, Son, and Holy Spirit, Whom we trust for life and salvation.

(5) As God's believing, baptized children we still battle against sins of thought, word, and deed. But God graciously hears our confession of sins and has given special authority to His Church on earth to forgive the sins of those who repent and to withhold forgiveness from those who do not repent (**Office of the Keys and Confession**).

(6) God welcomes His children, who know their weakness and hunger for His righteousness, to the **Sacrament of the Altar** (Lord's Supper), where Christ gives us His body to eat and His blood to drink for the forgiveness of our sins and to strengthen our faith.

Introduction to the Ten Commandments

11. What are the Ten Commandments?

The Ten Commandments summarize God's Law, namely, His good and loving will for the lives and well-being of all people within His creation.

12. What is God's will for our lives?

God wants us to love Him and love our neighbor.

> **18. Matthew 22:36-40** "Teacher, which is the great commandment in the Law?" And he said to him, "You shall love the Lord your God with all your heart and with all your soul and with all your mind. This is the great and first commandment. And a second is like it: You shall love your neighbor as yourself. On these two commandments depend all the Law and the Prophets."

> **19. Deuteronomy 6:1** Now this is the commandment—the statutes and the rules—that the LORD your God commanded me to teach you.

> **20. Leviticus 19:18** Love your neighbor as yourself: I am the LORD.

13. How did God give His Law to us?

First, God wrote these instructions upon the heart of every human creature.

> **21. Romans 2:14-16** For when Gentiles, who do not have the law, by nature do what the law requires, they are a law to themselves, even though they do not have the law. They show that the work of the law is written on their hearts, while their conscience also bears witness, and their conflicting thoughts accuse or even excuse them on that day when, according to my gospel, God judges the secrets of men by Christ Jesus.

Second, God wrote the Ten Commandments on stone tablets for the people of Israel.

Read about God giving the Ten Commandments to Israel in **Exodus 20:1-17; Deuteronomy 5:6-21;** and **Exodus 34:1, 27-28**.

Note: There are different ways of numbering the Ten Commandments. The Bible does not give us numbers for individual commands. Also note that there are other laws in the Old Testament that governed the affairs of state or pertained to the particular forms of religion and liturgy given specifically to Israel.

Third, God also gave these instructions in various ways throughout the Bible, for example, the Sermon the Mount.

Read Jesus' beatitudes in **Matthew 5:2-11** and his further commentary on the law in **Matthew 5:21-48**.

The First Commandment

You shall have no other gods.

What does this mean?

We should fear, love, and trust in God above all things.

The Central Thought

All people everywhere are constantly looking somewhere to find happiness, identity, security, and meaning in life.

Where do people today look to try to find these things?

Read **Matthew 6:25-34** and note the reasons Jesus gives for putting our trust in God.

✝ *As Christians, we look for all that we need to the God who created and redeemed us.*

In what ways does God generously provide me with all that I need for my daily life and my eternal salvation?

A Closer Reading of the *Small Catechism*

14. What does it mean to have a god?

    It means to trust in and rely on something or someone wholeheartedly to help us in times of need and to give us all good things.

    22. **Acts 17:16** In Athens, St. Paul was distressed when he "saw that the city was full of idols."

    23. **Proverbs 11:28** Whoever trusts in his riches will fall.

    24. **Matthew 10:37** [Jesus said,] "Whoever loves father or mother more than me is not worthy of me, and whoever loves son or daughter more than me is not worthy of me."

15. Why doesn't God want us to have any other gods besides Him?

    As our creator, God alone knows what is best for us. Only He can provide us with all that we need for time and eternity.

    25. **Isaiah 42:8** I am the LORD; that is my name; my glory I give to no other, nor my praise to carved idols.

    26. **Psalm 116:5** Gracious is the LORD, and righteous; our God is merciful.

    27. **Matthew 4:10** [Jesus said,] "You shall worship the Lord your God and Him only shall you serve."

    28. **Romans 1:22-23** Claiming to be wise, they became fools, and exchanged the glory of the immortal God for images resembling mortal man and birds and animals and creeping things.

16. What does God require of us in the first commandment?

    We should fear, love, and trust in Him.

    29. **Psalm 111:10** The fear of the LORD is the beginning of wisdom.

    30. **Deuteronomy 6:5** You shall love the LORD your God with all your heart, with all your soul and with all your might.

31. **Proverbs 3:5** Trust in the Lord with all your heart, and do not lean on your own understanding.

17. Should *all* people fear, love, and trust in God?

Yes. He created all people to live under His care and to trust and rely upon Him.

    32. **Psalm 22:27** All the ends of the earth shall remember and turn to the Lord, and all the families of the nations shall worship before you.

    33. **Malachi 2:10** Have we not all one Father? Has not one God created us? Why then are we faithless to one another, profaning the covenant of our fathers?

    34. **1 Corinthians 8:5-6** For although there may be so-called gods in heaven or on earth—as indeed there are many "gods" and many "lords"—yet for us there is one God, the Father, from whom are all things and for whom we exist, and one Lord, Jesus Christ, through whom are all things and through whom we exist.

18. What does it mean to fear God above all things?

It means to take God seriously as our creator and judge. He means what He says when He threatens to punish those who disobey.

    35. **Proverbs 8:13** The fear of the Lord is hatred of evil.

    36. **Matthew 10:28** And do not fear those who kill the body but cannot kill the soul. Rather fear him who can destroy both soul and body in hell.

Read **Psalm 96:4-13** which tells us to fear the only true God, who made all things and will judge the world.

19. What does it mean to love God above all things?

It means that we cherish and adore God more than anything else and gladly devote our lives to His service.

    37. **Psalm 73:25-26** Whom have I in heaven but you? And there is nothing on earth that I desire besides you. My flesh and my heart may fail, but God is the strength of my heart and my portion forever.

    38. **John 14:15** If you love me, you will keep my commandments.

Read **Mark 10:17-27** which warns about things that keep us from following Him.

20. What does it mean to trust *in* God above all things?

It means that we rely on God to take care of us and to keep all of His promises to us.

    39. **Isaiah 30:15** For thus said the Lord God, the Holy One of Israel, "In returning and rest you shall be saved; in quietness and in trust shall be your strength."

    40. **1 Peter 5:6-7** Humble yourselves, therefore, under the mighty hand of God so that at the proper time he may exalt you, casting all your anxieties on him, because he cares for you.

    41. **Philippians 4:5-6** The Lord is at hand; do not be anxious about anything, but in everything by prayer and supplication with thanksgiving let your requests be made known to God.

Read **Proverbs 3:5-10** and **Psalm 115:4** and note the various ways that we trust or do not trust God.

21. What does it mean to fear, love, and trust in God *above all things*?

It means that we look to God first and foremost for our well-being, rather than to:

- *human achievements such as intellect, technology, medical advances (**Genesis 11:1-9**);*
- *human goodness or religious devotion (**Luke 18:9-14**);*
- *money and possessions (**Luke 18:18-24**);*
- *pleasures such as food, drink, drugs, sex, sports, entertainment (**1 Corinthians 6:12-20**);*
- *family and friends (**Matthew 10:37-39**).*

22. What happens when we trust in these things rather than our creator?

We confuse the creator with His creation and thus break all the other commandments as well.

    42. **Matthew 6:19, 21** Do not lay up for yourselves treasures on earth, where moth and rust destroy and where thieves break in and steal…For where your treasure is, there your heart will be also.

Read **Exodus 32:1-10; Romans 1:18-25**; and **Ephesians 5:5.**

23. What is the relationship between the first and the other commandments?

When we fear, love, and trust in God, we gladly seek to keep all of His commandments. When we fear, love, and trust other things more than God, we will inevitably break the other commandments He has given us.

    43. **Matthew 6:33** But seek first the kingdom of God and his righteousness, and all these things will be added to you.

Read **Deuteronomy 30:19-20** and **Proverbs 11:28.**

Connections and Applications

24. Who is the only true God?

The only true God is the Triune God: Father, Son, and Holy Spirit, three distinct persons in one divine being (the Holy Trinity).

Read **Genesis 1:1-3; Matthew 3:16-17**; and **John 1:1-3.** Note how the three Persons of the Trinity are present and active.

    44. **Matthew 28:19** Go therefore and make disciples of all nations, baptizing them in the name of the Father and of the Son and of the Holy Spirit.

    45. **2 Corinthians 13:14** The grace of the Lord Jesus Christ and the love of God and the fellowship of the Holy Spirit be with you all.

    46. **Numbers 6:24-26** The LORD bless you and keep you; the LORD make his face to shine upon you and be gracious to you; the LORD lift up his countenance upon you and give you peace.

The First Commandment in Exodus

25. Read **Exodus 20:1-3**. Why do the commandments begin with the words, "I am the LORD Your God, who brought you out of the land of Egypt"?

*These words identify Israel's God, the one who rescued them from Egypt. The creator who rescued Israel is the one who also rescued us from sin and death by sending His Son to die and rise for us. (Read **John 3:16**).*

26. Read **Exodus 20:4**. What are graven (or carved) images?

They are statues of idols that are worshiped as gods.

27. Read **Exodus 20:5**. Why does God make these threats and promises?

God will not tolerate any other gods for no other "god" can give and sustain our life.

Non-Christian Religions

28. Do all religions worship the same God?

No. All religions do not worship the same god.

- *Some religions teach that life includes a spiritual dimension, but they reject the creator and His salvation in Jesus (for example, Animism, Hinduism, Buddhism, Shintoism). Read **Romans 1:16-25**.*

- *Some religions claim to worship the God of Abraham and may even regard the Old Testament as sacred writings, but they reject the Triune God by rejecting His salvation in Jesus Christ (for example, Islam and Judaism.) Read **John 5:19-23, 39-47**.*

- *Some religions claim to be Christian and hold the Bible sacred, but reject Scripture's witness that Jesus is the true Son of God, one with the Father, and therefore also deny the doctrine of the Trinity (for example, Mormonism and the Jehovah's Witnesses). Read **John 10:22-30**.*

- *Some religious practices involve seeking help from supernatural forces rather than God the creator who has revealed Himself in Jesus Christ (for example, Satanism, sorcery, superstitions, spirits of the dead, good luck charms, psychics). Read **1 Samuel 28** and note how Saul disobeyed God.*

- *Some religions or religious practices (for example, syncretism and moral therapeutic deism) combine elements of the above or simply believe in a generic deity. They reject God's exclusive revelation of salvation in Jesus Christ alone. Read **Psalm 53:1**; **Psalm 14:1**.*

Hymn (*LSB* 581, stanzas 1 and 2) and Prayer: *Lord God, author and source of all that is good, give us wisdom to fear Your wrath, strength to love You above all things, and faith to trust in Your promises alone, that by Your grace we may serve You all our days and finally come to inherit Your heavenly kingdom; through Jesus Christ, Your Son, our Lord who lives and reigns with You and the Holy Spirit, one God, now and forever. Amen.*

The Second Commandment

You shall not misuse the name of the Lord your God.

What does this mean?

We should fear and love God so that we do not curse, swear, use satanic arts, lie or deceive by His name, but call upon Him in every trouble, pray, praise and give thanks.

The Central Thought

When we trust God with our hearts, we use our lips to call upon Him as our creator and redeemer.

How is God's name used today? How does this reflect and affect the way people think about God?

Read **Luke 1:46-55**. How did Mary praise God's name?

✝ *As Christians, we treasure and honor God's name with our prayers, praise, and witness.*

How can I show that God is my creator and redeemer by the way I speak and in my daily conversations with others?

A Closer Reading of the *Small Catechism*

29. For what purpose did God reveal His name to us?

    God gave us His name so that we might

    - *know who created and redeemed us;*

        47. **Psalm 9:16** The LORD has made himself known; he has executed judgment; the wicked are snared in the work of their own hands.

        48. **Isaiah 44:24** Thus says the LORD, your Redeemer, who formed you from the womb: "I am the LORD, who made all things, who alone stretched out the heavens, who spread out the earth by myself."

        49. **Exodus 20:2** I am the LORD your God, who brought you out of the land of Egypt, out of the house of slavery.

    - *call upon Him personally as children do a father;*

        50. **Genesis 4:26** At that time people began to call upon the name of the LORD.

        51. **Luke 11:2** And [Jesus] said to them, "When you pray, say: 'Father, hallowed be your name.'"

    - *proclaim His name among all peoples.*

        52. **Isaiah 12:4** And you will say in that day: "Give thanks to the LORD, call upon his name, make known his deeds among the peoples, proclaim that his name is exalted."

        53. **Matthew 28:19-20** Go therefore and make disciples of all nations, baptizing them in the name of the Father and of the Son and of the Holy Spirit, teaching them to observe all that I have commanded you. And behold, I am with you always, to the end of the age.

30. How do we fear and love God in the second commandment?

    *First, we fear and love God by **not using** His name*

- *thoughtlessly or meaninglessly (in vain) as a "curse" word;*

    54. Exodus 20:7 For the Lord will not hold him guiltless who takes his name in vain.

- *to try and manipulate God for our purposes in sorcery, as a magic charm, or to curse others;*

    55. James 3:8-10 No human being can tame the tongue. It is a restless evil, full of deadly poison. With it we bless our Lord and Father, and with it we curse people who are made in the likeness of God. From the same mouth come blessing and cursing. My brothers, these things ought not to be so.

Read **Acts 19:11-20** the Sons of Sceva used Jesus' name superstitiously as a magical formula. Read **Luke 9:51-55** where Jesus rebukes the disciples' desire to curse a village so God would punish it; and **Acts 23:12-15** where the chief priests swore an oath to kill the apostle Paul.

- *to lie or to deceive others.*

    56. Matthew 7:21 Not everyone who says to me, "Lord, Lord," will enter the kingdom of heaven, but the one who does the will of my Father who is in heaven.

    57. Jeremiah 23:31-32 "Behold, I am against the prophets," declares the LORD, "who use their tongues and declare, 'declares the LORD'. Behold, I am against those who prophesy lying dreams," declares the LORD, "and who tell them and lead my people astray by their lies and their recklessness, when I did not send them or charge them. So they do not profit this people at all," declares the LORD.

Read **Matthew 26:69-74** where Peter swore that he did not know Jesus (also **Leviticus 19:12** and **Matthew 5:33-37**).

*Second, we fear and love God by **using** His name to*

- *seek from Him all good things for ourselves and others;*

    58. John 16:23 In that day you will ask nothing of me. Truly, truly, I say to you, whatever you ask of the Father in my name, he will give it to you.

    59. 1 Timothy 2:1 First of all, then, I urge that supplications, prayers, intercessions, and thanksgivings be made for all people.

Read **Luke 17:11-19** about the 10 lepers who all seek healing, even though only one returns to give thanks.

- *call upon Him in times of trouble;*

    60. Psalm 50:15 Call upon me in the day of trouble; I will deliver you, and you shall glorify me.

Read **Isaiah 36-37** where King Hezekiah prays to God when the overwhelming armies of Assyria are surrounding Jerusalem.

- *acknowledge in thanks and praise that all good things have come from Him alone.*

    61. Psalm 150:2 Praise him for his mighty deeds; praise him according to his excellent greatness!

    62. Psalm 118:1 Oh give thanks to the LORD, for he is good; for his steadfast love endures forever!

Read **Psalm 136, 138;** Mary's Magnificat in **Luke 1:46-55**; and Zechariah's prophecy in **Luke 1:58-79**

- *speak and teach truthfully about God in accordance with His Word.*

Read **John 17:11-19** and note the connection between God's name and the truthful speaking and teaching of His Word.

Connections and Applications

31. What "names" does God have in the Bible?

    The Bible refers to God by various titles (such as God, the Almighty, the Lord, etc.). This commandment applies to our use of all such terms. In the Old Testament, God primarily identified

*Himself by a personal name—Yahweh. ("Jehovah" is a mistaken pronunciation of Yahweh.) By New Testament times, Jews no longer spoke the name Yahweh, even when reading the Bible aloud, saying Adonai ("Lord") instead. Following this tradition, most English Bibles render Yahweh as "LORD." (all capitals). When God became a man, He revealed the fullness of His grace with a new personal name—Jesus, which means "Yahweh saves." The New Testament also reveals that God is rightly named as the Father, the Son, and the Holy Spirit (**Matthew 28:19**).*

32. What does God say about vulgar or coarse language?

    God calls His people to use wholesome speech (see also sixth and eighth commandments).

    63. **Proverbs 10:32** The lips of the righteous know what is acceptable, but the mouth of the wicked, what is perverse.

    64. **Ephesians 5:4** Let there be no filthiness nor foolish talk nor crude joking, which are out of place, but instead let there be thanksgiving.

    65. **Matthew 15:11** It is not what goes into the mouth that defiles a person, but what comes out of the mouth; this defiles a person.

33. Can we take oaths?

    Yes. We honor God's name by keeping the promises that we ask Him to witness, such as baptismal vows, confirmation vows, marriage vows, oaths of office, oaths in a court of law, oaths of citizenship.

    66. **Numbers 30:2** If a man vows a vow to the LORD, or swears an oath to bind himself by a pledge, he shall not break his word. He shall do according to all that proceeds out of his mouth.

    67. **Deuteronomy 6:13** It is the LORD your God you shall fear. Him you shall serve and by his name you shall swear.

    68. **Romans 13:1** Let every person be subject to the governing authorities.

    Note: Jesus testified under oath that he was the Messiah (**Mark 14:60-62**). Paul called upon God to bear witness the truth of his testimony about Christ (**Romans 1:9; 2 Corinthians 1:23;** and **Galatians 1:20**).

Hymn (*LSB* 581, stanza 3) and Prayer: *Holy Father, purify our lips from every misuse of Your name by cursing, swearing, superstition, lying, or deception. Open our mouths to reverence Your holy name, calling upon it in every time of trouble, praying for what You promise to give, praising You for Your glory, and giving thanks to You as the Giver of every good and perfect gift; this we ask in the name which gives us access to You, the name of Jesus Christ our Lord. Amen.*

The Third Commandment

Remember the Sabbath day by keeping it holy.

What does this mean?

We should fear and love God so that we do not despise preaching and His Word, but hold it sacred and gladly hear and learn it.

The Central Thought

God invites us to rest and reflect on His Word in order to strengthen our faith in Him.

When people today set aside time for rest, how do they spend that time?

Read **Luke 10:38-42**. Why does Jesus commend Mary and not hardworking Martha?

✝ *As Christians, God's Word leads us to delight in His wondrous works of creation and redemption.*

How does God's Word open our eyes to see all of His good works?

A Closer Reading of the *Small Catechism*

34. What is the Sabbath?

    The Sabbath is a day of rest that God set aside for His people to ponder

    - *the goodness of God's work of creation;*

        69. **Exodus 20:8-11** Remember the Sabbath day, to keep it holy. Six days you shall labor, and do all your work, but the seventh day is a Sabbath to the LORD your God…For in six days the LORD made heaven and earth, the sea, and all that is in them, and rested on the seventh day. Therefore the LORD blessed the Sabbath day and made it holy.

    Read **Matthew 6:24-34** and Jesus' observation about the flowers and the birds.

    - *the graciousness of God's work of redemption.*

        70. **Deuteronomy 5:12, 15** Observe the Sabbath day, to keep it holy, as the LORD your God commanded you…You shall remember that you were a slave in the land of Egypt, and the LORD your God brought you out from there with a mighty hand and an outstretched arm. Therefore the LORD your God commanded you to keep the Sabbath day.

35. What were some features of the Sabbath in the Old Testament?

    - *Physical rest was a part of the rhythm that God built into His creation.*

        71. **Psalm 104:19-23** He made the moon to mark the seasons; the sun knows its time for setting. You make darkness, and it is night, when all the beasts of the forest creep about. The young lions roar for their prey, seeking their food from God. When the sun rises, they steal away and lie down in their dens. Man goes out to his work and to his labor until the evening.

    - *Spiritual rest was provided by God appointing the Sabbath and holy festivals as a time for worship, and fellowship.*

    Read **Leviticus 23** and **Deuteronomy 6** where God gives days and seasons of worship to Israel for them to remember His saving deeds and His gracious care for them.

Note: Rest was part of the rhythm that God put in place for His Old Testament church. Every seventh day, people and animals were to rest from their work; Every seventh year the land was allowed to rest from planting and harvest. Every fiftieth year (the year after seven times seven years), all debts and burdens were cancelled (**Genesis 2:3; Leviticus 25;** and **Isaiah 61**).

36. How do we fear and love God in the third commandment?

*First, we fear God and love God by **not neglecting** His Word. We neglect God's Word by*

- *failing to gather together in worship to receive God's Word and sacraments;*

   72. Hebrews 10:25 [Do not neglect] to meet together, as is the habit of some, but [encourage] one another, and all the more as you see the Day drawing near.

- *rejecting or disregarding God's Word.*

   73. Luke 10:16 The one who hears you hears me, and the one who rejects you rejects me, and the one who rejects me rejects him who sent me.

Read **1 Samuel 15:10-23** noting that Saul rejected God's Word. In **John 8:42-47** certain Jews rejected God's Word. In **1 Timothy 4:11-16** Paul tells Timothy to hold fast to Scripture's teaching.

*Second, we fear and love God by **taking time to reflect** on God's Word. We do this by*

- *treasuring God's Word as sacred;*

   74. Psalm 119:105 Your word is a lamp to my feet and a light to my path.

   75. Colossians 3:16 Let the word of Christ dwell in you richly, teaching and admonishing one another in all wisdom, singing psalms and hymns and spiritual songs, with thankfulness in your hearts to God.

Read **Psalm 1** and **Luke 2:8-20**.

- *devoting ourselves to His Word (in private devotion and public worship).*

   76. Acts 2:42 And they devoted themselves to the apostles' teaching and the fellowship, to the breaking of bread and the prayers.

   77. Acts 17:10-11 The brothers immediately sent Paul and Silas away by night to Berea, and when they arrived they went into the Jewish synagogue. Now these Jews were more noble than those in Thessalonica; they received the word with all eagerness, examining the Scriptures daily to see if these things were so.

Read **Psalm 26:8; Luke 10:38-42;** and **Luke 11:28**.

Connections and Applications

37. What is the significance of the Sabbath for the Church today?

- *Physical rest remains important for us as God's creatures and children.*

   78. Mark 6:30-31 The apostles returned to Jesus and told him all that they had done and taught. And he said to them, "Come away by yourselves to a desolate place and rest a while." For many were coming and going, and they had no leisure even to eat.

Read **Psalm 127:2** and **Mark 4:35-41**.

- *The Sabbath was a sign pointing to Jesus, who gives us spiritual rest from the burden of our sins.*

   79. Matthew 11:28 Come to me, all who labor and are heavy laden, and I will give you rest.

   80. Revelation 14:13 And I heard a voice from heaven saying, "Write this: Blessed are the dead who die in the Lord from now on." "Blessed indeed," says the Spirit, "that they may rest from their labors, for their deeds follow them!"

Read **Psalm 23; John 5:1-17, 7:14-24;** and **Hebrews 4:1-13 (9-10)**.

Although God no longer requires us to observe the Sabbath and other holy days of the Old Testament, Christians ordinarily take time out to rest and hear God's Word by

- *worshiping on Sunday in commemoration of Jesus' resurrection (**Acts 20:7** and **John 20:19-31**).*

   81. **Colossians 2:16-17** Therefore let no one pass judgment on you in questions of food and drink, or with regard to a festival or a new moon or a Sabbath. These are a shadow of the things to come, but the substance belongs to Christ.

Read **Matthew 12:1-8.** The important thing about a day of worship is that we focus on what God has done for us, especially in His Son, who is Lord of the Sabbath.

- *recalling the wonders of our Triune God by observing the seasons and special holidays (holy days) of the church year (see pp. x-xi in* LSB*).*

   82. **Romans 14:5-6** One person esteems one day as better than another, while another esteems all days alike. Each one should be fully convinced in his own mind. The one who observes the day, observes it in honor of the Lord.

Hymn (*LSB* 581, stanza 4) and Prayer: *We thank You, kind Father, that You give us time to hear Your Holy Word. Grant that fearing and loving You, we may set aside our work to receive Your Son's words, which are spirit and life, and so, refreshed and renewed by the preaching of Your Gospel, we might live in the peace and quietness that come through faith alone; we ask it for the sake of Jesus Christ, our Lord. Amen.*

The Fourth Commandment

Honor your father and your mother.

What does this mean?

We should fear and love God so that we do not despise or anger our parents and other
authorities, but honor them, serve and obey them,
love and cherish them.

The Central Thought

God gives parents a unique task in the world that serves the well-being of all society.

What makes parents unique among all other people in our lives?

Read **John 19:25-27** Note how Jesus honored His mother as He was dying.

✝ *As Christians, we give parents special honor as God's representatives on earth—gifts of God
through whom He gave us the gift of life.*

How can I show that I honor and cherish my parents as gifts of God and as His representatives on earth?

A Closer Reading of the *Small Catechism*

38. Why does this commandment focus on parents and other authorities?

   • *A mother and father uniquely serve as God's representatives, those through whom He bestows
   and nurtures human life on earth.*

   • *Other authorities (pastors, teachers, employers, government officials) also serve as God's
   representatives for the support and protection of our life on earth.*

39. How do we fear and love God in the fourth commandment?

   *First, we fear and love God by **not despising** our parents or other authorities. Despising them
   includes*

   • *looking down upon them or making fun of them;*

      83. **Proverbs 23:22** Listen to your father who gave you life, and do not despise your mother when she is
      old.

   Read **Genesis 9:20-22**.

   • *rejecting or rebelling against their God-given authority.*

      84. **1 Samuel 2:23-24** And he said to them, "Why do you do such things? For I hear of your evil dealings
      from all these people. No, my sons; it is no good report that I hear the people of the LORD spreading
      abroad."

   Read **Deuteronomy 21:18-21** and **2 Samuel 15:1-12**.

   *Second, we fear and love God by **receiving and recognizing** parents and authorities as His
   representatives. We do this by*

- *honoring them;*

Read **Mark 7:10-12** where Jesus condemns those who used man-made religious traditions as an excuse for not honoring their father and mother .

- *serving and coming to the aid of our parents;*

85. **John 19:25-27** Standing by the cross of Jesus were his mother and his mother's sister, Mary the wife of Clopas, and Mary Magdalene. When Jesus saw his mother and the disciple whom he loved standing nearby, he said to his mother, "Woman, behold, your son!" Then he said to the disciple, "Behold, your mother!" And from that hour the disciple took her to his own home.

Read **Genesis 47:11-12** about how Joseph cared for his father and brothers.

- *obeying our parents, pastors and teachers, employers, and government authorities;*

86. **Luke 2:51** And [Jesus] went down with [Mary and Joseph] and came to Nazareth and was submissive to them. And his mother treasured up all these things in her heart.

87. **Ephesians 6:1-3** Children, obey your parents in the Lord, for this is right. "Honor your father and mother" (this is the first commandment with a promise), "that it may go well with you and that you may live long in the land."

88. **Hebrews 13:17** Obey your leaders and submit to them, for they are keeping watch over your souls, as those who will have to give an account. Let them do this with joy and not with groaning, for that would be of no advantage to you.

89. **Colossians 3:23-24** Whatever you do, work heartily, as for the Lord and not for men, knowing that from the Lord you will receive the inheritance as your reward. You are serving the Lord Christ.

90. **Romans 13:1** Let every person be subject to the governing authorities. For there is no authority except from God, and those that exist have been instituted by God.

- *loving and cherishing our parents and other authorities on account of their God-given vocations.*

91. **Ruth 1:16-17** But Ruth said, "Do not urge me to leave you or to return from following you. For where you go I will go, and where you lodge I will lodge. Your people shall be my people, and your God my God. Where you die I will die, and there will I be buried. May the LORD do so to me and more also if anything but death parts me from you."

Read **Leviticus 19:32; Proverbs 23:22-24; 1 Timothy 2:1-4;** and **Titus 3:1.**

Connections and Applications

40. What if my parents or other authorities poorly carry out their vocations from God?

   In faith and obedience to God's Word, we still respect them as those who have been given the privilege of representing God to us, even when they may not deserve such honor.

   (See the Table of Duties for the obligations of parents and other authorities.)

   92. **Ephesians 6:1** Children, obey your parents in the Lord, for this is right.

41. Am I always to obey my parents and other authorities without question?

   No. We must disobey them if they exceed the limits of their God-given authority by requiring us to disobey God's Word.

   93. **Acts 5:29** We must obey God rather than men.

   94. **Matthew 22:21** Then [Jesus] said to them, "Therefore render to Caesar the things that are Caesar's, and to God the things that are God's."

Read **1 Peter 2:18-19** and **1 Samuel 20:30-34.**

Note: We must distinguish between what a government permits people to do and what it compels them to do. When it compels us to act contrary to God's Word then we must disobey and live as God intends. When government permits activities contrary to God's Word (e.g., abortion, no-fault divorce, same sex marriage) we bear witness by living as God intended.

42. What promise does God give us with this commandment, and why does He give it?

God promises those who keep the fourth commandment "that it may go well with you and that you may live long in the land" (Ephesians 6:3; cf. Exodus 20:12). This promise highlights the vital importance of parents in raising children to grow up and become responsible members of society, wise caretakers of God's creation, and faithful witnesses to the Gospel.

Hymn (*LSB* 581, stanza 5) and Prayer: *Heavenly Father from whom all fatherhood on earth is given: Give unto us gratitude for the gifts of parents and others in authority and the humility to serve, obey, love and cherish them as they fulfill the duties and responsibilities You have assigned to them in this life; through Your Son, Jesus Christ, our Lord. Amen.*

The Fifth Commandment

You shall not murder.

What does this mean?

We should fear and love God so that we do not hurt or harm our neighbor in his body, but help and support him in every physical need.

The Central Thought

God created us to care about other people and to help them in their times of need.

What are some needs that people have in my immediate community and society?

Read **Luke 10:25-37**. Why did the Samaritan and lawyer view the beaten man differently?

✝ *As Christians, we look after our neighbors so that they may enjoy the life that God has given them.*

What opportunities does God give me to help my neighbor?

A Closer Reading of the *Small Catechism*

43. Who is our "neighbor"?

    Everyone, and especially those who need our help and assistance, for we all share God's gift of creaturely life.

44. How do we fear and love God in the fifth commandment?

    *First, we fear and love God by **not harming** our neighbor. Harming our neighbor includes*

    - *taking the life of another person (murder);*

        95. Psalm 10:8 [The wicked man] sits in ambush in the villages; in hiding places he murders the innocent.

    Read about Cain and Abel in **Genesis 4:8** and David and Uriah in **2 Samuel 11:15**.

    - *doing or saying anything that injures or endangers another's person's life;*

        96. Proverbs 24:1-2 Be not envious of evil men, nor desire to be with them, for their hearts devise violence, and their lips talk of trouble.

        97. Ephesians 4:31-32 Let all bitterness and wrath and anger and clamor and slander be put away from you, along with all malice. Be kind to one another, tenderhearted, forgiving one another, as God in Christ forgave you.

    Read about Joseph's brothers in **Genesis 37:31-35**; the physical oppression of the Israelites by the Egyptians in **Exodus 1 and 5.**

    Note: The Bible does not prohibit self-defense or defense of our neighbor when faced with imminent bodily harm or death.

    - *neglecting to assist people in bodily need;*

        98. Deuteronomy 15:11 For there will never cease to be poor in the land. Therefore I command you, "You shall open wide your hand to your brother, to the needy and to the poor, in your land."

99. Matthew 25:42-43 For I was hungry and you gave me no food, I was thirsty and you gave me no drink, I was a stranger and you did not welcome me, naked and you did not clothe me, sick and in prison and you did not visit me.

- *harboring anger or hatred in our hearts against our neighbor.*

  100. Matthew 5:22 But I say to you that everyone who is angry with his brother will be liable to judgment; whoever insults his brother will be liable to the council; and whoever says, 'You fool!' will be liable to the hell of fire.

  101. Romans 12:19 Beloved, never avenge yourselves, but leave it to the wrath of God, for it is written, "Vengeance is mine, I will repay, says the Lord."

  102. 1 John 4:19-21 We love because he first loved us. If anyone says, "I love God," and hates his brother, he is a liar; for he who does not love his brother whom he has seen cannot love God whom he has not seen. And this commandment we have from him: whoever loves God must also love his brother.

*Second, we fear and love God by **looking after** the physical well-being of our neighbor. We do this by*

- *coming to the aid of our neighbor;*

  103. Romans 12:20 If your enemy is hungry, feed him; if he is thirsty, give him something to drink.

Read about how Abraham rescues Lot in **Genesis 14:12-16**; how David protects Saul in **1 Samuel 26:1-12**; and the story of the Good Samaritan in **Luke 10:30-35**.

- *speaking in a way that helps and defends our neighbor;*

  104. Proverbs 31:8-9 Open your mouth for the mute, for the rights of all who are destitute. Open your mouth, judge righteously, defend the rights of the poor and needy.

Read about Joseph forgiving his brothers in **Genesis 45:1-16**.

- *treating our neighbor with kindness and compassion.*

  105. Ephesians 4:32 Be kind to one another, tenderhearted, forgiving one another, as God in Christ forgave you.

  106. Colossians 3:12-14 Put on then, as God's chosen ones, holy and beloved, compassionate hearts, kindness, humility, meekness, and patience, bearing with one another and, if one has a complaint against another, forgiving each other; as the Lord has forgiven you, so you also must forgive. And above all these put on love, which binds everything together in perfect harmony.

Read about how Jesus' obedience to this commandment by His compassion for the hungry (**Matthew 15:32**) and His mercy to 10 lepers (**Luke 17:11-19**). **Colossians 3:12-14** shows how love is the bond of harmony.

Connections and Applications

45. What do we need to remember about our neighbor when dealing with issues in society?

We need to remember that

- *God creates, preserves, and protects all life. He is caring and compassionate toward all He has made, and He calls us to be so also.*

- *God gives special dignity (or worth) and protection to every human life. God created humanity in His own image. God's Son became man and shared our human nature. God has redeemed every human life by the holy, precious blood of Christ.*

  107. Genesis 9:5-6 And for your lifeblood I will require a reckoning: from every beast I will require it and from man. From his fellow man I will require a reckoning for the life of man. "Whoever sheds the blood of man, by man shall his blood be shed, for God made man in his own image."

Read **Exodus 22:26-27** and **Matthew 5:42-45** for examples of God's care and commitment to our neighbor's well-being.

46. How does this commandment apply to some specific issues today?

It applies to any type of harming our own life or someone else's life such as

- *engaging in reckless and unhealthy behaviors (e.g., substance abuse);*

    108. 1 Corinthians 6:19-20 Do you not know that your body is a temple of the Holy Spirit within you, whom you have from God? You are not your own, for you were bought with a price. So glorify God in your body.

- *expressing hatred and lovelessness toward other groups of people (prejudice, racism, etc).;*

    109. Acts 17:26 And [God] made from one man every nation of mankind to live on all the face of the earth, having determined allotted periods and the boundaries of their dwelling place.

- *acting violently or abusively toward a spouse or child;*

    110. Colossians 3:19 Husbands love your wives and do not be harsh with them.

    111. Colossians 3:21 Fathers, do not provoke your children, lest they become discouraged.

- *killing ourselves (suicide) or seeking help in killing ourselves (assisted suicide);*

    112. Psalm 31:14-15 But I trust in you, O LORD; I say, "You are my God." My times are in your hand.

Note: When someone is near death, certain treatments may only prolong suffering and not enable either recovery or physical well-being. In such cases it is important to note that *allowing death to occur* when someone is irretrievably dying is different from *causing death* (which is forbidden by God).

- *aborting an unborn child.*

    113. Jeremiah 1:5 Before I formed you in the womb I knew you, and before you were born I consecrated you; I appointed you a prophet to the nations.

Read **Psalm 139:16** and **Luke 1:41-44**.

Note: In some rare and exceptional cases a medical procedure that is actually necessary to save a mother's life may (tragically) result in the death of her unborn child.

47. Does anyone have authority to take another person's life?

Government, acting justly as God's servant, may at times need to take life in order to protect the lives of others (e.g., just wars or capital punishment).

    114. Romans 13:4 For he is God's servant for your good. But if you do wrong, be afraid, for he does not bear the sword in vain. For he is the servant of God, an avenger who carries out God's wrath on the wrongdoer.

Note: Christians may in good conscience disagree about whether a particular war is just. They may also conscientiously disagree about whether capital punishment is always warranted or whether it is being administered in a just manner.

Hymn (*LSB* 581, stanza 6) and Prayer: *Lord God by Your Law You guard and defend every human life from violence and destruction. Give us wisdom never to hurt or harm our neighbors in their bodily life and give us hearts of mercy to help and support them in every physical need; through Jesus Christ, our Lord. Amen.*

The Sixth Commandment

You shall not commit adultery.

What does this mean?

We should fear and love God so that we lead a sexually pure and decent life in what we say and do, and husband and wife love and honor each other.

The Central Thought

God created us to live faithfully as male and female by respecting His purpose for sexual activity within the context of marriage.

Is marriage between a man and a woman held in high regard today? Why or why not?

Read **Genesis 2:15-24**. For what purpose(s) did God create us male and female?

✝ *As Christians, we cherish marriage as the union of our different yet complementary natures as male and female.*

How can I talk about marriage and sex in ways that reflect God's good purposes for it?

A Closer Reading of the *Small Catechism*

48. What is marriage?

    Marriage was created by God as the life-long union of a man and a woman for their mutual help and joy and for the procreation and nurturing of children. A man and a woman enter into marriage by the public promise to live faithfully together until death.

    > **115. Mark 10:6-12** But from the beginning of creation, "God made them male and female." "Therefore a man shall leave his father and mother and hold fast to his wife, and the two shall become one flesh." So they are no longer two but one flesh. What therefore God has joined together, let not man separate."

49. What is adultery?

    Adultery is the unfaithfulness of a spouse who engages in or desires sexual intercourse with someone to whom he or she is not married.

    Read **Matthew 19:4-6** to see that God intended marriage to be permanent and spouses to be faithful.

50. Does this commandment apply only to husbands and wives?

    No. The principle of sexual purity in this commandment applies to all human beings, whether married or not, and to all kinds of sexual desire and activity.

    > **116. Matthew 5:27-28** You have heard that it was said, "You shall not commit adultery." But I say to you that everyone who looks at a woman with lustful intent has already committed adultery with her in his heart.

51. How do we fear and love God in the sixth commandment?

    We fear and love God by living as men and women who respect God's purposes for marriage. We do so by

- *treating our bodies as holy—set apart for the purposes for which God created us as male and female—and and not as objects that serve our selfish desires;*

  117. 1 Thessalonians 4:3-5 For this is the will of God, your sanctification: that you abstain from sexual immorality; that each one of you know how to control his own body in holiness and honor, not in the passion of lust like the Gentiles who do not know God.

  118. 1 Corinthians 6:9-11 Or do you not know that the unrighteous will not inherit the kingdom of God? Do not be deceived: neither the sexually immoral, nor idolaters, nor adulterers, nor men who practice homosexuality, nor thieves, nor the greedy, nor drunkards, nor revilers, nor swindlers will inherit the kingdom of God. And such were some of you. But you were washed, you were sanctified, you were justified in the name of the Lord Jesus Christ and by the Spirit of our God.

Read **Genesis 1:26-28; Matthew 5:27-28;** and **1 Corinthians 6:13-18**.

Note: Human beings have often violated God's purposes for them as male and female by engaging in sexual sins such as fornication, pornography, rape, incest, sexual child abuse, homosexual behavior, etc.

- *speaking and acting in ways that build up rather than tear down each other as male and female (such as crude talk and derogatory comments about appearances; immodest dress; etc.);*

  119. Ephesians 5:4 Let there be no filthiness nor foolish talk nor crude joking, which are out of place, but instead let there be thanksgiving.

Read also **Philippians 4:8** and **1 Timothy 2:9.**

- *reserving sexual intercourse for the giving of one to another in marriage rather than before or outside of marriage;*

  120. Hebrews 13:4 Let marriage be held in honor among all, and let the marriage bed be undefiled, for God will judge the sexually immoral and adulterous.

Read the narrative of Joseph in **Genesis 39:6-10.** See also **1 Corinthians 6:9** and **6:18-20.**

- *refraining from lustful desire or activity of any kind, whether heterosexual, homosexual, bisexual, etc.;*

  121. Proverbs 11:6 The righteousness of the upright delivers them, but the treacherous are taken captive by their lust.

  122. Matthew 5:28 But I say to you that everyone who looks at a woman with lustful intent has already committed adultery with her in his heart.

  123. Colossians 3:5 Put to death therefore what is earthly in you: sexual immorality, impurity, passion, evil desire, and covetousness, which is idolatry.

- *treasuring our husband or wife as a gift of God (if we are married).*

  124. Ephesians 5:33. However, let each one of you love his wife as himself, and let the wife see that she respects her husband

Read **Genesis 2:23; 1 Corinthians 7:1-11;** and **Ephesians 5:21-33.**

52. Why are we (single or married) to respect the fact that God established marriage and created us as male and female?

Marriage is to be respected by all so that

- *individuals may flourish, in modesty and self-control;*

  125. Proverbs 25:28 A man without self-control is like a city broken into and left without walls.

  126. Galatians 5:22-23 But the fruit of the Spirit is love, joy, peace, patience, kindness, goodness, faithfulness, gentleness, self-control; against such things there is no law.

127. **2 Peter 1:5-6** Make every effort to supplement your faith with virtue, and virtue with knowledge, and knowledge with self-control, and self-control with steadfastness, and steadfastness with godliness.

Read **1 Timothy 2:8-10** where the Word describes our new life, emphasizing prayer with modesty, self-control, and other good works.

- *husbands and wives may flourish;*

128. **Genesis 2:21-24** So the LORD God caused a deep sleep to fall upon the man, and while he slept took one of his ribs and closed up its place with flesh. And the rib that the LORD God had taken from the man he made into a woman and brought her to the man. Then the man said, "This at last is bone of my bones and flesh of my flesh; she shall be called Woman, because she was taken out of Man." Therefore a man shall leave his father and his mother and hold fast to his wife, and they shall become one flesh.

Note: Since the fall, marriage also takes on a healing purpose to help keep each other from falling into sexual sin (see **1 Corinthians 7:2-5**).

- *families and societies may flourish through the procreation and the raising of children;*

129. **Genesis 1:28** And God said to them, "Be fruitful and multiply and fill the earth and subdue it, and have dominion over the fish of the sea and over the birds of the heavens and over every living thing that moves on the earth."

130. **Genesis 9:7** And you, be fruitful and multiply, increase greatly on the earth and multiply in it.

- *creation as a whole may flourish.*

131. **Genesis 1:26-27** Then God said, "Let us make man in our image, after our likeness. And let them have dominion over the fish of the sea and over the birds of the heavens and over the livestock and over all the earth and over every creeping thing that creeps on the earth." So God created man in his own image, in the image of God he created him; male and female he created them.

132. **Genesis 2:15-18** The LORD God took the man and put him in the garden of Eden to work it and keep it…Then the LORD God said, "It is not good that the man should be alone; I will make him a helper fit for him."

Read the narratives about the creation of man and woman in **Genesis 1:26-31** and **Genesis 2:15-25**.

Connections and Applications

53. What does the Bible affirm about people who are not married?

Our identity, worth, or completeness as human beings is not determined by our sexuality or marital status alone.

- *God created us and made us stewards of His creation, whether single or married.*

133. **Genesis 1:27-28** So God created man in his own image, in the image of God he created him; male and female he created them. And God blessed them. And God said to them, "Be fruitful and multiply and fill the earth and subdue it and have dominion over the fish of the sea and over the birds of the heavens and over every living thing that moves on the earth."

134. **Psalm 139:13-14** You formed my inward parts; you knitted me together in my mother's womb. I praise you, for I am fearfully and wonderfully made. Wonderful are your works; my soul knows it very well.

- *God has given all good things to all Christians, whether single or married.*

135. **Romans 8:32** He who did not spare his own Son but gave him up for us all, how will he not also with him graciously give us all things?

- *God calls unmarried persons to live in contentment as they trust in Him and serve their neighbor.*

   136. 1 Corinthians 7:8 To the unmarried and the widows I say that it is good for them to remain single as I am.

   137. 1 Corinthians 7:23-34 I want you to be free from anxieties. The unmarried man is anxious about the things of the Lord, how to please the Lord. But the married man is anxious about worldly things, how to please his wife, and his interests are divided. And the unmarried or betrothed woman is anxious about the things of the Lord, how to be holy in body and spirit. But the married woman is anxious about worldly things, how to please her husband.

- *People will not be married in the age to come after Jesus returns.*

   138. Matthew 22:30 For in the resurrection, they neither marry nor are given in marriage, but are like angels in heaven.

54. What does the Bible say about divorce and remarriage?

Divorce tears apart what God intends to be a lifelong union. Unfortunately, adultery (or desertion) already destroys that union. In such cases, the Bible allows for the possibility of divorce and remarriage.

   139. Matthew 19:7-9 They said to him, "Why then did Moses command one to give a certificate of divorce and to send her away?" He said to them, "Because of your hardness of heart Moses allowed you to divorce your wives, but from the beginning it was not so. And I say to you: whoever divorces his wife, except for sexual immorality, and marries another, commits adultery."

Read **Mark 10:6-12**; **1 Corinthians 7:10-11**; and **1 Corinthians 7:15**. See also the story of David and the wife of Uriah in **2 Samuel 11** and that of Herod taking his brother's wife in **Mark 6:18**.

Note: Sadly, divorce cannot be avoided in many circumstances that involve not only adultery and abandonment, but also domestic abuse.

55. What does the Bible say about same sex marriage?

God created us as male or female and established marriage as the union between a man and a woman. The differences between a man and a woman mean that they complement one another and are able, wherever God wills it, to bear children and nurture them. Same sex marriage rejects that intention.

   140. Romans 1:24, 26-27 Therefore God gave them up in the lusts of their hearts to impurity, to the dishonoring of their bodies among themselves…For this reason God gave them up to dishonorable passions. For their women exchanged natural relations for those that are contrary to nature; and the men likewise gave up natural relations with women and were consumed with passion for one another, men committing shameless acts with men and receiving in themselves the due penalty for their error.

Read **Leviticus 18:22** and **1 Timothy 1:8-11**.

56. What does nature (natural law) teach us about marriage?

Human beings are by nature male or female. According to the pattern of nature itself, a new human life cannot be conceived without a man and a woman. The most natural setting for the care of the baby who is born is for the child to be cared for by his or her mother and father, who have committed themselves to each other and to their child. This natural pattern has been the basis for marriages and families throughout all of human history in every human culture.

   141. Genesis 5:1-2 This is the book of the generations of Adam. When God created man, he made him in the likeness of God. Male and female he created them, and he blessed them and named them Man when they were created.

57. What should I do if I am confused about my sexual identity?

During adolescence most people come to realize a growing interest and attraction toward the opposite sex—a desire and attraction that God intended when He created us male and female and established marriage between man and woman. Christians realize that a desire and attraction for the opposite sex is the God-given basis for marriage, for the conception and birth of children, and for the future of earthly human life.

Some persons, however, may discover that they are attracted to others of the same sex. Still others may feel uncomfortable with their gender itself and wish they were, or believe they are, the opposite sex with the wrong body. Moreover, there are many human desires that are contrary to the will of God and result from our fallen nature.

Therefore we should

- *respect our identity as male or female as indicated by the body God gave us;*

- *respect God's intentions for us as male and female;*

- *remember and be obedient to God's command that all desires for genital sexual activity are to be curbed and disciplined until we are married;*

- *remember that while most people will marry, God's Word also praises and blesses those who serve Him by living chastely without marrying;*

- *seek the assistance of pastors, counselors, or other Christian professionals where that is needed or beneficial.*

142. **Genesis 1:27** So God created man in his own image, in the image of God he created him; male and female he created them.

143. **Romans 13:14** But put on the Lord Jesus Christ, and make no provision for the flesh, to gratify its desires.

144. **Romans 1:26-27** For this reason God gave them up to dishonorable passions. For their women exchanged natural relations for those that are contrary to nature; and the men likewise gave up natural relations with women and were consumed with passion for one another, men committing shameless acts with men and receiving in themselves the due penalty for their error.

145. **1 Corinthians 7:17** Only let each person lead the life that the Lord has assigned to him, and to which God has called him.

Note: In an extremely small number of cases, individuals may be born with bodies that are not clearly male or female. Their families will depend on the best medical advice available, seeking to treat the condition in a way that is both medically and morally responsible.

Hymn (*LSB* 581, stanza 7) and Prayer: *Holy Lord, You instituted marriage in Eden and by Your Word You uphold and protect this blessed union of man and woman in one flesh. Cause us to honor marriage and put away from us all sinful thoughts, words, and deeds which would dishonor and distort the gift of marriage. Bless all married couples with faithfulness. Hear the prayers of all who seek a godly spouse, and give to us all purity and decency in all things; through Jesus Christ, our Lord. Amen.*

The Seventh Commandment

You shall not steal.

What does this mean?

We should fear and love God so that we do not take our neighbor's money or possessions, or get them in any dishonest way, but help him to improve and protect his possessions and income.

The Central Thought

God created us to look after the earthly gifts that He has given to our neighbors for their life and well being.

What kinds of things do all people on earth need for their well-being?

Read **Luke 19:1-10**. What change did Jesus bring about in Zacchaeus?

✝ *As Christians, we rejoice in and look after the earthly goods that God has given us and our neighbor for the support of daily life.*

What are some ways that I can help to protect and care for the earthly goods of my neighbor?

A Closer Reading of the *Small Catechism*

58. Why are earthly goods such as money and possessions important?

    They are the gifts by which God provides for our own and our neighbor's needs and the enjoyment of life(see the first article of the Creed).

    > **146. Proverbs 19:17** Whoever is generous to the poor lends to the LORD, and he will repay him for his deed.

    > **147. Proverbs 14:21** Whoever despises his neighbor is a sinner, but blessed is he who is generous to the poor.

    Read **2 Corinthians 8:1-7** about the collection of money for poor Christians in Jerusalem.

59. How do we fear and love God in the seventh commandment?

    *First, we fear and love God by **not denying** our neighbor God's earthly gifts in such ways as*

    - *stealing our neighbor's possessions and money;*

      > **148. John 12:6** [Judas] said this, not because he cared about the poor, but because he was a thief, and having charge of the moneybag he used to help himself to what was put into it.

    - *laziness or sloppy work as employees;*

      > **149. Ephesians 4:28** Let the thief no longer steal, but rather let him labor, doing honest work with his own hands, so that he may have something to share with anyone in need.

    Read **2 Thessalonians 3:6-8**.

    - *acquiring goods by dishonesty, fraud, or taking advantage of others.*

      > **150. Psalm 37:21** The wicked borrows but does not pay back, but the righteous is generous and gives.

Read **Leviticus 19:36** about false measurements and **2 Kings 5:19-25** about trickery.

*Second, we fear and love God by **looking after** our neighbor's well-being. We do this by helping to protect and improve our neighbor's*

- *earthly possessions;*

    151. Genesis 14:12-16 [Enemies] took Lot…his possessions, and went their way. Then one who had escaped came and told Abram the Hebrew…When Abram heard that his kinsman had been taken captive, he led forth his trained men, born in his house, 318 of them, and went in pursuit as far as Dan. And he divided his forces against them by night, he and his servants, and defeated them and pursued them to Hobah, north of Damascus. Then he brought back all the possessions, and also brought back his kinsman Lot with his possessions, and the women and the people.

    152. Exodus 22:14 If a man borrows anything of his neighbor, and it is injured or dies, the owner not being with it, he shall make full restitution.

- *income and livelihood.*

    153. Philippians 2:4 Let each of you look not only to his own interests, but also to the interests of others.

    154. Exodus 23:4-5 If you meet your enemy's ox or his donkey going astray, you shall bring it back to him. If you see the donkey of one who hates you lying down under its burden, you shall refrain from leaving him with it; you shall rescue it with him.

Read **Genesis 13:8-12** and **Deuteronomy 22:1, 4**.

Connections and Applications

60. What else is considered to be our neighbor's possessions or property today?

    These include intellectual property such as ideas and writings (which can be stolen through patent infringement or plagiarism); music, software, movies, and personal information (which might be stolen through copyright violation, online piracy, computer hacking, identity theft), etc.

61. How does God provide us and others with our earthly goods?

    He provides for us through

- *the bounty of the earth (air, water, soil, food, minerals, etc);*

    155. Psalm 65:9-13 You visit the earth and water it; you greatly enrich it; the river of God is full of water; you provide their grain, for so you have prepared it. You water its furrows abundantly, settling its ridges, softening it with showers, and blessing its growth. You crown the year with your bounty; your wagon tracks overflow with abundance. The pastures of the wilderness overflow, the hills gird themselves with joy, the meadows clothe themselves with flocks, the valleys deck themselves with grain, they shout and sing together for joy.

Read **Deuteronomy 8:7-10**.

- *the vocation of parents, family, and neighbors;*

    156. Hebrews 11:20 By faith Isaac invoked future blessings on Jacob and Esau.

    157. Proverbs 1:8 Hear, my son, your father's instruction, and forsake not your mother's teaching.

Read **Matthew 1** and **Luke 2** about how Mary and Joseph cared for Jesus.

- *our jobs and careers.*

    158. 2 Thessalonians 3:10-12 For even when we were with you, we would give you this command: If anyone is not willing to work, let him not eat. For we hear that some among you walk in idleness, not busy at work, but busybodies. Now such persons we command and encourage in the Lord Jesus Christ to do their work quietly and to earn their own living.

159. Ephesians 4:28 Let the thief no longer steal, but rather let him labor, doing honest work with his own hands, so that he may have something to share with anyone in need.

62. How shall we use our own earthly goods?

We are to be good stewards of God's creaturely gifts so that

- *our family flourishes by our provision of shelter, food, education, healthcare, etc.;*

  160. 1 Timothy 5:8 But if anyone does not provide for his relatives, and especially for members of his household, he has denied the faith and is worse than an unbeliever.

- *others (especially, the poor) flourish by our grateful and charitable use of what God has given us at home, church, as neighbors and as citizens;*

  161. Matthew 5:42 Give to the one who begs from you, and do not refuse the one who would borrow from you.

  162. 1 John 3:17 If anyone has the world's goods and sees his brother in need, yet closes his heart against him, how does God's love abide in him?

  163. Hebrews 13:16 Do not neglect to do good and to share what you have, for such sacrifices are pleasing to God.

  Read **Proverbs 17:5** and **Leviticus 19:9-10**.

- *all creation flourishes by our care for the land, water, and air.*

  164. Genesis 2:15 The LORD God took the man and put him in the garden of Eden to work it and keep it.

  165. Leviticus 25:3-5 For six years you shall sow your field, and for six years you shall prune your vineyard and gather in its fruits, but in the seventh year there shall be a Sabbath of solemn rest for the land, a Sabbath to the LORD. You shall not sow your field or prune your vineyard. You shall not reap what grows of itself in your harvest, or gather the grapes of your undressed vine. It shall be a year of solemn rest for the land.

  166. Deuteronomy 22:6 If you come across a bird's nest in any tree or on the ground, with young ones or eggs and the mother sitting on the young or on the eggs, you shall not take the mother with the young.

Hymn (*LSB* 581, stanza 8) and Prayer: *Lord God, Giver of every good and perfect gift, teach us to rejoice in the bounty of Your gifts given to our neighbors and curb our appetite to claim for ourselves by theft or dishonesty the money or possessions You have bestowed on them. Instead give us cheerful hearts and willing hands to help our neighbors improve and protect their livelihood; through Jesus Christ, our Lord. Amen.*

The Eighth Commandment

You shall not give false testimony against your neighbor.

What does this mean?

We should fear and love God so that we do not tell lies about our neighbor, betray him, slander him, or hurt his reputation, but defend him, speak well of him, and explain everything in the kindest way.

The Central Thought

God calls upon us to speak truthfully and charitably about our neighbors, so that others view them in the best possible light.

What are some ways by which a person's reputation is damaged in our society?

Read **Mark 14:3-9**. See how Jesus defends and praises the woman who anointed Him.

✝ *As Christians, we seek to enhance the reputation of others so that people may think well of them.*

Who in my life or community needs me to speak well of them?

A Closer Reading of the *Small Catechism*

63. Why is a good reputation important?

    A good name or reputation is important so that each of us may enjoy the trust and respect of others.

    > **167. Proverbs 22:1** A good name is to be chosen rather than great riches, and favor is better than silver or gold.

    > **168. Ecclesiastes 7:1** A good name is better than precious ointment.

64. How do we fear and love God in the eighth commandment?

    *First, we fear and love God by **not speaking** about others in ways that harm them. Speaking in such damaging ways includes*

    - *telling lies about our neighbors in everyday life or in a court of law;*

      > **169. Matthew 26:59-61** Now the chief priests and the whole council were seeking false testimony against Jesus that they might put him to death, but they found none, though many false witnesses came forward. At last two came forward and said, "This man said, 'I am able to destroy the temple of God, and to rebuild it in three days.'"

      > **170. Colossians 3:9** Do not lie to one another, seeing that you have put off the old self with its practices.

    Read **1 Kings 21:13** about false testimony against Naboth; in **2 Kings 5:19-27** Gehazi tried to profit from a lie.

    - *betraying our neighbors by making public their private faults or secrets;*

      > **171. Proverbs 11:13** Whoever goes about slandering reveals secrets, but he who is trustworthy in spirit keeps a thing covered.

    Read **1 Samuel 22:6-19** about how Ahimelech was betrayed and Judas' betrayal of Jesus in **Matthew 26:14-16**.

    - *slandering our neighbors by complaining or spreading rumors.*

172. James 4:11 Do not speak evil against one another, brothers.

173. Zechariah 8:17 Do not devise evil in your hearts against one another, and love no false oath, for all these things I hate, declares the LORD.

Read **2 Samuel 15:1-6**. How did Absalom slander his father?

*Second, we fear and love God by **speaking constructively** about others. This includes*

- *defending our neighbors when others speak badly of them;*

    174. Proverbs 31:8-9 Open your mouth for the mute, for the rights of all who are destitute. Open your mouth, judge righteously, defend the rights of the poor and needy.

- *drawing attention to our neighbors' good qualities and deeds;*

    175. Luke 7:4-5 [The people of Capernaum spoke well of the centurion.] And when they came to Jesus, they pleaded with him earnestly, saying, "He is worthy to have you do this for him, for he loves our nation, and he is the one who built us our synagogue."

Read **1 Samuel 19:1-7**. How did Jonathan speak up for David to his father Saul?

- *explaining our neighbors' actions in the kindest possible way and putting the best possible construction on them.*

    176. 1 Peter 4:8 Above all, keep loving one another earnestly, since love covers a multitude of sins.

    177. Ephesians 4:15 Speaking the truth in love, we are to grow up in every way into him who is the head, into Christ.

    178. 1 Corinthians 13:7 Love bears all things, believes all things, hopes all things, endures all things.

Read **Acts 5:33-39** about Gamaliel defending the apostles and discouraging persecution.

Connections and Applications

65. What are some ways in which people's reputations are damaged or destroyed in our society?

    We may damage or destroy people's reputations when we ridicule them, gossip about them, label and demean them because of a particular fault or characteristic, or bully them in person or in social media by taunting them, isolating them, or inciting others against them.

66. The Bible tells us to speak the truth in love (**Ephesians 4:15**). What does this mean?

    It means to speak truthfully to others for their well-being, to build others up toward the mature fullness of life we have in Christ. It includes gently admonishing or encouraging someone to repent of their sin, and pointing out the dangers of false teachings and false teachers.

    179. 1 Thessalonians 5:14 And we urge you, brothers, admonish the idle, encourage the fainthearted, help the weak, be patient with them all.

Read **2 Samuel 12:1-14** where Nathan confronts David with his sin. Read **Ephesians 4:11-16** where Paul tells how speaking the truth in love prevents people from being deceived by false teaching and other dangers.

67. Are there times when not speaking the truth may be necessary?

    Yes, withholding the truth may be necessary when speaking the truth would result in injustice or harm.

    180. Exodus 1:15-20 Then the king of Egypt said to the Hebrew midwives, one of whom was named Shiphrah and the other Puah, "When you serve as midwife to the Hebrew women and see them on the birthstool, if it is a son, you shall kill him, but if it is a daughter, she shall live." But the midwives feared God and did not do as the king of Egypt commanded them, but let the male children live. So the king of Egypt called the midwives and said to them, "Why have you done this, and let the male children live?" The midwives said to Pharaoh, "Because the Hebrew women are not like the Egyptian women, for they are vigorous and give birth before the midwife comes to them." So God dealt well with the midwives. And the people multiplied and grew very strong.

Hymn (*LSB* 581, stanza 9) and Prayer: *Guard our lips, O Lord, and govern our unruly tongues so that our words about our neighbors are not tainted with falsehood, betrayal or slander which would damage their reputation. Instead, give us the wisdom to speak well of our neighbors, defend them, and explain their circumstances and actions in the kindest way; through Jesus Christ, our Lord. Amen.*

The Ninth Commandment

You shall not covet your neighbor's house.

What does this mean?

We should fear and love God so that we do not scheme to get our neighbor's inheritance or house, or get it in a way which only appears right, but help and be of service to him in keeping it.

The Tenth Commandment

You shall not covet your neighbor's wife, or his manservant or maidservant, his ox or donkey, or anything that belongs to your neighbor.

What does this mean?

We should fear and love God so that we do not entice or force away our neighbor's wife, workers, or animals or turn them against him, but urge them to stay and do their duty.

The Central Thought

God created us to be content with the gifts by which he sustains our life.

What are some of the reasons that people are not content with what God has given them?

Read **1 Kings 21:1-16**. How did Ahab acquire Naboth's vineyard?

✝ *As Christians, we seek to live a life of contentment by giving thanks for the creaturely gifts that God has given to us and to our neighbor.*

Name ten things for which you are grateful. Then offer a prayer of thanks to God.

A Closer Reading of the *Small Catechism*

68. What is coveting?

    Coveting is the desire in our hearts to acquire for ourselves anything that belongs to our neighbor. It is also the desire to draw away from our neighbor for our own benefit anyone who is important to our neighbor (a spouse, friends, etc.).

    181. Romans 7:8 But sin, seizing an opportunity through the commandment, produced in me all kinds of covetousness. For apart from the law, sin lies dead.

    182. James 4:1-2 What causes quarrels and what causes fights among you? Is it not this, that your passions are at war within you? You desire and do not have, so you murder. You covet and cannot obtain, so you fight and quarrel. You do not have, because you do not ask.

    183. Colossians 3:5 Put to death therefore what is earthly in you: sexual immorality, impurity, passion, evil desire, and covetousness, which is idolatry.

69. Is there a relationship between *coveting* and *envying?*

Envy involves dissatisfaction with what I have and resentfulness at what others have. Coveting involves craving that leads me to try to make my own what is my neighbor's.

    184. Genesis 30:1 When Rachel saw that she bore Jacob no children, she envied her sister. She said to Jacob, "Give me children, or I shall die!"

    185. Joshua 7:21 [Achan confessed:] "When I saw among the spoil a beautiful cloak from Shinar, and 200 shekels of silver, and a bar of gold weighing shekels, then I coveted them and took them. And see, they are hidden in the earth inside my tent, with the silver underneath."

    186. James 1:13-15 Let no one say when he is tempted, "I am being tempted by God," for God cannot be tempted with evil, and he himself tempts no one. But each person is tempted when he is lured and enticed by his own desire. Then desire when it has conceived gives birth to sin, and sin when it is fully grown brings forth death.

70. How do we fear and love God in the ninth and tenth commandments?

*First, we fear and love God by **not coveting** the gifts that He has given to our neighbor. This includes*

- *not plotting to acquire our neighbor's possessions in a way that appears proper or legal (see also the seventh commandment);*

    187. Isaiah 5:8 Woe to those who join house to house, who add field to field, until there is no more room, and you are made to dwell alone in the midst of the land.

    188. Micah 2:1-2 Woe to those who devise wickedness and work evil on their beds! When the morning dawns, they perform it, because it is in the power of their hand. They covet fields and seize them, and houses, and take them away; they oppress a man and his house, a man and his inheritance.

- *not plotting to lure away our neighbor's friends, spouse, or employees (or turn them against our neighbor).*

    189. Ephesians 5:3 But sexual immorality and all impurity or covetousness must not even be named among you, as is proper among saints.

*Read about how David coveted Bathsheba, Uriah's wife, in **2 Samuel 11:2-4**, and **2 Samuel 15:1-6** about how Absalom estranged the hearts of the people from David.*

*Second, we fear and love God by **being satisfied** with what God has provided us and others. This includes*

- *being thankful for all that God has given us;*

    190. Hebrews 13:5-6 Keep your life free from love of money, and be content with what you have, for he has said, "I will never leave you nor forsake you." So we can confidently say, "The Lord is my helper; I will not fear; what can man do to me?"

Read Proverbs 30:8-9; 1 Timothy 6:8-10; and Philippians 4:11-13.

- *helping others to retain what God has given them and encouraging their spouse and workers to remain faithful and loyal.*

    191. Philippians 2:4 Let each of you look not only to his own interests, but also to the interests of others.

Connections and Applications

71. How are we tempted to be dissatisfied with what we have?

Peer pressure often compels us to crave things in order to "fit in" or keep up appearances.

Advertising often encourages us to be dissatisfied with what we have, to keep craving more, and to seek happiness and satisfaction in new things.

> **192. Proverbs 10:3** The LORD does not let the righteous go hungry, but he thwarts the craving of the wicked.

72. Is all wanting, desiring, and ambition sinful?

No. God encourages us to seek His blessings of food, shelter, good jobs, health, success, etc. for ourselves and our family. Such desires become sinful when our seeking and desiring leads us to be ungrateful for what we have and dissatisfied with God's provision (first commandment). That can lead us to break the other commandments (e.g., the sixth and seventh commandments).

> **193. Psalm 107:6-9** Then they cried to the LORD in their trouble, and he delivered them from their distress. He led them by a straight way till they reached a city to dwell in. Let them thank the LORD for his steadfast love, for his wondrous works to the children of man! For he satisfies the longing soul, and the hungry soul he fills with good things.

Hymn (*LSB* 581, stanza 10) and Prayer: *Heavenly Father, You open Your hand and satisfy the desires of every living creature. Cause us to fear and love You above all things that our hearts would not covet that which You have given to our neighbors, but trusting in Your provision of daily bread learn contentment with Your provisions, rejecting every evil scheme or enticement which would secure for ourselves that which You have given to others. Enable us to serve our neighbors by helping them keep and guard all that You have given to them; through Jesus Christ, our Lord. Amen.*

The Close of the Commandments

What does God say about all these commandments?

He says: "I, the LORD your God, am a jealous God, punishing the children for the sin of the fathers to the third and the fourth generation of those who hate Me, but showing love to a thousand generations of those who love Me and keep My commandments.

What does this mean?

God threatens to punish all who break these commandments. Therefore, we should fear His wrath and not do anything against them. But He promises grace and every blessing to all who keep these commandments. Therefore, we should also love and trust in Him and gladly do all that he asks.

The Central Thought

God here shows how intensely He wants us to cling to Him alone.

Do people think that God cares about the way they live? Why or why not?

Read **Deuteronomy 30:1-10** Why is God making these threats and promises?

✝ *As Christians, we confess that God jealously guards His commandments so that all within His creation may prosper.*

How do God's threats and promises shape the way I view Him and His actions?

A Closer Reading of the *Small Catechism*

72. Why does God describe Himself as a "jealous God"?

    God refuses to share us with other gods.

    > **194. Isaiah 42:8** I am the LORD; that is my name; my glory I give to no other, nor my praise to carved idols.

    > **195. Exodus 19:5-6** Now therefore, if you will indeed obey my voice and keep my covenant, you shall be my treasured possession among all peoples, for all the earth is mine; and you shall be to me a kingdom of priests and a holy nation. These are the words that you shall speak to the people of Israel.

    Read **Ezekiel 6:9** and **Ezekiel 18:20-21**.

73. What moves God to punish or bless?

    - *Disobedience provokes God to righteous anger and acts of punishment. (This is God's "alien work.")*

    > **196. Judges 2:11-12** And the people of Israel did what was evil in the sight of the LORD and served the Baals. And they abandoned the LORD, the God of their fathers, who had brought them out of the land of Egypt. They went after other gods, from among the gods of the peoples who were around them, and bowed down to them. And they provoked the LORD to anger.

Read **2 Chronicles 36:17-21** and **Jeremiah 11:17**.

- *God's undeserved loving-kindness moves Him to forgive and bless us. (This is God's "proper work.")*

    197. Deuteronomy 7:6-9 For you are a people holy to the LORD your God. The LORD your God has chosen you to be a people for his treasured possession, out of all the peoples who are on the face of the earth. It was not because you were more in number than any other people that the LORD set his love on you and chose you, for you were the fewest of all peoples, but it is because the LORD loves you and is keeping the oath that he swore to your fathers, that the LORD has brought you out with a mighty hand and redeemed you from the house of slavery, from the hand of Pharaoh king of Egypt. Know therefore that the LORD your God is God, the faithful God who keeps covenant and steadfast love with those who love him and keep his commandments, to a thousand generations.

    198. Isaiah 54:7-8 "For a brief moment I deserted you, but with great compassion I will gather you. In overflowing anger for a moment I hid my face from you, but with everlasting love I will have compassion on you," says the LORD, your Redeemer.

Read **Exodus 34:6-7, Psalm 30:5; Lamentations 3:22-23, 3:31-33;** and **1 John 4:8-10**.

74. Why are those who break the commandments punished and those who keep them blessed?

    *Without faith it is impossible to please God (**Hebrews 11:6**). Keeping the commandments expresses faith in God and His provision for us; breaking the commandments expresses a lack of faith in God.*

    *From this perspective, read again the curses and blessings in **Deuteronomy 30:1-10** (see the Central Thought above).*

75. What is our proper response to God's warnings and promises?

    - *We should reject all other gods and strive not to break His commandments.*

        199. Ecclesiastes 12:13-14 The end of the matter; all has been heard. Fear God and keep his commandments, for this is the whole duty of man. For God will bring every deed into judgment, with every secret thing, whether good or evil.

    - *We should eagerly seek God and gladly do what He commands.*

        200. Psalm 119:2 Blessed are those who keep his testimonies, who seek him with their whole heart.

        201. Romans 7:22 For I delight in the law of God, in my inner being.

Read **Psalm 119:9**; **Psalm 40:8**; **Romans 12:1**, and **1 John 4:9**.

Connections and Applications

76. How does God's carry out His threats and blessings in this life?

    God carries out His threats by

    - *cursing the earth upon which we depend for the nourishment of life;*

        202. Genesis 3:16-19 To the woman he said, "I will surely multiply your pain in childbearing; in pain you shall bring forth children. Your desire shall be for your husband, and he shall rule over you." And to Adam he said, "Because you have listened to the voice of your wife and have eaten of the tree of which I commanded you, 'You shall not eat of it,' cursed is the ground because of you; in pain you shall eat of it all the days of your life; thorns and thistles it shall bring forth for you; and you shall eat the plants of the field. By the sweat of your face you shall eat bread, till you return to the ground, for out of it you were taken; for you are dust, and to dust you shall return."

Read **Leviticus 26:18-20**; **Jeremiah 12:4**; and **Romans 8:18-23**.

    - *authorizing parents and other authorities to punish when we have done wrong;*

203. Romans 13:1-4 Let every person be subject to the governing authorities. For there is no authority except from God, and those that exist have been instituted by God. Therefore whoever resists the authorities resists what God has appointed, and those who resist will incur judgment. For rulers are not a terror to good conduct, but to bad. Would you have no fear of the one who is in authority? Then do what is good, and you will receive his approval, for he is God's servant for your good. But if you do wrong, be afraid, for he does not bear the sword in vain. For he is the servant of God, an avenger who carries out God's wrath on the wrongdoer.

Read **Proverbs 13:24**; **2 Chronicles 36:17-21**.

Note: In the Old Testament, God often used foreign powers (e.g., Nebuchadnezzar, **2 Kings 25:1**) to punish Israel.

- *handing us over to our self-destructive habits and their consequences.*

  204. Romans 1:24-25, 28 Therefore God gave them up in the lusts of their hearts to impurity, to the dishonoring of their bodies among themselves, because they exchanged the truth about God for a lie and worshiped and served the creature rather than the creator, who is blessed forever! Amen...And since they did not see fit to acknowledge God, God gave them up to a debased mind to do what ought not to be done.

God fulfills his promises by

- *blessing the earth with water, crops, good weather, etc.;*

  205. Psalm 65:8-13 Those who dwell at the ends of the earth are in awe at your signs. You make the going out of the morning and the evening to shout for joy. You visit the earth and water it; you greatly enrich it; the river of God is full of water; you provide their grain, for so you have prepared it. You water its furrows abundantly, settling its ridges, softening it with showers, and blessing its growth. You crown the year with your bounty; your wagon tracks overflow with abundance. The pastures of the wilderness overflow, the hills gird themselves with joy, the meadows clothe themselves with flocks, the valleys deck themselves with grain, they shout and sing together for joy.

  206. Psalm 85:12 Yes, the LORD will give what is good, and our land will yield its increase.

Read a **Genesis 1:11-12, 19-30** and **Psalm 67:6**.

- *giving us parents and other authorities for the support of life;*

  207. Isaiah 38:19 The living, the living, he thanks you, as I do this day; the father makes known to the children your faithfulness.

  208. Joel 1:3 Tell your children of it, and let your children tell their children, and their children to another generation.

Read **Genesis 48:15**; **Psalm 78:4-7**; **Psalm 103:13-19**; and **1 Timothy 5:8**.

- *blessing us with health, talents, the ability to work, family, and possessions (house, food, etc).*

  209. Daniel 1:17 As for these four youths, God gave them learning and skill in all literature and wisdom, and Daniel had understanding in all visions and dreams.

  210. 1 Corinthians 15:58 Therefore, my beloved brothers, be steadfast, immovable, always abounding in the work of the Lord, knowing that in the Lord your labor is not in vain.

  211. Ecclesiastes 3:11-13 He has made everything beautiful in its time. Also, he has put eternity into man's heart, yet so that he cannot find out what God has done from the beginning to the end. I perceived that there is nothing better for them than to be joyful and to do good as long as they live; also that everyone should eat and drink and take pleasure in all his toil-this is God's gift to man.

77. Does this mean that when we live in a certain way, things will always go the way we want them to go?

No. We cling to God's promises and continue to seek to live obediently even in the face of trouble and difficulty (this has been called Scripture's "theology of the cross") rather than seeking assurance of God's love and blessing in outward, visible signs and manifestations (this is a man-made "theology of glory").

212. **Habakkuk 3:17-18** Though the fig tree should not blossom, nor fruit be on the vines, the produce of the olive fail and the fields yield no food, the flock be cut off from the fold and there be no herd in the stalls, yet I will rejoice in the LORD; I will take joy in the God of my salvation.

213. **1 Corinthians 10:13** No temptation has overtaken you that is not common to man. God is faithful, and he will not let you be tempted beyond your ability, but with the temptation he will also provide the way of escape, that you may be able to endure it.

214. **Romans 5:1-5** Therefore, since we have been justified by faith, we have peace with God through our Lord Jesus Christ. Through him we have also obtained access by faith into this grace in which we stand, and we rejoice in hope of the glory of God. Not only that, but we rejoice in our sufferings, knowing that suffering produces endurance, and endurance produces character, and character produces hope, and hope does not put us to shame, because God's love has been poured into our hearts through the Holy Spirit who has been given to us.

Read Jesus' words to Peter in **John 21:18-24** about the need to suffer for the sake of the Gospel.

78. What, ultimately, does God threaten against those who hate Him and break His commandments?

Ultimately, God threatens those who break His commandments not only with earthly punishments, but also with physical death and eternal damnation in hell.

215. **Romans 6:23** For the wages of sin is death.

216. **Matthew 25:41-43** Then [the King] will say to those on his left, "Depart from me, you cursed, into the eternal fire prepared for the devil and his angels. For I was hungry and you gave me no food, I was thirsty and you gave me no drink, I was a stranger and you did not welcome me, naked and you did not clothe me, sick and in prison and you did not visit me."

79. How carefully does God want us to keep His commandments?

God wants us to keep His commandments perfectly, in thoughts, desires, words, and deeds.

217. **Matthew 5:48** You therefore must be perfect, as your heavenly Father is perfect.

218. **James 2:10** For whoever keeps the whole law but fails in one point has become accountable for all of it.

80. Can anyone, then, be saved by keeping God's commandments?

No. God's holy Law condemns everyone, for we are all disobedient.

219. **Psalm 14:3** They have all turned aside; together they have become corrupt; there is none who does good, not even one.

220. **Ecclesiastes 7:20** Surely there is not a righteous man on earth who does good and never sins.

221. **Isaiah 64:6** We have all become like one who is unclean, and all our righteous deeds are like a polluted garment. We all fade like a leaf, and our iniquities, like the wind, take us away.

222. **Romans 3:23** For all have sinned and fall short of the glory of God.

223. **Galatians 3:10-11** For all who rely on works of the law are under a curse; for it is written, "Cursed be everyone who does not abide by all things written in the Book of the Law, and do them." Now it is evident that no one is justified before God by the law, for "The righteous shall live by faith."

224. **1 John 1:8** If we say we have no sin, we deceive ourselves, and the truth is not in us.

81. Where alone can we sinners find rescue from the condemnation of God?

Because of God's merciful kindness, He sent His only-begotten Son, Jesus, to rescue us from our sin and from the condemnation we deserved. As our substitute, Jesus kept God's holy Law perfectly, suffered, died, and rose again for us. Therefore, in our crucified and risen Lord Jesus, we are freed from the guilt, the punishment, and the power of sin, and we are saved eternally.

225. **John 3:16** For God so loved the world, that he gave his only Son, that whoever believes in him should not perish but have eternal life.

226. **Romans 8:1-2** There is therefore now no condemnation for those who are in Christ Jesus. For the law of the Spirit of life has set you free in Christ Jesus from the law of sin and death.

227. **Romans 5:19** For as by the one man's [Adam's] disobedience the many were made sinners, so by the one man's [Jesus'] obedience the many will be made righteous.

228. **Galatians 3:13** Christ redeemed us from the curse of the law by becoming a curse for us—for it is written, "Cursed is everyone who is hanged on a tree."

229. **Colossians 1:13-14** He has delivered us from the domain of darkness and transferred us to the kingdom of his beloved Son, in whom we have redemption, the forgiveness of sins.

Hymn (*LSB* 581, stanzas 11 and 12) and Prayer: *Holy and merciful God, You have taught us what You would have us do and not do. Pour out Your Holy Spirit on us so that He may bear fruit in our lives and that, remembering your mercies and Your laws, we may grow in obedience to Your will and in love for You and our neighbor. Help us to follow the example of Your dear Son, Jesus Christ, our Lord, in whose name we pray. Amen.*

Sin and Our Human Condition

82. What is sin?

Sin is any thought, desire, word, or work that is contrary to God's will as summarized in the Ten Commandments.

> **230. 1 John 3:4** Everyone who makes a practice of sinning also practices lawlessness; sin is lawlessness.

Note: Other names for sin are unbelief (**John 3:18**); disobedience (**Romans 5:19**); debts (**Matthew 6:12**); rebellion (**Exodus 34:7**); fault (**Matthew 18:15**); trespass (**Romans 5:17**); wickedness (**Romans 6:13**); and wrong (**Colossians 3:25**).

83. How did sin enter God's good creation?

The devil brought sin into the world by tempting Adam and Eve, who willingly yielded to the temptation.

Read **Genesis 3:1-6** about the fall into sin of our first parents.

> **231. 1 John 3:8** Whoever makes a practice of sinning is of the devil, for the devil has been sinning from the beginning. The reason the Son of God appeared was to destroy the works of the devil.

> **232. Romans 5:12** Therefore, just as sin came into the world through one man, and death through sin, and so death spread to all men because all sinned.

84. How did Adam and Eve's disobedience affect us?

In Adam and Eve's fall into sin the entire human race fell into sin. We call this original sin.

> **233. Psalm 51:5**. Behold, I was brought forth in iniquity, and in sin did my mother conceive me.

Read **John 3:6** and **Ephesians 4:22**.

85. How does original sin affect every human creature?

It means that every person is born

- *without the ability to fear and love God. This has left us spiritually blind and dead.*

> **234. 1 Corinthians 2:14** The natural person does not accept the things of the Spirit of God, for they are folly to him, and he is not able to understand them because they are spiritually discerned.

Read **Romans 8:7** and **Ephesians 2:1-3**.

- *with an incessant desire to sin. This has made us enemies of God.*

> **235. Genesis 8:21** And when the LORD smelled the pleasing aroma, the LORD said in his heart, "I will never again curse the ground because of man, for the intention of man's heart is evil from his youth. Neither will I ever again strike down every living creature as I have done."

Read **Matthew 7:17-20** and **Galatians 5:19**.

- *deserving of God's temporal and eternal death sentence.*

> **236. Romans 5:12** Therefore just as sin came into the world through one man and death through sin, and so death spread to all men because all sinned.

> **237. Ephesians 2:3** [We] were by nature children of wrath, like the rest of mankind.

Read **Romans 5:12-19**.

- *enslaved in a lifelong sinful condition from which we cannot free ourselves. Even as Christians (who are simultaneously sinners and "saints" through faith in Christ), we must struggle daily against sin and the power of the devil.*

  238. John 8:34 Jesus answered them, "Truly, truly, I say to you, everyone who practices sin is a slave to sin."

Read **Romans 7:14-25**, where Paul describes the ongoing struggle against sin that we experience as Christians.

The Law and the Gospel

86. How does God use the Ten Commandments in our lives and the lives of others in this world?

    God uses the Ten Commandments (the Law) in three different ways. We call these the three uses of the Law.

    First, He uses the Law to limit or prevent the outbreak of sin for the good of His creation (**a curb**).

    239. 1 Timothy 1:8-10 Now we know that the law is good, if one uses it lawfully, understanding this, that the law is not laid down for the just but for the lawless and disobedient, for the ungodly and sinners, for the unholy and profane, for those who strike their fathers and mothers, for murderers, the sexually immoral, men who practice homosexuality, enslavers, liars, perjurers, and whatever else is contrary to sound doctrine.

    Second, He uses the Law to reveal and condemn our sin (**a mirror**).

    240. Romans 3:20 For by works of the law no human being will be justified in his sight, since through the law comes knowledge of sin.

    241. Romans 7:7 What then shall we say? That the law is sin? By no means! Yet if it had not been for the law, I would not have known sin. For I would not have known what it is to covet if the law had not said, "You shall not covet."

    242. 1 John 1:10 If we say we have not sinned, we make him a liar, and his word is not in us.

    Third, He uses the Law to guide and direct our thoughts, words, and deeds as Christians in God-pleasing ways (**a guide**).

    243. Psalm 119:105 Your word is a lamp to my feet and a light to my path.

    244. Proverbs 6:23 For the commandment is a lamp and the teaching a light, and the reproofs of discipline are the way of life.

87. Why is the second use of the Law so important?

    It makes known our need for the Gospel of Christ, who is the fulfillment of the Law.

    245. Romans 10:4 For Christ is the end of the law for righteousness to everyone who believes.

    246. Galatians 3:13-14 Christ redeemed us from the curse of the law by becoming a curse for us—for it is written, "Cursed is everyone who is hanged on a tree"—so that in Christ Jesus the blessing of Abraham might come to the Gentiles, so that we might receive the promised Spirit through faith.

    247. Colossians 1:13 He has delivered us from the domain of darkness and transferred us to the kingdom of his beloved Son.

88. How does the Gospel differ from the Law?

    - *The Law teaches what God expects from us; the Gospel teaches what God has done to rescue and restore us.*

- *The Law shows us our sin and reveals God's wrath; the Gospel shows our Savior and brings God's grace and favor.*

- *The Law must be proclaimed especially to sinners who refuse to repent; the Gospel must be proclaimed to sinners who seek freedom from their sin.*

In summary, each and every one of us is born as a lost and condemned person, in dire need of the rescue and redemption which our Lord Jesus has won for us, which we learn about and confess in the next chief part of the catechism: the Apostles' Creed.

89. Why does the Creed follow the Ten Commandments?

The Ten Commandments are written on the hearts of all people by virtue of their creation. They reveal our sin and prepare us to receive the gifts of salvation confessed in the Creed. "The Commandments teach what we ought to do. But the Creed tells what God does for us and gives to us" (LC II, 67).

> **248. Romans 2:15** They show that the work of the law is written on their hearts, while their conscience also bears witness, and their conflicting thoughts accuse or even excuse them.

> **249. Romans 3:19, 21-22** Now we know that whatever the law says it speaks to those who are under the law, so that every mouth may be stopped, and the whole world may be held accountable to God...But now the righteousness of God has been manifested apart from the law, although the Law and the Prophets bear witness to it—the righteousness of God through faith in Jesus Christ for all who believe.

90. What is the Creed?

The Creed provides a summary of all of God's work in creation and human history as set forth in the Bible.

91. Can one learn about God outside the Bible?

To some extent we can learn about God as our creator from what we see in the creation around us. Creation witnesses to its creator and His goodness and power.

> **250. Psalm 19:1** The heavens declare the glory of God, and the sky above proclaims his handiwork.

> **251. Acts 14:17** Yet he did not leave himself without witness, for he did good by giving you rains from heaven and fruitful seasons, satisfying your hearts with food and gladness.

> **252. Romans 1:20** For his invisible attributes, namely, his eternal power and divine nature, have been clearly perceived, ever since the creation of the world, in the things that have been made.

Note: Sometimes creation's witness is referred to as natural revelation in distinction from the special revelation of God in Scripture.

92. Then why do we need the Bible or a summary of the Bible such as the Creed?

Although creation gives witness to its creator, it does not reveal His identity and name. In some ways, creation gives us the first chapter of the story. The Bible (and its summary in the creed) gives us the rest of that story. The Bible teaches us to know God more fully and for our salvation (LC II, 1).

93. How many creeds do we have?

The Christian church has long used three creeds, the Apostles' Creed, Nicene Creed, and Athanasian Creed. We use the Apostles' Creed in the catechism. Each of them clarifies specific areas of doctrinal controversy and confusion.

94. Why do we use the Apostles' Creed?

It is the one most commonly used in Baptism. We were baptized in the name of the Father, Son, and Holy Spirit. In three articles or parts the Creed expresses the divine work most commonly associated with each person: the Father (creation), the Son (redemption), and the Holy Spirit (sanctification).

95. Why does the creed begin with the words, "I believe…"

The English word creed comes from the Latin word credo—*"I believe." A creed is a statement of faith, a statement of what I believe. To say "I believe" is to say what God has done **for me**. "I am convinced that God has made **me**, redeemed **me**, and sanctified **me**."*

The First Article (Part 1)

I believe in God the Father Almighty, maker of heaven and earth.

What does this mean?

I believe that God has made me and all creatures, that He has given me my body and soul, eyes, ears, and all my members, my reason and all my senses, and still takes care of them.

He also gives me clothing and shoes, food and drink, house and home, wife and children, land, animals, and all I have. He richly and daily provides me with all that I need to support this body and life. He defends me against all danger and guards and protects me from all evil.

All this He does only out of fatherly, divine goodness and mercy, without any merit or worthiness in me. For all this it is my duty to thank and praise, serve and obey Him.

This is most certainly true.

The Central Thought

No one but God "could create heaven and earth" (LC II, 11)—this truth determines how I understand myself and how I relate to God and His world.

How might people answer the question "What is a human being?"

Read **Genesis 2:7-25**. How were we created in relationship to God and to the rest of the world?

✝ *As Christians, we confess, "I am God's creature!" (LC II, 13).*

How does seeing myself as God's creature shape my relationship to Him and to His world?

A Closer Reading of the *Small Catechism*

96. Why does the Creed begin by confessing God as the "maker" of heaven and earth?

- *Only the one who made heaven and earth can rightly be called God.*

    253. Genesis 1:1 In the beginning, God created the heavens and the earth.

    254. 2 Kings 19:15 And Hezekiah prayed before the LORD and said: "O LORD, the God of Israel, enthroned above the cherubim, you are the God, you alone, of all the kingdoms of the earth; you have made heaven and earth."

Read **Psalm 115:15-16; Job 38-41**; and **Isaiah 36-37**.

- *Only the one who made heaven and earth can make His creation new again.*

    255. John 1:1-3 In the beginning was the Word, and the Word was with God, and the Word was God. He was in the beginning with God. All things were made through him, and without him was not anything made that was made.

    256. 1 Corinthians 8:6 Yet for us there is one God, the Father, from whom are all things and for whom we exist, and one Lord, Jesus Christ, through whom are all things and through whom we exist.

    257. Revelation 21:5 And [Jesus] who was seated on the throne said, "Behold, I am making all things new."

97. What is included in the phrase "heaven and earth"?

God created everything that exists, namely, "all things visible and invisible" (Nicene Creed).

> **258. Colossians 1:16** For by him all things were created, in heaven and on earth, visible and invisible, whether thrones or dominions or rulers or authorities—all things were created through him and for him.

98. Why does the catechism say that God created "me and all creatures"?

It is another way of saying that God made the universe and everything in it.

> **259. Nehemiah 9:6** You are the LORD, you alone. You have made heaven, the heaven of heavens, with all their host, the earth and all that is on it, the seas and all that is in them; and you preserve all of them; and the host of heaven worships you.

99. What does it mean to confess that God made "me"?

I am a creature of God. My life is a gift from Him. I am accountable to Him.

> **260. 1 Corinthians 4:7** What do you have that you did not receive? If then you received it, why do you boast as if you did not receive it?

> **261. Psalm 139:13-14** For you formed my inward parts; you knitted me together in my mother's womb. I praise you, for I am fearfully and wonderfully made. Wonderful are your works; my soul knows it very well.

> **262. James 1:17-18** Every good and perfect gift comes down from above…Of his own will he brought us forth by the word of truth, that we should be a kind of first fruits of his creatures.

Read also **Psalm 100** and **Job 10:8-11**.

100. What does it mean to confess that God made me "and all creatures."

- *All human creatures (regardless of sex, race, and ethnicity) receive life from God just as I do.*

> **263. Acts 17:26-27** And he made from one man every nation of mankind to live on all the face of the earth, having determined allotted periods and the boundaries of their dwelling place, that they should seek God, and perhaps feel their way toward him and find him.

- *All other living creatures receive life from God and depend upon God's care just as I do.*

> **264. Genesis 1:30** And to every beast of the earth and to every bird of the heavens and to everything that creeps on the earth, everything that has the breath of life, I have given every green plant for food. And it was so.

> **265. Genesis 2:19** Now out of the ground the LORD God had formed every beast of the field and every bird of the heavens and brought them to the man to see what he would call them. And whatever the man called every living creature, that was its name.

> **266. Psalm 145:15-16** The eyes of all look to you, and you give them their food in due season. You open your hand; you satisfy the desire of every living thing.

> **267. Matthew 6:26** Look at the birds of the air: they neither sow nor reap nor gather into barns, and yet your heavenly Father feeds them. Are you not of more value than they?

- *All that exists—the universe, this planet, land, sea, and the whole material world—depends upon God for its ongoing existence just as I do.*

> **268. Psalm 65:5-7** By awesome deeds you answer us with righteousness, O God of our salvation, the hope of all the ends of the earth and of the farthest seas; the one who by his strength established the mountains, being girded with might; who stills the roaring of the seas, the roaring of their waves, the tumult of the peoples.

269. Psalm 95:4-5 In his hand are the depths of the earth, the heights of the mountains are his also. The sea is his, for he made it, and his hands formed the dry land.

101. What does it mean that God has given me both a body and a soul?

I am not only a body. I am not only a soul. I am a body into which God has breathed life.

270. Genesis 2:7 Then the LORD God formed the man of dust from the ground and breathed into his nostrils the breath of life, and the man became a living creature.

271. Ecclesiastes 11:5. As you do not know the way the spirit comes to the bones in the womb of a woman with child, so you do not know the work of God who makes everything.

102. What is the significance of having a body and soul for my personal identity and relationships?

- *In giving me a particular body and soul, God has made me either a male or a female.*

  272. Genesis 1:27 So God created man in his own image, in the image of God he created him; male and female he created them.

- *It is with my body ("eyes, ears, and all my members") and with my soul ("reason and all my senses") that I relate to God, to other people, to other living things, and to this world.*

  273. Psalm 103:1 Bless the LORD, O my soul, and all that is within me, bless his holy name!

  274. Romans 12:1 I appeal to you therefore, brothers, by the mercies of God, to present your bodies as a living sacrifice, holy and acceptable to God, which is your spiritual worship.

  275. 1 Corinthians 6:19-20 Or do you not know that your body is a temple of the Holy Spirit within you, whom you have from God? You are not your own, for you were bought with a price. So glorify God in your body.

  276. Matthew 22:37 And he said to him, "You shall love the Lord your God with all your heart and with all your soul and with all your mind."

Connections and Applications

103. Why is the first person of the Trinity called God the "Father"?

- *He is the eternal Father of the Son of God, Christ our Savior.*

  277. John 3:16 For God so loved the world, that he gave his only Son, that whoever believes in him should not perish but have eternal life.

- *He is the Father of all people as their creator.*

  278. Acts 17:29 Being then God's offspring, we ought not to think that the divine being is like gold or silver or stone, an image formed by the art and imagination of man.

- *He is our gracious Father, having adopted us in Jesus Christ.*

  279. Galatians 4:4-6 But when the fullness of time had come, God sent forth his Son, born of woman, born under the law, to redeem those who were under the law, so that we might receive adoption as sons. And because you are sons, God has sent the Spirit of his Son into our hearts, crying, "Abba! Father!"

THE CREATION OF ALL THINGS

104. How did God create everything?

- *By His Word God spoke creation into existence. By His Word He formed it and filled it over six days.*

280. Genesis 1:3-11 And God said, "Let there be light," and there was light…And God said, "Let there be an expanse in the midst of the waters, and let it separate the waters from the waters." And God made the expanse and separated the waters that were under the expanse from the waters that were above the expanse. And it was so…And God said, "Let the waters under the heavens be gathered together into one place, and let the dry land appear." And it was so…And God said, "Let the earth sprout vegetation, plants yielding seed, and fruit trees bearing fruit in which is their seed, each according to its kind, on the earth." And it was so.

281. Psalm 33:6-9 By the word of the LORD the heavens were made, and by the breath of his mouth all their host. He gathers the waters of the sea as a heap; he puts the deeps in storehouses. Let all the earth fear the LORD; let all the inhabitants of the world stand in awe of him! For he spoke, and it came to be; he commanded, and it stood firm.

Read **Hebrews 11:3** and **2 Peter 3:5-7**.

- *By His Word He blessed it and declared it to be very good (just right, orderly, harmonious, beautiful, morally pure, etc).*

  282. Genesis 1:31 And God saw everything that he had made, and behold, it was very good.

105. Where should we begin when assessing other competing accounts of how the world came into existence?

We should evaluate the assumptions with which they work, determine where these assumptions come from, and consider whether they lead to unbiblical conclusions.

Many ancient and modern views assume that the universe always existed and thus all gods and beings arise from it and exist on a spectrum of deity. This leads one to assume that everything is in some way divine or part of divinity, thus confusing the creator and His creation (e.g. animism, pantheism, polytheism).

Atheistic evolutionary theories assume that the Bible is not the Word of God and the universe is closed with no possibility of outside intervention. This invites the conclusion that the world and universe have no special meaning or purpose.

Some theistic evolutionists and evolutionary creationists may hold to a view of Scripture as God's Word but wrongly assume that, in light of current scientific claims, Genesis 1-3 should not be read as historical accounts. Thus they will affirm that God is the creator, but see evolution as the means by which God made the world as we know it. This can lead to the questioning of certain truths in Scripture that are dependent upon the special creation of God.

GOD'S HUMAN CREATURES

106. What distinguishes humans from all other creatures?

- *God created all living things, but He uniquely made humanity in His image.*

  283. Genesis 1:26-27 Then God said, "Let us make man in our image, after our likeness. And let them have dominion over the fish of the sea and over the birds of the heavens and over the livestock and over all the earth and over every creeping thing that creeps on the earth." So God created man in his own image, in the image of God he created him; male and female he created them.

- *God's Son became a man—a human being.*

  284. John 1:14, 16 And the Word became flesh and dwelt among us, and we have seen his glory, glory as of the only Son from the Father, full of grace and truth…For from his fullness we have all received, grace upon grace.

  285. Philippians 2:5-7 Have this mind among yourselves, which is yours in Christ Jesus, who, though he was in the form of God, did not count equality with God a thing to be grasped, but made himself nothing, taking the form of a servant, being born in the likeness of men.

- *Jesus Christ, who is God and Man, suffered, shed His blood, died, and rose bodily from the dead for the salvation of humanity.*

  286. Ephesians 1:7 In him we have redemption through his blood, the forgiveness of our trespasses, according to the riches of his grace.

  287. Hebrews 9:12 [Christ, our high priest,] entered once for all into the holy places, not by means of the blood of goats and calves but by means of his own blood, thus securing an eternal redemption.

107. Do we still have the image of God?

- *Since the Fall into sin, we lost the ability to live by faith in God, in perfect love toward one another, and in a proper relationship to creation (original righteousness). In this sense, we have lost the image of God.*

  288. Genesis 5:3 When Adam had lived 130 years, he fathered a son in his own likeness, after his image, and named him Seth.

  289. 1 Corinthians 2:14 The natural person does not accept the things of the Spirit of God, for they are folly to him, and he is not able to understand them because they are spiritually discerned.

- *However, we still possess unique dignity (or worth) as those who were created in the image of God and were given dominion in creation.*

  290. Genesis 9:6 Whoever sheds the blood of man, by man shall his blood be shed, for God made man in his own image.

  291. James 3:9 With it we bless our Lord and Father, and with it we curse people who are made in the likeness of God.

108. Will we ever regain the image of God that was lost?

Yes. In Christ, the restoration of God's image in us has begun, but in this life it is only a beginning, and will be fully restored on the last day.

  292. Colossians 3:10 [You] have put on the new self, which is being renewed in knowledge after the image of its creator.

  293. Ephesians 4:24 Put on the new self, created after the likeness of God in true righteousness and holiness.

  294. 2 Corinthians 3:18 And we all, with unveiled face, beholding the glory of the Lord, are being transformed into the same image from one degree of glory to another. For this comes from the Lord who is the Spirit.

GOD'S NON-HUMAN CREATURES

109. What other living creatures did God create?

- *God made other creatures from the earth, including plants, birds, animals, and fish, etc.*

  295. Genesis 2:19 Now out of the ground the LORD God had formed every beast of the field and every bird of the heavens and brought them to the man to see what he would call them.

  296. Genesis 1:20 And God said, "Let the waters swarm with swarms of living creatures, and let birds fly above the earth across the expanse of the heavens."

- *God also made non-physical creatures called angels.*

  297. Nehemiah 9:6 You are the LORD, you alone. You have made heaven, the heaven of heavens, with all their host [angels], the earth and all that is on it, the seas and all that is in them; and you preserve all of them; and the host of heaven worships you.

Read **Luke 1:1-20; Luke 1:26-38; Matthew 1:18-21; Luke 24:4-7; and Acts 1:10-22**

110. For what purpose did God create nonhuman creatures on earth?

- *God created them for beauty, joy, and delight.*

  298. Psalm 104:31 May the glory of the LORD endure forever; may the LORD rejoice in his works.

- *God created them to offer Him praise and thanks.*

  299. Psalm 150:6 Let everything that has breath praise the LORD! Praise the LORD!

- *God created them for the sustenance of life.*

  300. Genesis 1:29 And God said, "Behold, I have given you every plant yielding seed that is on the face of all the earth, and every tree with seed in its fruit. You shall have them for food."

  301. Genesis 9:3 Every moving thing that lives shall be food for you. And as I gave you green plants, I give you everything.

Read **Psalm 148**.

111. For what purpose did God create the angels?

- *God created angels to be His messengers and servants.*

  302. Luke 1:13 The angel said to him, "Do not be afraid, Zechariah, for your prayer has been heard, and your wife Elizabeth will bear you a son, and you shall call his name John."

  303. Luke 1:26-28 In the sixth month the angel Gabriel was sent from God to a city of Galilee named Nazareth, to a virgin betrothed to a man whose name was Joseph, of the house of David. And the virgin's name was Mary. And he came to her and said, "Greetings, O favored one, the Lord is with you!"

- *God created angels to protect the people of God.*

  304. Psalm 91:11-12 For he will command his angels concerning you to guard you in all your ways. On their hands they will bear you up, lest you strike your foot against a stone.

  305. Hebrews 1:14 Are they not all ministering spirits sent out to serve for the sake of those who are to inherit salvation?

- *God created angels to lead His people in worship and to praise Him continually.*

  306. Luke 2:13-14 And suddenly there was with the angel a multitude of the heavenly host praising God and saying, "Glory to God in the highest, and on earth peace among those with whom he is pleased!"

  307. Psalm 103:20-21 Bless the LORD, O you his angels, you mighty ones who do his word, obeying the voice of his word! Bless the LORD, all his hosts, his ministers, who do his will!

Read **2 Kings 19:35; 2 Kings 6:15-17; Acts 12:5-11, and Daniel 7:10**

112. Do all the angels serve these purposes of God?

No. Some angels (e.g., the devil and his minions) rebelled against God and now seek to destroy everything that is good, especially faith in Christ.

  308. Jude 6 And the angels who did not stay within their own position of authority, but left their proper dwelling, he has kept in eternal chains under gloomy darkness until the judgment of the great day.

  309. John 8:44 You are of your father the devil, and your will is to do your father's desires. He was a murderer from the beginning, and does not stand in the truth, because there is no truth in him. When he lies, he speaks out of his own character, for he is a liar and the father of lies.

310. Ephesians 6:12 For we do not wrestle against flesh and blood, but against the rulers, against the authorities, against the cosmic powers over this present darkness, against the spiritual forces of evil in the heavenly places.

311. 1 Peter 5:8-9 Be sober-minded; be watchful. Your adversary the devil prowls around like a roaring lion, seeking someone to devour. Resist him, firm in your faith, knowing that the same kinds of suffering are being experienced by your brotherhood throughout the world.

Read **Mark 4:15 and 5:9, Genesis 3:1-5; Job 2; Matthew 4:1-11;** and **2 Peter 2:4**.

113. What are some common questions about angels?

- *Do we become angels when we die? No. We will be raised from the dead as glorified human creatures.*

   312. Philippians 3:20-21 But our citizenship is in heaven, and from it we await a Savior, the Lord Jesus Christ, who will transform our lowly body to be like his glorious body, by the power that enables him even to subject all things to himself.

- *Are we to look to angels for direction in our lives or pray to them? No. We pray only to God.*

   313. Colossians 2:18 Let no one disqualify you, insisting on asceticism and worship of angels, going on in detail about visions, puffed up without reason by his sensuous mind,

- *Do I have a personal guardian angel? Scripture does not directly answer this question, but it does speak of angels protecting His people.*

   314. Psalm 91:9-12 Because you have made the LORD your dwelling place—the Most High, who is my refuge—no evil shall be allowed to befall you, no plague come near your tent. For he will command his angels concerning you to guard you in all your ways. On their hands they will bear you up, lest you strike your foot against a stone.

   315. Matthew 18:10 See that you do not despise one of these little ones. For I tell you that in heaven their angels always see the face of my Father who is in heaven.

Hymn (*LSB* 811) and Prayer: *Almighty Father, Maker of heaven and earth: I praise You for having fashioned me in love and set me within this world which You have also created. For all that You have given me in body and soul and for the wondrous ways in which You take care of me, I give You thanks. Keep me mindful of Your bountiful gifts, ever looking to You for all good things in this earthly life, and teach me to receive them as Your child and heir; through Jesus Christ, Your Son. Amen.*

The First Article (Part 2)

I believe in God the Father Almighty, maker of heaven and earth.

What does this mean?

I believe that God has made me and all creatures, that He has given me my body and soul, eyes, ears, and all my members, my reason and all my senses, and still takes care of them.

He also gives me clothing and shoes, food and drink, house and home, wife and children, land, animals, and all I have. He richly and daily provides me with all that I need to support this body and life. He defends me against all danger and guards and protects me from all evil.

All this He does only out of fatherly, divine goodness and mercy, without any merit or worthiness in me. For all this it is my duty to thank and praise, serve and obey Him.

This is most certainly true.

The Central Thought

As creatures, we need certain basic necessities to nourish and support our life on earth. God Himself provides these necessities for me, as He does for all His creatures (LC II, 14).

Where would most people say that the basic necessities of their life come from?

Read **Psalm 104**. How does the psalmist describe God's relationship to creation?

✝ *As Christians, we confess that God provides for us each and every day by working in and through His creation.*

Who or what are the "hands, channels, and means" (LC I, 26) through which God provides my daily needs?

A Closer Reading of the *Small Catechism*

114. Does God continue to be involved with His creation?

    Yes. God remains present and active within His creation, constantly looking after it, and creating new life within it.

    316. Psalm 139:7-10 Where shall I go from your Spirit? Or where shall I flee from your presence? If I ascend to heaven you are there! if I make my bed in Sheol, you are there! If I take the wings of the morning and dwell in the uttermost parts of the sea, even there your hand shall lead me, and your right hand shall hold me.

    317. Jeremiah 23:23-24 "Am I a God at hand," declares the LORD, "and not a God far away? Can a man hide himself in secret places so that I cannot see him?" declares the LORD. "Do I not fill heaven and earth?" declares the LORD.

    318. Acts 17:27-28 That they should seek God, and perhaps feel their way toward him and find him. Yet he is actually not far from each one of us, for "In him we live and move and have our being"; as even some of your own poets have said, "For we are indeed his offspring."

    319. Nehemiah 9:6 You are the LORD, you alone. You have made heaven, the heaven of heavens, with all their host, the earth and all that is on it, the seas and all that is in them; and you preserve all of them; and the host of heaven worships you.

320. Job 12:10 In his hand is the life of every living thing and the breath of all mankind.

321. Colossians 1:17 And he is before all things, and in him all things hold together.

322.Hebrews 1:2-3. In these last days he has spoken to us by his Son, whom he appointed the heir of all things, through whom also he created the world. He is the radiance of the glory of God and the exact imprint of his nature, and he upholds the universe by the word of his power.

Read **Genesis 8:22; Psalm 65; Psalm 139; Proverbs 15:3; Isaiah 40:12;** and **Deuteronomy 11:12**.

115. For whom does God care and provide within His creation?

God cares for His entire creation and everything and everyone within it. In other words

- *God cares for and provides for His entire nonhuman creation;*

  323. Psalm 104:10-13 You make springs gush forth in the valleys; they flow between the hills; they give drink to every beast of the field; the wild donkeys quench their thirst. Beside them the birds of the heavens dwell; they sing among the branches. From your lofty abode you water the mountains; the earth is satisfied with the fruit of your work.

  324. Psalm 147:8-9 He covers the heavens with clouds; he prepares rain for the earth; he makes grass grow on the hills. He gives to the beasts their food, and to the young ravens that cry.

  325. Job 38:25-29 Who has cleft a channel for the torrents of rain and a way for the thunderbolt, to bring rain on a land where no man is, on the desert in which there is no man, to satisfy the waste and desolate land, and to make the ground sprout with grass?

  326. Psalm 145:15-16 The eyes of all look to you, and you give them their food in due season. You open your hand; you satisfy the desire of every living thing.

  327. Matthew 6:26 Look at the birds of the air: they neither sow nor reap nor gather into barns, and yet your heavenly Father feeds them.

Read **Job 38:41; Jonah 4:11; Matthew 10:29-31;** and **Luke 12:6-7**.

- *God cares and provides for all people, even those who fail to acknowledge Him.*

  328. Psalm 104:14-15 You cause the grass to grow for the livestock and plants for man to cultivate, that he may bring forth food from the earth and wine to gladden the heart of man, oil to make his face shine and bread to strengthen man's heart.

  329. Matthew 5:45 For he makes his sun rise on the evil and on the good, and sends rain on the just and on the unjust.

  330. Acts 14:16-17 In past generations he allowed all the nations to walk in their own ways. Yet he did not leave himself without witness, for he did good by giving you rains from heaven and fruitful seasons, satisfying your hearts with food and gladness.

- *God cares and provides for us, who are His children in Christ.*

  331. Philippians 4:19 And my God will supply every need of yours according to his riches in glory in Christ Jesus.

  332. 1 Peter 3:12 For the eyes of the Lord are on the righteous, and his ears are open to their prayer. But the face of the Lord is against those who do evil."

  333. 1 Peter 5:7 [Cast] all your anxieties on him, because he cares for you.

  334. Ephesians 1:22 And he put all things under his feet and gave him as head over all things to the church.

  335. Psalm 121:4 Behold, he who keeps Israel will neither slumber nor sleep.

Read **Jeremiah 31:12-13**.

116. What does God provide for our body and life?

- *God provides food and drink to give us energy, health, community, and enjoyment.*

    336. Psalm 104:14-15 You cause the grass to grow for the livestock and plants for man to cultivate, that he may bring forth food from the earth and wine to gladden the heart of man, oil to make his face shine and bread to strengthen man's heart.

- *God provides clothing and shoes for protection against the elements and for modesty.*

    337. Genesis 3:21 And the LORD God made for Adam and for his wife garments of skins and clothed them.

    338. Deuteronomy 10:18 He executes justice for the fatherless and the widow, and loves the sojourner, giving him food and clothing.

- *God provides house and home for shelter, security, and hospitality.*

    339. Psalm 68:6 God settles the solitary in a home.

- *God provides spouse and child (families and also friends) to bear each other's burdens.*

    340. Genesis 2:23 Then the man said, "This at last is bone of my bones and flesh of my flesh; she shall be called Woman, because she was taken out of Man."

    341. Proverbs 18:22 He who finds a wife finds a good thing and obtains favor from the LORD.

    342. Psalm 127:3 Behold, children are a heritage from the LORD, the fruit of the womb a reward.

    343. Ruth 1:16-17 But Ruth said, "Do not urge me to leave you or to return from following you. For where you go I will go, and where you lodge I will lodge. Your people shall be my people, and your God my God. Where you die I will die, and there will I be buried. May the LORD do so to me and more also if anything but death parts me from you."

    344. Proverbs 17:17 A friend loves at all times, and a brother is born for adversity.

    345. Proverbs 18:24 A man of many companions may come to ruin, but there is a friend who sticks closer than a brother.

- *God provides land and animals (that is, work and livelihood).*

    346. Genesis 30:29-30 Jacob said to him, "You yourself know how I have served you, and how your livestock has fared with me. For you had little before I came, and it has increased abundantly, and the LORD has blessed you wherever I turned."

117. What else does God do to take care of us?

- *God protects us from danger and evil.*

    347. Psalm 121:1-8 I lift up my eyes to the hills. From where does my help come? My help comes from the LORD, who made heaven and earth. He will not let your foot be moved; he who keeps you will not slumber. Behold, he who keeps Israel will neither slumber nor sleep. The LORD is your keeper; the LORD is your shade on your right hand. The sun shall not strike you by day, nor the moon by night. The LORD will keep you from all evil; he will keep your life. The LORD will keep your going out and your coming in from this time forth and forevermore.

    348. Psalm 147:6 The LORD lifts up the humble; he casts the wicked to the ground.

See **Genesis 19; Exodus 13:14; Psalm 147:6; Psalm 37** and **73**.

- *God is at work in all things for our good.*

    349. Romans 8:28 And we know that for those who love God all things work together for good.

118. How does God provide for me and protect me each day?

God's word of blessing enlists other creatures as His co-workers in caring for me. These include the entire creation, including angels, parents, government, land, weather, and animals.

> **350. Genesis 1:11** And God said, "Let the earth sprout vegetation, plants yielding seed, and fruit trees bearing fruit in which is their seed, each according to its kind, on the earth." And it was so.

> **351. Genesis 9:3** Every moving thing that lives shall be food for you. And as I gave you the green plants, I give you everything.

> **352. Romans 13:1** For there is no authority except from God, and those that exist have been instituted by God.

Connections and Applications

119. If our gracious creator provides for all of our needs and protects us from all evil, why do suffering and death exist in the world (such as poverty, homelessness, war, disease, natural disasters)?

- *Our first parents (prompted by the devil) brought evil and suffering into the world by rebelling against God. Sinful activity continues to cause tremendous suffering throughout the world.*

> **353. James 1:13-15** Let no one say when he is tempted, "I am being tempted by God," for God cannot be tempted with evil, and he himself tempts no one. But each person is tempted when he is lured and enticed by his own desire. Then desire when it has conceived gives birth to sin, and sin when it is fully grown brings forth death.

> **354. John 8:44** You are of your father the devil, and your will is to do your father's desires. He was a murderer from the beginning, and does not stand in the truth, because there is no truth in him. When he lies, he speaks out of his own character, for he is a liar and the father of lies.

> **355. Romans 5:12** As sin came into the world through one man…death spread to all men for all have sinned.

- God punished His human creatures for their rebellion by cursing the earth. That curse erupts from the earth in ways that cause suffering (earthquakes, floods, diseases, etc) for human and non-human creatures just as God's blessing on the earth supports and sustains life for all.

> **356. Genesis 3:17-19** Cursed is the ground because of you; in pain you shall eat of it all the days of your life; thorns and thistles it shall bring forth for you; and you shall eat the plants of the field. By the sweat of your face you shall eat bread, till you return to the ground, for out of it you were taken; for you are dust, and to dust you shall return.

> **357. Romans 8:20-22** For the creation was subjected to futility, not willingly, but because of him who subjected it, in hope that the creation itself will be set free from its to corruption and obtain the freedom of the glory of the children of God. For we know that the whole creation has been groaning together in the pains of childbirth until now.

- *Therefore, we need to repent of human sin and the destruction it brings into the world, ask for God's forgiveness, care for those who suffer, and pray for God's restoration of all things when suffering and death will be ended.*

Read **Luke 13:1-5** where Jesus urges repentance in response to tragic suffering.

120. Why do some of us experience more suffering and misfortune than others?

- *In some cases, we bring the suffering upon ourselves as a consequence of our sins.*

> **358. Galatians 6:7** Do not be deceived: God is not mocked, for whatever one sows, that will he also reap.

> **359. James 4:1-2** What causes quarrels and what causes fights among you? Is it not this, that your passions are at war within you? You desire and do not have, so you murder. You covet and cannot obtain, so you fight and quarrel.

Read **2 Samuel 12:1-15** about how David suffered for his sin.

- *In many cases, we do not know why God allows some to suffer more than others. Those reasons remain hidden in God whose purposes within creation are often beyond our understanding.*

  360. Isaiah 55:8-9 "For my thoughts are not your thoughts, neither are your ways my ways," declares the LORD. "For as the heavens are higher than the earth, so are my ways higher than your ways and my thoughts than your thoughts."

  361. Romans 9:19-23 You will say to me then, "Why does he still find fault? For who can resist his will?" But who are you, O man, to answer back to God? Will what is molded say to its molder, "Why have you made me like this?" Has the potter no right over the clay, to make out of the same lump one vessel for honorable use and another for dishonorable use? What if God, desiring to show his wrath and to make known his power, has endured with much patience vessels of wrath prepared for destruction, in order to make known the riches of his glory for vessels of mercy, which he has prepared beforehand for glory.

  362. Ecclesiastes 11:5 As you do not know the way the spirit comes to the bones in the womb of a woman with child, so you do not know the work of God who makes everything.

Read **Genesis 50:15-21; Isaiah 45:9**; and **Job 42:1-6**.

- *Therefore, we should lament our suffering to God, pray for His help, care for those who suffer, and commend ourselves and others into His merciful hands.*

  363. Psalm 130:1-2 Out of the depths I cry to you, O LORD! O LORD, hear my voice! Let your ears be attentive to the voice of my pleas for mercy!

  364. Psalm 90:13-15 Return, O LORD! How long? Have pity on your servants! Satisfy us in the morning with your steadfast love, that we may rejoice and be glad all our days. Make us glad for as many days as you have afflicted us, and for as many years as we have seen evil.

  365. 1 Peter 4:12-19 Beloved, do not be surprised at the fiery trial when it comes upon you to test you, as though something strange were happening to you. But rejoice insofar as you share Christ's sufferings, that you may also rejoice and be glad when his glory is revealed. If you are insulted for the name of Christ, you are blessed, because the Spirit of glory and of God rests upon you. But let none of you suffer as a murderer or a thief or an evildoer or as a meddler. Yet if anyone suffers as a Christian, let him not be ashamed, but let him glorify God in that name. For it is time for judgment to begin at the household of God; and if it begins with us, what will be the outcome for those who do not obey the gospel of God? And "If the righteous is scarcely saved, what will become of the ungodly and the sinner?" Therefore let those who suffer according to God's will entrust their souls to a faithful creator while doing good.

121. What is God doing about all the suffering and death in the world?

- *God does not allow evil to have the final word. He daily brings forth new life in the midst of and in spite of all the sin and death in the world.*

  366. Genesis 8:21-22 And when the LORD smelled the pleasing aroma, the LORD said in his heart, "I will never again curse the ground because of man, for the intention of man's heart is evil from his youth. Neither will I ever again strike down every living creature as I have done. While the earth remains, seedtime and harvest, cold and heat, summer and winter, day and night, shall not cease."

  367. Matthew 5:45 so that you may be sons of your Father who is in heaven. For he makes his sun rise on the evil and on the good, and sends rain on the just and on the unjust.

  368. Acts 14:16-17 In past generations he allowed all the nations to walk in their own ways. Yet he did not leave himself without witness, for he did good by giving you rains from heaven and fruitful seasons, satisfying your hearts with food and gladness.

- *Christ's death has overcome suffering and death, and in His resurrection eternal life begins.*

369. Romans 5:8 but God shows his love for us in that while we were still sinners, Christ died for us.

370. John 10:27-28 My sheep hear my voice, and I know them, and they follow me. I give them eternal life, and they will never perish, and no one will snatch them out of my hand.

371. 1 John 3:2 Beloved, we are God's children now, and what we will be has not yet appeared; but we know that when he appears we shall be like him, because we shall see him as he is.

- *God will work out all things for His gracious purposes and for the well-being of His Church.*

  372. Genesis 50:20 As for you, you meant evil against me, but God meant it for good, to bring it about that many people should be kept alive, as they are today.

  373. Romans 5:1-5 Therefore, since we have been justified by faith, we have peace with God through our Lord Jesus Christ. Through him we have also obtained access by faith into this grace in which we stand, and we rejoice in hope of the glory of God. Not only that, but we rejoice in our sufferings, knowing that suffering produces endurance, and endurance produces character, and character produces hope, and hope does not put us to shame, because God's love has been poured into our hearts through the Holy Spirit who has been given to us.

  374. Romans 8:28-30 And we know that for those who love God all things work together for good, for those who are called according to his purpose. For those whom he foreknew he also predestined to be conformed to the image of his Son, in order that he might be the firstborn among many brothers. And those whom he predestined he also called, and those whom he called he also justified, and those whom he justified he also glorified.

- *When Jesus returns He will free the children of God from all suffering and, with them, the entire creation.*

  375. Romans 8:18-21 I consider that the sufferings of this present time are not worth comparing with the glory that is to be revealed to us. For the creation waits with eager longing for the revealing of the sons of God. For the creation was subjected to futility, not willingly, but because of him who subjected it, in hope that the creation itself will be set free from its bondage to corruption and obtain the freedom of the glory of the children of God.

  376. Revelation 21:4 He will wipe away every tear from their eyes, and death shall be no more, neither shall there be mourning, nor crying, nor pain anymore, for the former things have passed away.

122. What are some false beliefs about God's presence and activity within the world?

Atheism denies the existence, presence, and activity of God within the world.

Agnosticism expresses uncertainty about whether there is a God or how God is present and active in the world.

Deism denies God's daily activity within the world by contending that once He created the world, He then left it alone to run like a machine.

Pantheism maintains that everything is God, thus denying the redemptive intervention of God from outside of creation.

These various philosophies manifest themselves in a wide variety of forms.

Hymn (*LSB* 876) and Prayer: *Gracious Father, You open Your hand to satisfy the desires of every living creature and provide me with all that I need to support my body and life. I thank You for the provisions You have given me in clothing and shoes to wear, food and drink to nourish and refresh my body, a place to live, the love and companionship of family, and daily work. Give me the grace to acknowledge Your goodness and live with gratitude and contentment, confident in Your love for the sake of Jesus Christ, my Lord, who lives and reigns with You and Holy Spirit, one God now and forever. Amen.*

The First Article (Part 3)

I believe in God the Father Almighty, maker of heaven and earth.

What does this mean?

I believe that God has made me and all creatures, that He has given me my body and soul, eyes, ears, and all my members, my reason and all my senses, and still takes care of them.

He also gives me clothing and shoes, food and drink, house and home, wife and children, land, animals, and all I have. He richly and daily provides me with all that I need to support this body and life. He defends me against all danger and guards and protects me from all evil.

All this He does only out of fatherly, divine goodness and mercy, without any merit or worthiness in me. For all this it is my duty to thank and praise, serve and obey Him.

This is most certainly true.

The Central Thought

No one is self-sufficient. Each one of us receives life and support as a gift from outside of ourselves.

Is the gratitude of Christians different from that of those who do not know God as their gracious Father?

Read **Psalm 65:5-13**. How does this psalm depict the generosity of God?

✝ *As Christians, we confess that every good thing (however small) within our lives is an undeserved gift from God.*

What are some examples of God's generosity in my life?

A Closer Reading of the *Small Catechism*

123. Why does the catechism use the word "all" nine times in its explanation of the first article?

    This emphasizes the comprehensiveness of God's creative work. It is another way of saying, God created the "heavens and the earth."

    377. John 3:27 John answered, "A person cannot receive even one thing unless it is given him from heaven."

    378. James 1:17 Every good gift and every perfect gift is from above, coming down from the Father of lights with whom there is no variation or shadow due to change.

    379. 1 Corinthians 4:7 What do you have that you did not receive? if then you received it why do you boast as if you did not receive it?

124. What is the significance of confessing that God did all of this out of "fatherly, divine goodness and mercy, without any merit or worthiness in me"?

    • *God did not have to create the world. He created the world freely, out of love.*

    380. Psalm 136:4-9 To him who alone does great wonders, for his steadfast love endures forever; to him who by understanding made the heavens, for his steadfast love endures forever; to him who spread out the earth above the waters, for his steadfast love endures forever; to him who made the great lights, for his steadfast love endures forever; the sun to rule over the day, for his steadfast love endures forever; the moon and stars to rule over the night, for his steadfast love endures forever.

- *God created each one of us and mercifully sustains us in spite of our sinfulness.*

  381. Luke 7:6-7 When [Jesus] was not far from the house, the centurion sent friends, saying to him, "Lord, do not trouble yourself, for I am not worthy to have you come under my roof. Therefore I did not presume to come to you. But say the word, and let my servant be healed."

  382. Genesis 32:10 I am not worthy of the least of all the deeds of steadfast love and all the faithfulness that you have shown to your servant, for with only my staff I crossed this Jordan, and now I have become two camps.

- *Life in this world remains a good gift even when we feel that life is more of a curse than a gift, more of a burden than a delight, more tearful than joyful.*

  383. 1 Timothy 4:4 For everything created by God is good, and nothing is to be rejected if it is received with thanksgiving, for it is made holy by the word of God and prayer.

  384. Habakkuk 3:17-19 Though the fig tree should not blossom, nor fruit be on the vines, the produce of the olive fail and the fields yield no food, the flock be cut off from the fold and there be no herd in the stalls, yet I will rejoice in the LORD; I will take joy in the God of my salvation. God, the LORD, is my strength; he makes my feet like the deer's; he makes me tread on my high places.

  385. Philippians 4:11-13 Not that I am speaking of being in need, for I have learned in whatever situation I am to be content. I know how to be brought low, and I know how to abound. In any and every circumstance, I have learned the secret of facing plenty and hunger, abundance and need. I can do all things through him who strengthens me.

  Read **Jonah 2, Jeremiah 20:18; Jeremiah 31:3, 31-33; Psalm 13:6.**

- *Creation and redemption are bound closely together. It is by God's goodness and mercy that we are created, and it is by God's goodness and mercy that we are made new again.*

  386. Psalm 136:1, 5, 11, 24- 25 Give thanks to the LORD…who by understanding made the heavens, for his steadfast love endures forever…and brought Israel out from among [the Egyptians], for his steadfast love endures forever…and rescued us from our foes, for his steadfast love endures forever; he who gives food to all flesh, for his steadfast love endures forever.

  387. Isaiah 43:1 But now thus says the LORD, he who created you, O Jacob, he who formed you, O Israel: "Fear not, for I have redeemed you; I have called you by name, you are mine."

  Read **Psalm 103** and **Jeremiah 31:9-12**.

125. Why do we say that it is our duty to thank and praise, serve and obey?

It is only right and proper for creatures to respond to the gifts of their creator in word ("thank and praise") and deed ("serve and obey").

  388. Luke 17:10 So you also, when you have done all that you were commanded, say, "We are unworthy servants; we have only done what was our duty."

  389. Deuteronomy 13:4 You shall walk after the LORD your God and fear him and keep his commandments and obey his voice, and you shall serve him and hold fast to him.

  390. Joshua 24:15 But as for me and my house, we will serve the LORD.

  Read **Psalm 71** noting that despite many troubles, the psalmist sings praise.

126. How do I thank and praise God?

- *I thank God by expressing my gratitude for all that He has done for me.*

  391. Psalm 118:1 Oh give thanks to the LORD, for he is good; for his steadfast love endures forever!

392. 1 Timothy 4:4-5 For everything created by God is good, and nothing is to be rejected if it is received with thanksgiving, for it is made holy by the word of God and prayer.

393. 1 Thessalonians 5:16-18 Rejoice always, pray without ceasing, give thanks in all circumstances; for this is the will of God in Christ Jesus for you.

- *I praise God by recounting and extolling His works.*

394. Psalm 40:5 You have multiplied, O LORD my God, your wondrous deeds and your thoughts toward us; none can compare with you! I will proclaim and tell of them, yet they are more than can be told.

Read **Psalm 136** and **Psalm 145**.

- *I thank and praise God within the rhythms of my daily life (see "Daily Prayers").*

395. Daniel 6:10 When Daniel knew that the document had been signed, he went to his house where he had windows in his upper chamber open toward Jerusalem. He got down on his knees three times a day and prayed and gave thanks before his God, as he had done previously.

396. Philippians 4:6 Do not be anxious about anything, but in everything by prayer and supplication with thanksgiving let your requests be made known to God.

127. How do I serve and obey God?

I serve and obey God when I use all of these gifts for the well-being of myself, my neighbor, and the wider creation within my various walks of life (vocations; see the Ten Commandments and the Table of Duties).

Connections and Applications

128. How should I think of my calling as a human creature in God's creation?

God cares about His creation and has called us to care for it as His stewards.

397. Genesis 1:28 And God blessed them. And God said to them, "Be fruitful and multiply and fill the earth and subdue it, and have dominion over the fish of the sea and over the birds of the heavens and over every living thing that moves on the earth."

398. Genesis 2:15 The LORD God took the man and put him in the garden of Eden to work it and keep it.

399. Psalm 8:5-6 Yet you have made him a little lower than the heavenly beings and crowned him with glory and honor. You have given him dominion over the works of your hands; you have put all things under his feet.

400. Psalm 24:1-2 The earth is the LORD's and the fullness thereof, the world and those who dwell therein, for he has founded it upon the seas and established it upon the rivers.

401. Psalm 115:16 The heavens are the LORD's heavens, but the earth he has given to the children of man.

129. What does it mean to be a steward?

We have been entrusted to look after God's creation so that it may flourish.

402. Luke 12:42-44, 48 And the Lord said, "Who then is the faithful and wise manager, whom his master will set over his household, to give them their portion of food at the proper time? Blessed is that servant whom his master will find so doing when he comes. Truly, I say to you, he will set him over all his possessions…Everyone to whom much was given, of him much will be required, and from him to whom they entrusted much, they will demand the more."

403. 1 Corinthians 4:2 Moreover, it is required of stewards that they be found faithful.

Read **Matthew 5:13-16**.

130. What are some of our stewardship responsibilities?

- *We are responsible for the care of our bodies.*

    404. 1 Corinthians 6:19-20 Or do you not know that your body is a temple of the Holy Spirit within you, whom you have from God? You are not your own, for you were bought with a price. So glorify God in your body.

- *We are responsible for the care of our possessions and finances.*

    405. Proverbs 10:4-5 A slack hand causes poverty, but the hand of the diligent makes rich. He who gathers in summer is a prudent son, but he who sleeps in harvest is a son who brings shame.

Read **Ephesians 4:28; Hebrews 13:16;** and **1 Timothy 6:17-19**.

- *We are responsible for the care of our neighbors.*

    406. 1 Peter 4:10-11 As each has received a gift, use it to serve one another, as good stewards of God's varied grace: whoever speaks, as one who speaks oracles of God; whoever serves, as one who serves by the strength that God supplies—in order that in everything God may be glorified through Jesus Christ. To him belong glory and dominion forever and ever. Amen.

Read **2 Corinthians 9:6-11**.

- *We are responsible for the care of the church, church workers, and church property.*

    407. 1 Chronicles 29:11-13, 16 Yours, O LORD, is the greatness and the power and the glory and the victory and the majesty, for all that is in the heavens and in the earth is yours. Yours is the kingdom, O LORD, and you are exalted as head above all. Both riches and honor come from you, and you rule over all. In your hand are power and might, and in your hand it is to make great and to give strength to all. And now we thank you, our God, and praise your glorious name…O LORD our God, all this abundance that we have provided for building you a house for your holy name comes from your hand and is all your own.

    408. 1 Timothy 5:17-18 Let the elders who rule well be considered worthy of double honor, especially those who labor in preaching and teaching. For the Scripture says,"You shall not muzzle an ox when it treads out the grain," and,"The laborer deserves his wages."

Read **Malachi 3:8; John 12:3-8;** and **Philippians 4:14-20**.

- *We are responsible for the care of the rest of God's creation: the earth, its bounty, and all life.*

    409. Genesis 2:15 The LORD God took the man and put him in the garden of Eden to work it and keep it.

    410. Leviticus 25:4-7 In the seventh year there shall be a Sabbath of solemn rest for the land, a Sabbath to the LORD. You shall not sow your field or prune your vineyard. You shall not reap what grows of itself in your harvest, or gather the grapes of your undressed vine. It shall be a year of solemn rest for the land. The Sabbath of the land shall provide food for you, for yourself and for your male and female slaves and for your hired worker and the sojourner who lives with you, and for your cattle and for the wild animals that are in your land: all its yield shall be for food.

    411. Genesis 6:19-22 And of every living thing of all flesh, you shall bring two of every sort into the ark to *keep them alive with you*. They shall be male and female. Of the birds according to their kinds, and of the animals according to their kinds, of every creeping thing of the ground, according to its kind, two of every sort shall come in to you *to keep them alive*. Also take with you every sort of food that is eaten, and store it up. It shall serve as food for you and for them. Noah did this; he did all that God commanded him.

    412. Proverbs 12:10 Whoever is righteous has regard for the life of his beast.

Read **Exodus 23:5-6; Deuteronomy 11:13-14;** and **Deuteronomy 22:6-7**.

> Hymn (*LSB* 895) and Prayer: *Heavenly Father, out of your fatherly, divine goodness and mercy, You have created me, endowed me with all that I have in this body and life, and You continue to defend me from all danger and guard and protect me from all evil. Receive now my thanks and praise for all of Your gifts and shape my life to serve and obey You in the callings which You have given me; through Jesus Christ, my Lord. Amen.*

The Second Article (Part 1)

And [I believe] in Jesus Christ, His only Son, our Lord, who was conceived by the Holy Spirit, born of the virgin Mary, suffered under Pontius Pilate, was crucified, died and was buried. He descended into hell. The third day He rose again from the dead. He ascended into heaven and sits at the right hand of God the Father Almighty. From thence He will come to judge the living and the dead.

What does this mean?

I believe that Jesus Christ, true God, begotten of the Father from eternity, and also true man born of the Virgin Mary, is my Lord,

who has redeemed me, a lost and condemned person, purchased and won me from all sins, from death, and from the power of the devil; not with gold or silver, but with His holy, precious blood and with His innocent suffering and death,

that I may be His own and live under Him in His kingdom and serve Him in everlasting righteousness, innocence, and blessedness, just as He is risen from the dead, lives and reigns to all eternity.

This is most certainly true.

The Central Thought

Jesus once asked, "Who do people say that I am?" Many different answers were given.

What do people today think of Jesus? Who or what do they say that He is?

Read **John 20:24-29**. Note what Thomas concludes about Jesus.

✝ *As Christians, we confess: "This man Jesus is my Lord: He is both my creator and my redeemer."*

How can I acknowledge in my words and actions that Jesus is my Lord?

A Closer Reading of the *Small Catechism*

131. What does it mean to confess that Jesus is Lord?

> *It means to acknowledge that He rules over all things as our creator and redeemer.*

> **413. Romans 10:9-10** If you confess with your mouth that Jesus is Lord and believe in your heart that God raised him from the dead, you will be saved. For with the heart one believes and is justified, and with the mouth one confesses and is saved.

> **414. Colossians 1:16-20** For by him [Jesus] all things were created, in heaven and on earth, visible and invisible, whether thrones or dominions or rulers or authorities—all things were created through him and for him. And he is before all things, and in him all things hold together. And he is the head of the body, the church. He is the beginning, the firstborn from the dead, that in everything he might be preeminent. For in him all the fullness of God was pleased to dwell, and through him to reconcile to himself all things, whether on earth or in heaven, making peace by the blood of his cross.

Read **John 4:42**; **John 20:20-24**; and **Acts 4:12**.

132. Why do I confess that Jesus Christ is *my* Lord?

Jesus has given me eternal life and taken me under His eternal care and protection.

    415. John 3:36 Whoever believes in the Son has eternal life; whoever does not obey the Son shall not see life, but the wrath of God remains on him.

    416. John 17:3-5 And this is eternal life, that they know you the only true God, and Jesus Christ whom you have sent. I glorified you on earth, having accomplished the work that you gave me to do. And now, Father, glorify me in your own presence with the glory that I had with you before the world existed.

    417. 2 Timothy 1:12 I am not ashamed, for I know whom I have believed, and I am convinced that he is able to guard until that Day what has been entrusted to me.

133. Who is this Jesus that I confess as my Lord?

He is the eternal Son of God who entered human history by taking upon Himself a human body and soul as the fulfillment of God's Old Testament promises. Thus He is both creator and creature, God and man, in one person.

134. What does it mean to confess that Jesus is true God?

The Son is God in the very same sense that the Father is God—namely, He existed from all eternity and, together with the Father and the Spirit, created the entire universe and everything within it.

    418. John 1:3 All things were made through him [the Word], and without him was not anything made that was made.

    419. 1 Corinthians 8:6 Yet for us there is one God, the Father, from whom are all things and for whom we exist, and one Lord, Jesus Christ, through whom are all things and through whom we exist.

    420. Colossians 1:16-17 For by him all things were created, in heaven and on earth, visible and invisible, whether thrones or dominions or rulers or authorities—all things were created through him and for him. And he is before all things, and in him all things hold together.

The Nicene Creed says of the Lord Jesus Christ: "by whom all things were made."

135. What does it mean to confess that Jesus is "begotten of the Father from eternity"?

The Son has no beginning. He eternally receives life from the Father. Thus in the Nicene Creed we confess Jesus as "begotten, not made."

    421. John 1:1-2, 14 In the beginning was the Word, and the Word was with God, and the Word was God. He was in the beginning with God...And the Word became flesh and dwelt among us, and we have seen his glory, glory as of the only Son from the Father, full of grace and truth.

    422. Hebrews 1:3 He is the radiance of the glory of God and the exact imprint of his nature, and he upholds the universe by the word of his power. After making purification for sins, he sat down at the right hand of the Majesty on high.

The Nicene Creed also says of the Lord Jesus Christ: "the only-begotten Son of God, begotten of His Father before all worlds, God of God, Light of Light, very God of very God, begotten, not made, being of one substance with the Father."

136. What does it mean to confess that Jesus is true man?

Jesus is human in the very same sense that we are human, except without sin.

    423. Hebrews 4:15 For we do not have a high priest who is unable to sympathize with our weaknesses, but one who in every respect has been tempted as we are, yet without sin.

    424. 1 Timothy 2:5-6 For there is one God, and there is one mediator between God and men, the man

Christ Jesus, who gave himself as a ransom for all, which is the testimony given at the proper time.

137. What does it mean to confess that Jesus was conceived by the Holy Spirit?

Jesus was conceived in Mary's womb by the will and act of God apart from a human father.

425. Matthew 1:18-25 Now the birth of Jesus Christ took place in this way. When his mother Mary had been betrothed to Joseph, before they came together she was found to be with child from the Holy Spirit. And her husband Joseph, being a just man and unwilling to put her to shame, resolved to divorce her quietly. But as he considered these things, behold, an angel of the Lord appeared to him in a dream, saying, "Joseph, son of David, do not fear to take Mary as your wife, for that which is conceived in her is from the Holy Spirit. She will bear a son, and you shall call his name Jesus, for he will save his people from their sins." All this took place to fulfill what the Lord had spoken by the prophet: "Behold, the virgin shall conceive and bear a son, and they shall call his name Immanuel" (which means, God with us). When Joseph woke from sleep, he did as the angel of the Lord commanded him: he took his wife, but knew her not until she had given birth to a son. And he called his name Jesus.

Read **Luke 1:26-38**.

Connections and Applications

138. What do we call the event by which the Son of God became man?

We call this the incarnation, the unfathomable mystery that the very Son of God, who created the universe, entered His creation and became a part of it by becoming a human creature.

426. John 1:14 And the Word became flesh and dwelt among us, and we have seen his glory, glory as of the only Son from the Father, full of grace and truth.

427. Colossians 2:9 For in him the whole fullness of deity dwells bodily.

428. 1 Timothy 3:16 Great indeed, we confess, is the mystery of godliness: He was manifested in the flesh, vindicated by the Spirit, seen by angels, proclaimed among the nations, believed on in the world, taken up in glory.

139. How did the incarnation take place?

The Holy Spirit fashioned from Mary (that is, from her very DNA) a human body and soul for the Son of God.

429. Luke 1:35 And the angel answered her, "The Holy Spirit will come upon you, and the power of the Most High will overshadow you; therefore the child to be born will be called holy—the Son of God."

430. Matthew 1:20 But as he considered these things, behold, an angel of the Lord appeared to him in a dream, saying, "Joseph, son of David, do not fear to take Mary as your wife, for that which is conceived in her is from the Holy Spirit."

431. Isaiah 7:14 Therefore the Lord himself will give you a sign. Behold, the virgin shall conceive and bear a son, and shall call his name Immanuel.

Note: The Athanasian Creed (*LSB* 320) speaks of the incarnation: "He is God, begotten from the substance of the Father before all ages; and He is man, born from the substance of his mother in this age…Although He is God and man, He is not two, but one Christ…not by the conversion of the divinity into flesh, but by the assumption of the humanity into God."

140. What can we say about Jesus as a result of the incarnation?

The Son of God (the creator of the universe) has become our brother in this man named Jesus. And this man Jesus is the very Son of God who created the universe.

432. Hebrews 2:11 For he who sanctifies and those who are sanctified all have one source. That is why he is not ashamed to call them brothers.

141. What does it mean for us *as human creatures* that the Son of God has become our brother?

As our brother,

- *Jesus has a human ancestry;*

    433. Romans 1:3 The Gospel concerns God's Son, "who was descended from David according to the flesh."

    434. 1 Timothy 2:5 For there is one God, and there is one mediator between God and men, the man Christ Jesus.

    Read the genealogy of Christ in **Matthew 1:1-17** and **Luke 3:23-38**.

- *Jesus has a human body and soul.*

    435. Luke 24:39 See my hands and my feet, that it is I myself. Touch me, and see. For a spirit does not have flesh and bones as you see that I have.

    436. Matthew 26:38 Then he said to them, "My soul is very sorrowful, even to death; remain here, and watch with me."

- *Jesus has a human gender;*

    437. Matthew 1:22-23 All this took place to fulfill what the Lord had spoken by the prophet: "Behold, the virgin shall conceive and bear a son, and they shall call his name Immanuel"

    438. Luke 2:21 And at the end of eight days, when he was circumcised, he was called Jesus, the name given by the angel before he was conceived in the womb.

- *Jesus has human feelings and actions.*

    439. Matthew 4:2 And after fasting forty days and forty nights, he was hungry.

    440. John 11:35 Jesus wept.

    441. John 19:28 Jesus, knowing that all was now finished, said (to fulfill the Scripture), "I thirst."

    442. Hebrews 4:14-16 Since then we have a great high priest who has passed through the heavens, Jesus, the Son of God, let us hold fast our confession. For we do not have a high priest who is unable to sympathize with our weaknesses, but one who in every respect has been tempted as we are, yet without sin. Let us then with confidence draw near to the throne of grace, that we may receive mercy and find grace to help in time of need.

    Read about how Jesus was born (**Luke 2**); slept (**Mark 4:38**); suffered and died (**Matthew 26-27**).

142. What does it mean for us *as sinners* that the Son of God has become our brother?

As our brother,

- *Jesus fulfilled our obligation to keep the Law (His active obedience);*

    443. Romans 5:19 For as by the one man's [Adam] disobedience the many were made sinners, so by the one man's [Jesus] obedience the many will be made righteous.

    444. Galatians 4:4-7 But when the fullness of time had come, God sent forth his Son, born of woman, born under the law, to redeem those who were under the law, so that we might receive adoption as sons. And because you are sons, God has sent the Spirit of his Son into our hearts, crying, "Abba! Father!" So you are no longer a slave, but a son, and if a son, then an heir through God.

- *Jesus suffered and died to pay the penalty of our sin (His passive obedience).*

    445. Mark 10:45 For even the Son of Man came not to be served but to serve, and to give his life as a ransom for many."

    446. Galatians 3:13 Christ redeemed us from the curse of the law by becoming a curse for us-for it is written, "Cursed is everyone who is hanged on a tree."

447. 1 Peter 1:18-19 Knowing that you were ransomed from the futile ways inherited from your forefathers, not with perishable things such as silver or gold, but with the precious blood of Christ, like that of a lamb without blemish or spot.

448. Hebrews 2:14 Since therefore the children share in flesh and blood, he himself likewise partook of the same things, that through death he might destroy the one who has the power of death, that is, the devil.

Read **Romans 3:22-24** and **Colossians 1:22**.

- *Jesus overcame death thus becoming the firstfruits of our resurrection.*

    449. 1 Corinthians 15:57 But thanks be to God, who gives us the victory through our Lord Jesus Christ.

    450. 2 Timothy 1:10 It is Christ Jesus "who abolished death and brought life and immortality to light through the gospel."

    451. Hebrews 2:14 Since therefore the children share in flesh and blood, he himself likewise partook of the same things, that through death he might destroy the one who has the power of death, that is, the devil.

143. What does it mean for us that the man Jesus, our brother, is also the very Son of God who created the universe?

Because Jesus, our brother is the very Son of God,

- *He is always with us;*

    452. Matthew 28:20 And behold, I am with you always, to the end of the age.

Read about the miraculous catch of fish (**Luke 5:4-6**); Jesus knowing the character of Nathaniel (**John 1:48**); Jesus and a Samaritan woman (**John 4:17-28**). Also, **Matthew 21:1-7; 26:20-25** and **Luke 18:31-33; 22:8-13**.

- *He intercedes for us before the Father;*

    453. 1 Timothy 2:5-6 For there is one God, and there is one mediator between God and men, the man Christ Jesus, who gave himself as a ransom for all, which is the testimony given at the proper time.

- *He rules over creation and the Church;*

    454. Matthew 28:18 And Jesus came and said to them, "All authority in heaven and on earth has been given to me."

    455. Hebrews 2:8-9 Now in putting everything in subjection to him, he left nothing outside his control. At present, we do not yet see everything in subjection to him. But we see him who for a little while was made lower than the angels, namely Jesus, crowned with glory and honor because of the suffering of death, so that by the grace of God he might taste death for everyone.

    456. Ephesians 4:10 He who descended is the one who also ascended far above all heavens that he might fill all things.

    457. 1 John 4:4 He who is in you is greater than he who is in the world.

Read the temptation narrative in **Matthew 4:1-11** and also about the wedding feast in Cana (**John 2:1-22**); Jesus rebuking the storm (**Luke 8:22-25**); healing a paralytic (**Matthew 9:1-8**); calling Lazarus back to life (**John 11:38-44**); and His resurrection from the dead (**Matthew 28:6-7**).

- *He has the authority to judge and forgive;*

    458. John 5:27 And he has given him authority to execute judgment, because he is the Son of Man.

    459. Matthew 9:6 "That you may know that the Son of Man has authority on earth to forgive sins"—he then said to the paralytic—"Rise, pick up your bed and go home."

    460. Acts 17:31 He has fixed a day on which he will judge the world in righteousness by a man whom he has appointed; and of this he has given assurance to all by raising him from the dead.

- *He is worthy of divine honor and glory;*

    461. John 20:28 Thomas answered him, "My Lord and my God!"

    462. John 5: 21-23 For as the Father raises the dead and gives them life, so also the Son gives life to whom he will. The Father judges no one, but has given all judgment to the Son, that all may honor the Son, just as they honor the Father. Whoever does not honor the Son does not honor the Father who sent him.

Read **Hebrews 1:6; Revelation 5:12-13; Romans 9:5;** and **1 John 5:20.**

- *He loves us with an everlasting love.*

    463. John 17: 25-26 O righteous Father, even though the world does not know you, I know you, and these know that you have sent me. I made known to them your name, and I will continue to make it known, that the love with which you have loved me may be in them, and I in them.

Hymn (*LSB* 954, stanza 1) and Prayer: *Lord Jesus Christ, begotten of the Father from eternity and also true man born of the virgin Mary, I give You thanks that You have become my brother. Give me the confidence and boldness to confess You as my Lord and so live and die within Your loving care; for You live and reign with the Father and the Holy Spirit, one God now and forever. Amen.*

The Second Article (Part 2)

And [I believe] in Jesus Christ, His only Son, our Lord, who was conceived by the Holy Spirit, born of the virgin Mary, suffered under Pontius Pilate, was crucified, died and was buried. He descended into hell. The third day He rose again from the dead. He ascended into heaven and sits at the right hand of God the Father Almighty. From thence He will come to judge the living and the dead.

What does this mean?

I believe that Jesus Christ, true God, begotten of the Father from eternity, and also true man born of the Virgin Mary, is my Lord,

who has redeemed me, a lost and condemned person, purchased and won me from all sins, from death, and from the power of the devil; not with gold or silver, but with His holy, precious blood and with His innocent suffering and death,

that I may be His own and live under Him in His kingdom and serve Him in everlasting righteousness, innocence, and blessedness, just as He is risen from the dead, lives and reigns to all eternity.

This is most certainly true.

The Central Thought

Human history has been constantly characterized by hatred and violence.

Despite all our scientific and technological progress, why have we not overcome these deep-seated problems that plague our human race?

Read **Genesis 3**. Identify the reasons for and the results of Adam and Eve's downfall.

✝ *As Christians, we confess that Jesus became our Lord by dying on the cross in order to rescue us from our captivity to sin, death, and the devil.*

What does it say about Jesus that He willingly gave His life for me? What does it say about me?

A Closer Reading of the *Small Catechism*

144. What are we saying when we confess that Jesus has redeemed us?

   We acknowledge that Jesus has rescued and reclaimed us from powers we cannot overcome.

   464. Colossians 1:13-14 He has delivered us from the domain of darkness and transferred us into the kingdom of his beloved Son in whom we have redemption, the forgiveness of sins.

   465. Titus 2:14 [Jesus] gave himself for us to redeem us from all lawlessness and to purify for himself a people for his own possession who are zealous for good works.

   466. Hebrews 2:14-15 Since therefore the children share in flesh and blood now, he himself likewise partook of the same things, so that through death he might destroy the one who has the power of death, that is, the devil, and deliver all those who through fear of death were subject to lifelong slavery.

467. 1 John 3:8 Whoever makes a practice of sinning is of the devil, for the devil has been sinning from the beginning. The reason the Son of God appeared was to destroy the works of the devil.

Read **1 Peter 1:18-21**.

145. Why did we need to be rescued? What was our situation?

- *The entire human race (including us) lived under the tyranny of sin, death, and the devil.*

  468. John 8:34-36 Jesus answered them, "Truly, truly, I say to you, everyone who practices sin is a slave to sin. The slave does not remain in the house forever; the son remains forever. So if the Son sets you free, you will be free indeed."

  469. Psalm 51:5 Behold, I was brought forth in iniquity, and in sin did my mother conceive me.

  470. 1 John 5:19 The whole world lies in the power of the evil one.

  471. Galatians 4:8 Formerly, when you did not know God, you were enslaved to those that by nature are not gods.

Read **Genesis 4:1-12**; **Genesis 6:5-12**; **John 8**; and **Romans 3:9-18**.

- *The entire human race (including us) stood under the judgment of God.*

  472. Ephesians 2:1 You were dead in the trespasses and sins.

  473. Romans 1:18 For the wrath of God is revealed from heaven against all ungodliness and unrighteousness of men, who by their unrighteousness suppress the truth.

  474. Ephesians 2:3 We all once lived in the passions of our flesh, carrying out the desires of the body and the mind, and were by nature children of wrath, like the rest of mankind.

146. How did we come to be lost and condemned?

The devil led Adam and Eve into rebellion by sowing in them the seeds of doubt with the desire to become like God. We all have inherited their addiction to sin and the resulting punishment.

  475. Romans 5:12 Therefore, just as sin came into the world through one man, and death through sin, and so death spread to all men because all sinned.

  476. Genesis 8:21 And when the LORD smelled the pleasing aroma, the LORD said in his heart, "I will never again curse the ground because of man, for the intention of man's heart is evil from his youth."

Read **Genesis 3**. Note how doubt about God's Word leads to the denial of God's Word, which leads to disbelief, which leads to disobedience, which resulted in death.

147. Why did God send His Son to rescue us?

As our loving creator, He had compassion on us.

  477. Genesis 3:15 I will put enmity between you [Satan] and the woman, and between your offspring and her offspring; he shall bruise your head, and you shall bruise his heel.

  478. John 3:16 For God so loved the world, that he gave his only Son, that whoever believes in him should not perish but have eternal life.

  479. Ephesians 2:8-9 For by grace you have been saved through faith. And this is not your own doing; it is the gift of God, not a result of works, so that no one may boast.

  480. 1 John 4:10 In this is love, not that we have loved God but that he loved us and sent his Son to be the propitiation for our sins.

148. How did Jesus rescue me from sin?

- *By His death on the cross, He paid the entire penalty of my sin and guilt.*

  481. Mark 10:45 For even the Son of Man came not to be served but to serve, and to give his life as a ransom for many.

482. Romans 5:19 For as by the one man's disobedience the many were made sinners, so by the one man's obedience the many will be made righteous.

483. 2 Corinthians 5:21 For our sake he made him to be sin who knew no sin, so that in him we might become the righteousness of God.

484. Galatians 3:13 Christ redeemed us from the curse of the law by becoming a curse for us—for it is written, "Cursed is everyone who is hanged on a tree."

485. 1 Peter 1:18-19 You were ransomed from the futile ways inherited from your forefathers, not with perishable things such as silver or gold, but with the precious blood of Christ, like that of a lamb without blemish or spot.

486. Romans 4:25 [Jesus] was delivered up for our trespasses and raised for our justification.

- *By His death on the cross, He fully endured and appeased (propitiated) the wrath of God toward us, thereby reconciling us to God.*

    487. Romans 3:25 God put forward [Jesus] as a propitiation by his blood, to be received by faith. This was to show God's righteousness, because in his divine forbearance he had passed over former sins.

    488. Hebrews 2:17 Therefore he had to be made like his brothers in every respect, so that he might become a merciful and faithful high priest in the service of God, to make propitiation for the sins of the people.

    489. 1 John 2:2 He is the propitiation for our sins, and not for ours only but also for the sins of the whole world.

    490. Ephesians 1:7 In him we have redemption through his blood, the forgiveness of our trespasses, according to the riches of his grace.

    491. 2 Corinthians 5:19 That is, in Christ God was reconciling the world to himself, not counting their trespasses against them, and entrusting to us the message of reconciliation.

    492. Romans 5:10 For if while we were enemies we were reconciled to God by the death of his Son, much more, now that we are reconciled, shall we be saved by his life.

- *By His death on the cross, He destroyed the power of sin to enslave me.*

    493. John 8:34-36 Jesus answered them: Truly, truly, I say to you, everyone who practices sin is a slave to sin. The slave does not remain in the house forever; the son remains forever. So if the Son sets you free, you will be free indeed."

    494. 1 Peter 2:24 He himself bore our sins in his body on the tree, that we might die to sin and live to righteousness. By his wounds you have been healed.

    495. Romans 6:4 We were buried therefore with him by baptism into death, in order that, just as Christ was raised from the dead by the glory of the Father, we too might walk in newness of life.

    496. Romans 6:8-9 Now if we have died with Christ, we believe that we will also live with him. We know that Christ, being raised from the dead, will never die again; death no longer has dominion over him.

149. How did Jesus rescue me from the devil?

    He defeated Satan by obeying His Father's will throughout His earthly life, even going all the way to the cross.

    497. Philippians 2:8 Being found in human form, he humbled himself by becoming obedient to the point of death, even death on a cross.

    498. Hebrews 12:2 [Look] to Jesus, the founder and perfecter of our faith, who for the joy that was set before him endured the cross, despising the shame, and is seated at the right hand of the throne of God.

499. Genesis 3:15 I will put enmity between you and the woman, and between your offspring and her offspring; he shall bruise your head, and you shall bruise his heel.

500. 1 John 3:8 The reason the Son of God appeared was to destroy the works of the devil.

Read **Matthew 4:1-11** about Jesus' temptation.

Read also: **Luke 8:26-39; Romans 8:31-24; Philippians 2:6-11; Colossians 2:15; Hebrews 2:14; James 4:7,** and **1 Peter 5:8-9**.

150. How did Jesus rescue me from death?

He put death to death by His own death and resurrection.

501. Hebrews 2:14-15 Since therefore the children share in flesh and blood, he himself likewise partook of the same things, that through death he might destroy the one who has the power of death, that is, the devil, and deliver all those who through fear of death were subject to lifelong slavery.

502. 1 Peter 1:3-5 Blessed be the God and Father of our Lord Jesus Christ! According to his great mercy, he has caused us to be born again to a living hope through the resurrection of Jesus Christ from the dead, to an inheritance that is imperishable, undefiled, and unfading, kept in heaven for you, who by God's power are being guarded through faith for a salvation ready to be revealed in the last time.

503. 1 Corinthians 15:54-57 When the perishable puts on the imperishable, and the mortal puts on immortality, then shall come to pass the saying that is written: "Death is swallowed up in victory." "O death, where is your victory? O death, where is your sting?" The sting of death is sin, and the power of sin is the law. But thanks be to God, who gives us the victory through our Lord Jesus Christ.

504. 2 Timothy 1:10 Our Savior Jesus "abolished death and brought life and immortality to light through the gospel."

Connections and Applications

151. Why did it not always seem that Jesus possessed divine majesty as the Son of God during His earthly life?

As man, Christ did not always or fully use or manifest His divine powers and majesty. This began with the lowly manner of His incarnation, continued in the manner of His birth and life, and culminated with His death and burial. We call this His state of humiliation.

505. Philippians 2:5-8 Have this mind among yourselves, which is yours in Christ Jesus, who, though he was in the form of God, did not count equality with God a thing to be grasped, but emptied himself, by taking the form of a servant, being born in the likeness of men. And being found in human form, he humbled himself by becoming obedient to the point of death, even death on a cross.

506. 2 Corinthians 8:9 For you know the grace of our Lord Jesus Christ, that though he was rich, yet for your sake he became poor, so that you by his poverty might become rich.

152. What does this state of humiliation mean for our understanding of Jesus' life?

It highlights the full and deep sense in which Jesus, as our brother, became like us with very real human feelings and struggles. For example:

- *as our brother, Jesus was born in humble circumstances;*

  507. Luke 2:7 And she gave birth to her firstborn son and wrapped him in swaddling cloths and laid him in a manger, because there was no place for them in the inn.

- *as our brother, Jesus chose not to know everything;*

  508. Matthew 24:36 But concerning that day and hour no one knows, not even the angels of heaven, nor the Son, but the Father only.

- *as our brother, Jesus was faced with real human dilemmas;*

Read **John 2:1-11**. Consider how Jesus was confronted with a true human dilemma. His time had not come to reveal His glory, yet He was also subject to His mother. What will He do? He had to make a real life decision and He decided to give in to His mother.

- as our brother, Jesus experienced sadness and loss;

Read **John 11:38-44**. Consider Jesus' very real human reaction when He learned about the death of His friend Lazarus.

- as our brother, Jesus struggled to carry out God's will;

Read **Matthew 4:1-11**. Consider how Jesus struggled to resist the Satan's temptations.

Read **Matthew 26:36-46**. Consider how in the Garden of Gethsemane Jesus was agonized between His desire to stay alive and His desire to carry out God's will that He die.

- as our brother, Jesus suffered a shameful and agonizing death;

Read **John 19:28-42**. Consider the various details that show the type of suffering and death Jesus experienced.

Read also **Luke 2:7; Matthew 2:13; Luke 4:29; John 8:50; Matthew 8:20; Isaiah 53:3; John 8:40; John 19:1-3; John 19:16-18; Matthew 27:46;** and **Mark 15:1-20**.

- *as our brother, Jesus was a pauper buried in a borrowed tomb.*

   509. Luke 23:50-53 Now there was a man named Joseph, from the Jewish town of Arimathea. He was a member of the council, a good and righteous man, who had not consented to their decision and action; and he was looking for the kingdom of God. This man went to Pilate and asked for the body of Jesus. Then he took it down and wrapped it in a linen shroud and laid him in a tomb cut in stone, where no one had ever yet been laid.

153. What comfort does the state of humiliation bring us?

Jesus promises us "that not only His mere divinity would be with them (which to us poor sinners is like a consuming fire on dry stubble). But Christ promised that He—He, the man who has spoken with them, who has experienced all tribulations in His received human nature, and who can therefore have sympathy with us, as with men and His brethren—He will be with us in our troubles also according to the nature by which He is our brother and we are flesh of His flesh" (FC SD VIII, 87).

154. When does Jesus, as our brother, manifest the divine majesty that is His as the Son of God?

- *Jesus made His divine power and majesty visible at times during His earthly life with miracles, and especially at the Transfiguration.*

   510. John 2:11 This, the first of his signs, Jesus did at Cana in Galilee, and manifested his glory.

   511. Matthew 28:18 And Jesus came and said to them, "All authority in heaven and on earth has been given to me."

   512. Luke 6:8 But he knew their thoughts, and he said to the man with the withered hand, "Come and stand here." And he rose and stood there.

   513. Matthew 17:1-2 And after six days Jesus took with him Peter and James, and John his brother, and led them up a high mountain by themselves. And he was transfigured before them, and his face shone like the sun, and his clothes became white as light.

- *Jesus manifests His divine power and majesty fully and constantly in His victorious descent into hell, His resurrection from the dead, His ascension into heaven, His present reign at the right hand of God, and His future return for judgment. We call this His state of exaltation.*

   514. Philippians 2:9-11 Therefore God has highly exalted him and bestowed on him the name that is above every name, so that at the name of Jesus every knee should bow, in heaven and on earth and under the earth, and every tongue confess that Jesus Christ is Lord, to the glory of God the Father.

155. What does the state of exaltation mean for our understanding of who Jesus is and what He has done?

It highlights the full and deep sense in which Jesus, as our brother, has been exalted by God the Father over sin, death, and the devil so that our future in Him is secure. For example, as our brother

- *Jesus descended into hell and declared victory over Satan for us;*

  515. 1 Peter 3:18-20 For Christ also suffered once for sins, the righteous for the unrighteous, that he might bring us to God, being put to death in the flesh but made alive in the spirit, in which he went and proclaimed to the spirits in prison, because they formerly did not obey, when God's patience waited in the days of Noah, while the ark was being prepared, in which a few, that is, eight persons, were brought safely through water.

  516. Colossians 2:15 He disarmed the rulers and authorities and put them to open shame, by triumphing over them in him.

- *Jesus rose triumphantly over death and the grave for us;*

  517. Mark 16:6 And he said to them, "Do not be alarmed. You seek Jesus of Nazareth, who was crucified. He has risen; he is not here. See the place where they laid him."

  518. Luke 24:6 He is not here, but has risen. Remember how he told you, while he was still in Galilee.

- *Jesus ascended to the right hand of God and now rules for our benefit;*

  519. Luke 24:50-51 Then he led them out as far as Bethany, and lifting up his hands he blessed them. While he blessed them, he parted from them and was carried up into heaven.

  520. Hebrews 1:3 He is the radiance of the glory of God and the exact imprint of his nature, and he upholds the universe by the word of his power. After making purification for sins, he sat down at the right hand of the Majesty on high.

  521. Ephesians 4:9-10 (In saying, "He ascended," what does it mean but that he had also descended into the lower regions, the earth? He who descended is the one who also ascended far above all the heavens, that he might fill all things.)

  522. Hebrews 8:1 Now the point in what we are saying is this: we have such a high priest, one who is seated at the right hand of the throne of the Majesty in heaven.

- *Jesus will return in glory for judgment on the last day and bring us into His new creation.*

  523. Acts 1:11 [The angel] said, "Men of Galilee, why do you stand looking into heaven? This Jesus, who was taken up from you into heaven, will come in the same way as you saw him go into heaven."

  524. Hebrews 9:28 So Christ, having been offered once to bear the sins of many, will appear a second time, not to deal with sin but to save those who are eagerly waiting for him.

  525. Acts 17:31 Because he has fixed a day on which he will judge the world in righteousness by a man whom he has appointed; and of this he has given assurance to all by raising him from the dead.

156. What comfort does the state of exaltation bring us?

"There He forever reigns and has dominion over all creatures. He sanctifies those who believe in Him, by sending the Holy Spirit into their hearts to rule, comfort, and make them alive. He defends them against the devil and the power of sin" (AC III, 4-5; see also FC SD VIII, 27).

> Hymn (*LSB* 556, stanzas 1-5) and Prayer: *Lord Jesus Christ, my brother and Savior, I praise You for rescuing me from sin, death, and the power of the devil by Your innocent suffering and death. Thank You for Your great love and Your undeserved sacrifice that won me, a lost and condemned creature, to be Your own. Give me faith always to trust Your reconciling work and so live in the knowledge of Your salvation; for You live and reign with the Father and the Holy Spirit one God now and forever. Amen.*

The Second Article (Part 3)

And [I believe] in Jesus Christ, His only Son, our Lord, who was conceived by the Holy Spirit, born of the virgin Mary, suffered under Pontius Pilate, was crucified, died and was buried. He descended into hell. The third day He rose again from the dead. He ascended into heaven and sits at the right hand of God the Father Almighty. From thence He will come to judge the living and the dead.

What does this mean?

I believe that Jesus Christ, true God, begotten of the Father from eternity, and also true man born of the Virgin Mary, is my Lord,

who has redeemed me, a lost and condemned person, purchased and won me from all sins, from death, and from the power of the devil; not with gold or silver, but with His holy, precious blood and with His innocent suffering and death,

that I may be His own and live under Him in His kingdom and serve Him in everlasting righteousness, innocence, and blessedness, just as He is risen from the dead, lives and reigns to all eternity.

This is most certainly true.

The Central Thought

Our lives are meaningless without some sense of purpose.

What do people live for today?

Read **Matthew 4:18–22**. How did Jesus give the disciples the defining purpose for their lives?

✝ *As Christians, we confess that "Our salvation and all our happiness rests" on Jesus our Lord (LC II, 33). He set us free so we may be governed "by His righteousness, wisdom, power, life, and blessedness" (LC II, 30).*

How does confessing Jesus as my Lord give my life direction and purpose?

A Closer Reading of the *Small Catechism*

157. For what purpose has Christ freed me from sin, death, and the devil?

Jesus did all this to be my Lord, in other words, so that I might live with Him and for Him in peace and joy, now and forever.

> **526. 2 Corinthians 5:15** He died for all, that those who live might no longer live for themselves but for him who for their sake died and was raised.

> **527. Jude 24–25** Now to him who is able to keep you from stumbling and to present you blameless before the presence of his glory with great joy, to the only God, our Savior, through Jesus Christ our Lord, be glory, majesty, dominion, and authority, before all time and now and forever. Amen.

> **528. Revelation 5:9** And they sang a new song, saying, "Worthy are you to take the scroll and to open its seals, for you were slain, and by your blood you ransomed people for God from every tribe and language and people and nation."

158. What does it mean to confess that I belong to Christ?

I am united with Him by faith so that He is mine and I am His.

> **529. Galatians 2:20** I have been crucified with Christ. It is no longer I who live, but Christ who lives in me. And the life I now live in the flesh I live by faith in the Son of God, who loved me and gave himself for me.
>
> **530. Romans 14:7-9** For none of us lives to himself, and none of us dies to himself. For if we live, we live to the Lord, and if we die, we die to the Lord. So then, whether we live or whether we die, we are the Lord's. For to this end Christ died and lived again, that he might be Lord both of the dead and of the living.
>
> **531. Philippians 3:12** Not that I have already obtained this or am already perfect, but I press on to make it my own, because Christ Jesus has made me his own.
>
> **532. 1 Peter 2:9** But you are a chosen race, a royal priesthood, a holy nation, a people for his own possession, that you may proclaim the excellencies of him who called you out of darkness into his marvelous light.
>
> **533. Titus 2:14** [Christ] gave himself for us to redeem us from all lawlessness and to purify for himself a people for his own possession who are zealous for good works.

159. What does it mean to confess that I live under Him in His kingdom?

- *As our Lord, Jesus graciously rules to defend me, protect me, and give me rest.*

> **534. Psalm 24:8** Who is this King of glory? The LORD, strong and mighty, the LORD, mighty in battle!
>
> **535. Psalm 84:3** Even the sparrow finds a home, and the swallow a nest for herself, where she may lay her young, at your altars, O LORD of hosts, my King and my God.
>
> **536. Matthew 11:28** Come to me, all who labor and are heavy laden, and I will give you rest.
>
> **537. John 14:27** Peace I leave with you; my peace I give to you. Not as the world gives do I give to you. Let not your hearts be troubled, neither let them be afraid.

Read **Psalm 23** about the Lord who rules as a kind shepherd.

- *As our Lord, Jesus sends the Holy Spirit to be with me, to teach me, and to sanctify me.*

> **538. Mark 1:14-15** Jesus came into Galilee, proclaiming the gospel of God, and saying, "The time is fulfilled, and the kingdom of God is at hand; repent and believe in the gospel."
>
> **539. John 14:16-17** And I will ask the Father, and he will give you another Helper, to be with you forever, even the Spirit of truth, whom the world cannot receive, because it neither sees him nor knows him. You know him, for he dwells with you and will be in you.
>
> **540. John 14:26** But the Helper, the Holy Spirit, whom the Father will send in my name, he will teach you all things and bring to your remembrance all that I have said to you.
>
> **541. John 16:13** When the Spirit of truth comes, he will guide you into all the truth, for he will not speak on his own authority, but whatever he hears he will speak, and he will declare to you the things that are to come.

160. What does it mean that we will serve Him in everlasting righteousness, innocence, and blessedness?

We serve Jesus now as those who belong to Him and live under Him in His kingdom. At the same time, we also look forward to the day when sin, death, and the devil will no longer hinder us from serving Him with complete devotion in peace and joy forever.

> **542. Colossians 2:6** Therefore, as you received Christ Jesus the Lord, so walk in him.
>
> **543. Philippians 1:6** He who began a good work in you will bring it to completion on the day of Christ.
>
> **544. Romans 14:17** For the kingdom of God is not a matter of eating and drinking but of righteousness and peace and joy in the Holy Spirit.

545. Romans 16:20 The God of peace will soon crush Satan under your feet. The grace of our Lord Jesus Christ be with you.

546. Revelation 21:4 He will wipe away every tear from their eyes and death will be no more, neither will there be crying and pain anymore for the former things have passed away.

See **Luke 1:69-75; Matthew 25:31-46**.

161. What is the basis for my confession and confidence that I will live forever in His eternal kingdom?

The resurrection of Christ is the basis for everything that we confess in this article.

547. 1 Corinthians 15:3-5 For I delivered to you as of first importance what I also received: that Christ died for our sins in accordance with the Scriptures, that he was buried, that he was raised on the third day in accordance with the Scriptures, and that he appeared to Cephas, then to the twelve.

548. 1 Corinthians 15:17-20 And if Christ has not been raised, your faith is futile and you are still in your sins. Then those also who have fallen asleep in Christ have perished. If in Christ we have hope in this life only, we are of all people most to be pitied. But in fact Christ has been raised from the dead, the firstfruits of those who have fallen asleep.

549. Colossians 3:1-4 If then you have been raised with Christ, seek the things that are above, where Christ is, seated at the right hand of God. Set your minds on things that are above, not on things that are on earth. For you have died, and your life is hidden with Christ in God. When Christ who is your life appears, then you also will appear with him in glory.

550. Acts 1:3 He presented himself alive to them after his suffering by many proofs, appearing to them during forty days and speaking about the kingdom of God.

Note: The evidence for Jesus' resurrection is well attested by numerous eye-witnesses. The four Gospels all attest to Jesus' bodily resurrection. John and Peter both emphasize the role of the apostles as eye-witnesses of the risen Lord (**Acts 1:3; 2:32; 1 John 1:1-4**). Paul refers to over 500 witnesses to the resurrection of Jesus (**1 Corinthians 15:5-9**). The New Testament term for witness came to mean martyr—since many of the eye-witnesses gave their lives for their testimony to Jesus' resurrection.

Connections and Applications

162. What does it mean that our Lord Jesus is called the Christ?

In the Old Testament, God set certain people apart as prophets, priests, and kings by anointing them with oil. The title Christ or Messiah means Anointed One. In the New Testament, Jesus was anointed with the Holy Spirit to be our Prophet, Priest, and King.

Note: Other titles for the Son include: Redeemer (**Isaiah 59:20**); Immanuel (**Matthew 1:23**); Son of the living God (**Matthew 16:16**); Son of Man (**Matthew 25:31**); the Word (**John 1:14**); Lord and God (**John 20:28**).

163. What does it mean for us to speak of Jesus as our prophet?

As our prophet, Jesus proclaims the Word of God to us.

551. Luke 4:18-19 The Spirit of the Lord is upon me, because he has anointed me to proclaim good news to the poor. He has sent me to proclaim liberty to the captives and recovering of sight to the blind, to set at liberty those who are oppressed, to proclaim the year of the Lord's favor.

552. Acts 10:38 God anointed Jesus of Nazareth with the Holy Spirit and with power. He went about doing good and healing all who were oppressed by the devil, for God was with him.

553. Matthew 17:5 He was still speaking when, behold, a bright cloud overshadowed them, and a voice from the cloud said, "This is my beloved Son, with whom I am well pleased; listen to him."

554. Hebrews 1:1-2 Long ago, at many times and in many ways, God spoke to our fathers by the prophets, but in these last days he has spoken to us by his Son.

Read **Deuteronomy 18:15; John 1:17-18; John 6:68; Mark 16:15; Luke 10:16; 2 Corinthians 5:20; Mark 1:38;** and **John 3:34.**

164. What does it mean for us to speak of Jesus as our priest?

As our priest, Jesus offered Himself as the sacrifice for our sin and still intercedes with the Father on our behalf.

> **555. Hebrews 7:26-27** For it was indeed fitting that we should have such a high priest, holy, innocent, unstained, separated from sinners, and exalted above the heavens. He has no need, like those high priests, to offer sacrifices daily, first for his own sins and then for those of the people, since he did this once for all when he offered up himself.

> **556. 1 John 2:1-2** My little children, I am writing these things to you so that you may not sin. But if anyone does sin, we have an advocate with the Father, Jesus Christ the righteous. He is the propitiation for our sins, and not for ours only but also for the sins of the whole world.

> **557. Romans 8:34** Who is to condemn? Christ Jesus is the one who died—more than that, who was raised—who is at the right hand of God, who indeed is interceding for us.

165. What does it mean for us to speak of Jesus as our king?

As our king, Jesus rules over all creation, especially for the good of His Church.

> **558. Colossians 1:17-18** And he is before all things, and in him all things hold together. And he is the head of the body, the church. He is the beginning, the firstborn from the dead, that in everything he might be preeminent.

> **559. Hebrews 1:3-4** He is the radiance of the glory of God and the exact imprint of his nature, and he upholds the universe by the word of his power. After making purification for sins, he sat down at the right hand of the Majesty on high, having become as much superior to angels as the name he has inherited is more excellent than theirs.

> **560. John 18:36** Jesus answered, "My kingdom is not of this world. If my kingdom were of this world, my servants would have been fighting, that I might not be delivered over to the Jews. But my kingdom is not from the world."

> **561. Ephesians 1:22-23** [When God raised Christ Jesus and seated him at his right hand,] he put all things under his feet and gave him as head over all things to the church, which is his body, the fullness of him who fills all in all.

> **562. 2 Timothy 4:18** The Lord will rescue me from every evil deed and bring me safely into his heavenly kingdom. To him be the glory forever and ever. Amen.

Read **Matthew 28:18; Psalm 45:7; John 3:34;** and **Acts 10:38.**

Hymn (*LSB 556*, stanzas 6-10) and Prayer: *King of Glory, by Your mercy and compassion, You gave Yourself over to death on the cross to obtain everlasting righteousness, innocence, and blessedness for me and all believers. By Your Spirit keep me firm in this faith that I might always live under You in Your Kingdom and serve You in joy and peace even as You have been raised from the dead and live and reign to all eternity. Amen.*

The Third Article (Part 1)

I believe in the Holy Spirit, the holy Christian Church, the communion of saints, the forgiveness of sins, the resurrection of the body, and the life everlasting.

What does this mean?

I believe that I cannot by my own reason or strength believe in Jesus my Lord or come to Him; but the Holy Spirit has called me by the Gospel, enlightened me with His gifts, sanctified and kept me in the true faith.

In the same way He calls, gathers, enlightens, and sanctifies the whole Christian church on earth, and keeps it with Jesus Christ in the one true faith. In this Christian church He daily and richly forgives all my sins and the sins of all believers.

On the Last Day He will raise me and all the dead, and give eternal life to me and all believers in Christ.

This is most certainly true.

The Central Thought

"I believe… that I cannot believe." As fallen people, we are unable to find God on our own let alone choose to entrust our lives to Him.

Which is harder to accept—that I choose to believe or that I am brought to saving faith apart from my own efforts?

Read **Acts 9:1-22** about Paul's conversion. What role did Paul play in his conversion?

✝ *As Christians, we confess that the Holy Spirit has made us new creatures by bringing us to saving faith in Jesus Christ. Such faith is "granted to our hearts by the Holy Spirit through the preaching of the Gospel" (LC II, 38).*

Say a brief prayer of thanks to the Holy Spirit for the gift of faith.

A Closer Reading of the *Small Catechism*

166. How was I brought under the gracious lordship of Jesus?

The Holy Spirit brought me to Jesus by bringing the promise of the Gospel to me and by giving me faith in Christ through that Gospel.

563. John 6:65 And he said, "This is why I told you that no one can come to me unless it is granted him by the Father."

564. Acts 16:14 One who heard us was a woman named Lydia, from the city of Thyatira, a seller of purple goods, who was a worshiper of God. The Lord opened her heart to pay attention to what was said by Paul.

565. Romans 10:20 Then Isaiah is so bold as to say, "I have been found by those who did not seek me; I have shown myself to those who did not ask for me."

566. Ephesians 2:8-9 For by grace you have been saved through faith. And this is not your own doing; it is the gift of God, not a result of works, so that no one may boast.

567. 1 Corinthians 12:3 Therefore I want you to understand that no one speaking in the Spirit of God ever says "Jesus is accursed!" and no one can say "Jesus is Lord" except in the Holy Spirit.

167. Why can I not come to faith in Jesus by my own own reason or strength?

- *Apart from the Holy Spirit, I am spiritually blind and dead and thus cannot trust in Christ.*

    568. 1 Corinthians 2:14 The natural person does not accept the things of the Spirit of God, for they are folly to him, and he is not able to understand them because they are spiritually discerned.

    569. Ephesians 2:1 And you were dead in the trespasses and sins.

    570. 1 Corinthians 12:3 Therefore I want you to understand that no one speaking in the Spirit of God ever says "Jesus is accursed!" and no one can say "Jesus is Lord" except in the Holy Spirit.

- *Apart from the Holy Spirit, I actively resist the Gospel's call to faith in Christ.*

    571. Jeremiah 17:9 The heart is deceitful above all things, and desperately sick; who can understand it?

    572. Acts 7:51 You stiff-necked people, uncircumcised in heart and ears, you always resist the Holy Spirit. As your fathers did, so do you.

    573. Romans 8:7 For the mind that is set on the flesh is hostile to God, for it does not submit to God's law; indeed, it cannot.

    574. Galatians 5:17 For the desires of the flesh are against the Spirit, and the desires of the Spirit are against the flesh, for these are opposed to each other, to keep you from doing the things you want to do.

    575. Romans 7:23 I see in my members another law waging war against the law of my mind and making me captive to the law of sin that dwells in my members.

168. What does it mean that the Holy Spirit has called me by the Gospel?

Through the Gospel, the Spirit both invites and enables me to believe by promising me a new life on the basis of Christ's death and resurrection.

    576. 2 Thessalonians 2:14 To this he called you through our gospel, so that you may obtain the glory of our Lord Jesus Christ.

    577. John 17:20 I do not ask for these only, but also for those who will believe in me through their word.

    578. Romans 1:16 For I am not ashamed of the gospel, for it is the power of God for salvation to everyone who believes.

    579. Romans 10:17 So faith comes from hearing, and hearing through the word of Christ.

    580. 1 Corinthians 4:15 For though you have countless guides in Christ, you do not have many fathers. For I became your father in Christ Jesus through the gospel.

    581. 1 Peter 1:23 You have been born again, not of perishable seed but of imperishable, through the living and abiding word of God.

    582. Titus 3:5 He saved us, not because of works done by us in righteousness, but according to his own mercy, by the washing of regeneration and renewal of the Holy Spirit.

169. What does it mean that I am enlightened with His gifts?

Christ is made known to me by means of the Spirit's gifts of the Word, Baptism, and the Lord's Supper.

    583. 2 Corinthians 4:6 For God, who said, "Let light shine out of darkness," has shone in our hearts to give the light of the knowledge of the glory of God in the face of Jesus Christ.

584. Colossians 3:1-3 If then you have been raised with Christ, seek the things that are above, where Christ is, seated at the right hand of God. Set your minds on things that are above, not on things that are on earth. For you have died, and your life is hidden with Christ in God.

170. What does it mean to be sanctified by the Spirit?

- *The Spirit first sanctifies me (makes me holy) by bringing me "to the Lord Jesus to receive His gifts" through faith (LC III:13).*

    585. 1 Corinthians 6:11 And such were some of you. But you were washed, you were sanctified, you were justified in the name of the Lord Jesus Christ and by the Spirit of our God.

    586. Hebrews 10:10 And by that will we have been sanctified through the offering of the body of Jesus Christ once for all.

    587. 1 Corinthians 1:2 To the church of God that is in Corinth, to those sanctified in Christ Jesus, called to be saints together with all those who in every place call upon the name of our Lord Jesus Christ, both their Lord and ours.

- *The Holy Spirit then sanctifies me (makes me holy) by strengthening my faith and increasing its fruits within my life. This includes giving me new desires so that I strive to overcome sin and do good works.*

    588. Psalm 51:10 Create in me a clean heart, O God, and renew a right spirit within me.

    589. Romans 8:9 You, however, are not in the flesh but in the Spirit, if in fact the Spirit of God dwells in you. Anyone who does not have the Spirit of Christ does not belong to him.

    590. 2 Corinthians 5:17 Therefore, if anyone is in Christ, he is a new creation. The old has passed away; behold, the new has come.

    591. Galatians 5:22-23 But the fruit of the Spirit is love, joy, peace, patience, kindness, goodness, faithfulness, gentleness, self-control; against such things there is no law.

    592. Ephesians 2:10 For we are his workmanship, created in Christ Jesus for good works, which God prepared beforehand, that we should walk in them.

    593. Titus 2:14 [Jesus] gave himself for us to redeem us from all lawlessness and to purify for himself a people for his own possession who are zealous for good works.

171. What are good works in God's sight?

Our activities and works are good in God's sight when

- *they flow from our faith in Christ as children of God;*

    594. Psalm 103:1 Bless the LORD, O my soul, and all that is within me, bless his holy name!

    595. Hebrews 11:6. And without faith it is impossible to please him, for whoever would draw near to God must believe that he exists and that he rewards those who seek him.

    596. John 15:5 I am the vine; you are the branches. Whoever abides in me and I in him, he it is that bears much fruit, for apart from me you can do nothing.

    597. Galatians 5:13 For you were called to freedom, brothers. Only do not use your freedom as an opportunity for the flesh, but through love serve one another.

- *they are carried out within our callings in accord with the Ten Commandments.*

    598. Exodus 20:9 Six days you shall labor and do all your work.

    599. John 14:15 If you love me, you will keep my commandments.

    600. Colossians 3:17 And whatever you do, in word or deed, do everything in the name of the Lord Jesus, giving thanks to God the Father through him.

601. Matthew 15:9 In vain do they worship me, teaching as doctrines the commandments of men.

602. Ephesians 2:10 For we are his workmanship, created in Christ Jesus for good works, which God prepared beforehand, that we should walk in them.

603. 1 Corinthians 10:31 So, whether you eat or drink, or whatever you do, do all to the glory of God.

Read **Psalm 119** and notice the psalmist's attitude toward God's Law; **Mark 12:41-44** about a widow's offering; **Mark 14:3-9** about expensive perfume poured on Jesus' head; and **Luke 10:38-42,** the story of Mary and Martha.

172. What does it mean to be kept in the true faith?

Through His Word, the Holy Spirit continually directs my faith to God's works of creation and redemption in Christ.

604. John 8:31-32 So Jesus said to the Jews who had believed him, "If you abide in my word, you are truly my disciples, and you will know the truth, and the truth will set you free."

605. 1 Thessalonians 2:13 And we also thank God constantly for this, that when you received the word of God, which you heard from us, you accepted it not as the word of men but as what it really is, the word of God, which is at work in you believers.

606. Philippians 1:6 I am sure of this, that he who began a good work in you will bring it to completion at the day of Jesus Christ.

607. 1 Peter 1:5 [We] who by God's power are being guarded through faith for a salvation ready to be revealed in the last time.

608. 2 Timothy 4:18 The Lord will rescue me from every evil deed and bring me safely into his heavenly kingdom. To him be the glory forever and ever. Amen.

Read **Jude 22-25**.

Connections and Applications

173. Who is the Holy Spirit?

The Holy Spirit is God. He is one of the three persons within the Trinity.

174. Why do we speak of the Holy Spirit as God?

The Bible speaks of the Holy Spirit as the creator of the universe together with the Father and the Son.

609. Genesis 1:2 The earth was without form and void, and darkness was over the face of the deep. And the Spirit of God was hovering over the face of the waters.

610. Psalm 104:30 When you send forth your Spirit, they are created, and you renew the face of the ground.

611. Job 26:13 By His Spirit He adorned the heavens. (NKJV)

175. What is the special role of the Holy Spirit in our salvation?

The Spirit turns people from bondage to sin and brings them to Christ by giving them faith. We call this conversion or regeneration (new birth).

612. Psalm 51:13 Then I will teach transgressors your ways, and sinners will return to you.

613. John 3:5-6 Jesus answered, "Truly, truly, I say to you, unless one is born of water and the Spirit, he cannot enter the kingdom of God. That which is born of the flesh is flesh, and that which is born of the Spirit is spirit."

614. John 15:26 But when the Helper comes, whom I will send to you from the Father, the Spirit of truth, who proceeds from the Father, he will bear witness about me.

615. Acts 26:18 Paul was sent "to open their eyes, so that they may turn from darkness to light and from the power of Satan to God, that they may receive forgiveness of sins and a place among those who are sanctified by faith in me."

176. Does the Holy Spirit want to bring everyone to faith in Jesus?

Yes. The Spirit wants to create faith in everyone and bring them under the gracious lordship of Jesus.

616. Ezekiel 33:11 Say to them, "As I live, declares the Lord GOD, I have no pleasure in the death of the wicked, but that the wicked turn from his way and live; turn back, turn back from your evil ways, for why will you die, O house of Israel?"

617. 1 Timothy 2:4 [God] who desires all people to be saved and to come to the knowledge of the truth.

618. 2 Peter 3:9 The Lord is not slow to fulfill his promise as some count slowness, but is patient toward you, not wishing that any should perish, but that all should reach repentance.

177. Why doesn't everyone who hears the Gospel believe in Jesus as their Lord?

Many reject the Gospel and resist the Holy Spirit.

619. Matthew 23:37 O Jerusalem, Jerusalem, the city that kills the prophets and stones those who are sent to it! How often would I have gathered your children together as a hen gathers her brood under her wings, and you were not willing!

620. Acts 7:51 You stiff-necked people, uncircumcised in heart and ears, you always resist the Holy Spirit. As your fathers did, so do you.

621. Luke 7:30 The Pharisees and the lawyers rejected the purpose of God for themselves, not having been baptized by him.

Read **Matthew 22:1-10** or **Luke 14:16-24** where the guests invited to the feast refuse to come.

178. Do people believe in Jesus because they decide to follow Him of their own free will?

No. All who come to faith do so because the Holy Spirit works faith in them. If some do not have faith it is because they have rejected the Spirit.

622. John 15:16 You did not choose me, but I chose you.

623. 1 Corinthians 12:3 Therefore I want you to understand that no one speaking in the Spirit of God ever says, "Jesus is accursed!" And no one can say, "Jesus is Lord" except by the Holy Spirit.

624. 1 Thessalonians 4:8 Therefore whoever disregards this, disregards not man but God, who gives his Holy Spirit to you.

179. Did God determine in advance that He would not convert some people?

No. While God chose some from eternity to be brought to faith, He did not select or predestine others to be unbelievers. This scriptural teaching about predestination is a mystery that defies human logic and understanding.

625. Ephesians 1:3-6 Blessed be the God and Father of our Lord Jesus Christ, who has blessed us in Christ with every spiritual blessing in the heavenly places, even as he chose us in him before the foundation of the world, that we should be holy and blameless before him. In love he predestined us for adoption as sons through Jesus Christ, according to the purpose of his will, to the praise of his glorious grace, with which he has blessed us in the Beloved.

180. Can we be truly spiritual without the Holy Spirit and the Gospel?

"Spirituality" can have different meanings. For example, some may find benefit in the enjoyment of nature or contemplating life's deeper meanings and refer to that as spirituality. This reflects the truth

that life in the world is more than mere material reality. Such human spirituality, however, does not enable us truly to know God and His grace. That is an impossible task for human contemplation or imagination. "The whole world with all diligence has struggled to figure out what God is, what He has in mind and does" (LC II, 63). Only the Holy Spirit, working through the Word, shows us the incarnate Son and, through Him, the Father. Because God has revealed the truth about Himself in this way, only Christian faith and life is authentic spirituality.

626. John 1:18 No one has ever seen God; the only God, who is at the Father's side, he has made him known.

627. John 3:31-32 He who comes from above is above all. He who is of the earth belongs to the earth and speaks in an earthly way. He who comes from heaven is above all. He bears witness to what he has seen and heard, yet no one receives his testimony.

628. Romans 10:17 So faith comes from hearing, and hearing through the word of Christ.

629. 1 Corinthians 2:9-11 But, as it is written, "What no eye has seen, nor ear heard, nor the heart of man imagined, what God has prepared for those who love him"—these things God has revealed to us through the Spirit. For the Spirit searches everything, even the depths of God. For who knows a person's thoughts except the spirit of that person, which is in him? So also no one comprehends the thoughts of God except the Spirit of God.

Read **1 Corinthians 1:18-25** and **Ephesians 3:14-19.**

Hymn (*LSB* 497) and Prayer: *Holy Spirit, I give You thanks that You have called me to saving faith in my Lord Jesus Christ through His Gospel, for without Your work I could never come to Him. By Your words which are spirit and life, keep me united with my Savior in the true faith, always enlightening me with Your gifts, and sanctifying me in body and soul to live for Christ alone; through my Lord Jesus Christ who lives and reigns with You and the Father forever one God. Amen.*

The Third Article (Part 2)

I believe in the Holy Spirit, the holy Christian church, the communion of saints, the forgiveness of sins, the resurrection of the body, and the life everlasting.

What does this mean?

I believe that I cannot by my own reason or strength believe in Jesus my Lord or come to Him; but the Holy Spirit has called me by the Gospel, enlightened me with His gifts, sanctified and kept me in the true faith.

In the same way He calls, gathers, enlightens, and sanctifies the whole Christian church on earth, and keeps it with Jesus Christ in the one true faith. In this Christian church He daily and richly forgives all my sins and the sins of all believers.

On the Last Day He will raise me and all the dead, and give eternal life to me and all believers in Christ.

This is most certainly true.

The Central Thought

God did not create us to live in isolation from each other.

What kind of a community is the church perceived to be by many people in society?

Read **Acts 2:42-47**. How is the church described here?

✝ *As Christians, we confess that the Holy Spirit has brought us into a community we call the church— gathered "in one faith, one mind, and understanding, with many different gifts" (LC II, 51).*

I should seek out those who also confess Jesus for they are truly my brothers and sisters in Christ.

A Closer Reading of the *Small Catechism*

181. What did the Holy Spirit do when He brought me to faith?

    The Holy Spirit made me a member of the Church.

    630. 1 Corinthians 12:13 For in one Spirit we were all baptized into one body—Jews or Greeks, slaves or free—and all were made to drink of one Spirit.

    631. Ephesians 2:19-22 So then you are no longer strangers and aliens, but you are fellow citizens with the saints and members of the household of God, built on the foundation of the apostles and prophets, Christ Jesus himself being the cornerstone, in whom the whole structure, being joined together, grows into a holy temple in the Lord. In him you also are being built together into a dwelling place for God by the Spirit.

182. What is the Church?

    It is the body of Christ, that is, all people whom the Spirit has gathered to Christ in faith throughout the world.

632. **John 10:16** And I have other sheep that are not of this fold. I must bring them also, and they will listen to my voice. So there will be one flock, one shepherd.

633. **1 Corinthians 12:27** Now you are the body of Christ and individually members of it.

634. **Matthew 18:20** For where two or three are gathered in my name, there am I among them.

635. **Revelation 5:9** And they sang a new song, saying, "Worthy are you to take the scroll and to open its seals, for you were slain, and by your blood you ransomed people for God from every tribe and language and people and nation."

Note: The Creed in its original words speaks of the Church as "catholic" (universal), that is, existing throughout all time and throughout the world, including people who confess and believe in Jesus Christ from every background ("people and nation" **Revelation 5:9**). Another way to say this is to speak of the "Christian Church."

While the word Church, properly speaking, refers to all those who believe in Christ, it is also used in a variety of other ways (such as a building, a congregation, a denomination, etc.). The reason we do this is because confessing Christians are found within them.

183. How is the Church different from all other communities?

- *Christ is the Head of the Church, for which reason it is called the "Christian" Church.*

    636. **Colossians 1:18** And he [Christ Jesus] is the head of the body, the church.

    637. **Ephesians 5:23** For the husband is the head of the wife even as Christ is the head of the church, his body, and is himself its Savior.

    638. **Acts 22:8** [When Saul persecuted the church, Jesus said] "I am Jesus of Nazareth, whom you are persecuting."

- *The Church is the only community in the world in which God "daily and richly forgives my sins and the sins of all believers." Therefore it is called "holy" and a "communion of saints."*

    639. **Colossians 1:13-14** He has delivered us from the domain of darkness and transferred us to the kingdom of his beloved Son, in whom we have redemption, the forgiveness of sins.

    640. **John 20:23** If you forgive the sins of any, they are forgiven them; if you withhold forgiveness from any, it is withheld."

184. What is the forgiveness of sins?

God promises that, for Christ's sake, He will not hold our many sins against us.

641. **1 John 1:7** But if we walk in the light, as he is in the light, we have fellowship with one another, and the blood of Jesus his Son cleanses us from all sin.

642. **1 John 2:1** My little children, I am writing these things to you so that you may not sin. But if anyone does sin, we have an advocate with the Father, Jesus Christ the righteous.

643. **Romans 8:33-34** Who shall bring any charge against God's elect? It is God who justifies. Who is to condemn? Christ Jesus is the one who died—more than that, who was raised—who is at the right hand of God, who indeed is interceding for us.

644. **Isaiah 1:18** "Come now, let us reason together," says the LORD: "though your sins are like scarlet, they shall be as white as snow; though they are red like crimson, they shall become like wool."

645. **Micah 7:18-19** Who is a God like you, pardoning iniquity and passing over transgression for the remnant of his inheritance? He does not retain his anger forever, because he delights in steadfast love. He will again have compassion on us; he will tread our iniquities underfoot. You will cast all our5 sins into the depths of the sea.

646. **Psalm 130:3-4** If you, O LORD, should mark iniquities, O LORD, who could stand? But with you there is forgiveness, that you may be feared.

647. 2 Corinthians 5:19 In Christ God was reconciling the world to himself, not counting their trespasses against them, and entrusting to us the message of reconciliation.

Read **Matthew 18:23-35** where the king forgave the debts of his servant.

185. Why does God forgive our sins?

God is merciful and forgives us on account of Christ's sacrifice for our sins.

648. Psalm 86:15 But you, O LORD, are a God merciful and gracious, slow to anger and abounding in steadfast love and faithfulness.

649. John 3:16 For God so loved the world, that he gave his only Son, that whoever believes in him should not perish but have eternal life.

650. Ephesians 1:7 In him we have redemption through his blood, the forgiveness of our trespasses, according to the riches of his grace,

651. 1 John 2:2 He is the propitiation for our sins, and not for ours only but also for the sins of the whole world.

186. Why can and should I be sure of the forgiveness of my sins?

I can be sure because God always keeps His promises in Christ.

652. Romans 8:38-39 For I am sure that neither death nor life, nor angels nor rulers, nor things present nor things to come, nor powers, nor height nor depth, nor anything else in all creation, will be able to separate us from the love of God in Christ Jesus our Lord.

653. 2 Timothy 1:12 But I am not ashamed, for I know whom I have believed, and I am convinced that he is able to guard until that Day what has been entrusted to me.

654. 2 Corinthians 1:20 For all the promises of God find their Yes in him. That is why it is through him that we utter our Amen to God for his glory.

655. 1 John 1:9 If we confess our sins, he is faithful and just to forgive us our sins and to cleanse us from all unrighteousness.

Connections and Applications

187. Where can I find the Church within the world? How do I recognize the Church?

Even though I cannot see the Church (as a community of believers), I can see identifying characteristics (also called "marks") of the Church.

188. What are the identifying characteristics of the Church?

The identifying marks that guarantee the presence of the Church are the pure proclamation of the Gospel and the right administration of the sacraments. Where these are, the Spirit creates faith.

656. Isaiah 55:10-11 For as the rain and the snow come down from heaven and do not return there but water the earth, making it bring forth and sprout, giving seed to the sower and bread to the eater, so shall my word be that goes out from my mouth; it shall not return to me empty, but it shall accomplish that which I purpose, and shall succeed in the thing for which I sent it.

657. Matthew 18:20 For where two or three are gathered in my name, there am I among them.

189. What are some other outward indications that the Church is present?

Such things as gatherings for prayer and worship, fruits of faith, suffering for Christ, also serve as good outward indications that the Church is present without guaranteeing it.

658. Matthew 7:21 Not everyone who says to me, "Lord, Lord," will enter the kingdom of heaven, but the one who does the will of my Father who is in heaven.

659. John 13:35 By this all people will know that you are my disciples, if you have love for one another.

660. 1 Peter 2:21 For to this you have been called, because Christ also suffered for you, leaving you an example, so that you might follow in his steps.

661. 2 Timothy 1:8 Therefore do not be ashamed of the testimony about our Lord, nor of me his prisoner, but share in suffering for the gospel by the power of God.

662. Acts 2:42-43 And they devoted themselves to the apostles' teaching and the fellowship, to the breaking of bread and the prayers. And awe came upon every soul, and many wonders and signs were being done through the apostles.

663. Hebrews 10:24-25 And let us consider how to stir up one another to love and good works, not neglecting to meet together, as is the habit of some, but encouraging one another, and all the more as you see the Day drawing near.

664. Romans 12:14 Bless those who persecute you; bless and do not curse them.

665. Matthew 10: 32 So everyone who acknowledges me before men, I also will acknowledge before my Father who is in heaven.

190. What are some of the privileges and responsibilities of members of the church?

- *We should regularly receive the Word and sacraments within the community of believers.*

    666. John 8:31-32 So Jesus said to the Jews who had believed him, "If you abide in my word, you are truly my disciples, and you will know the truth, and the truth will set you free."

    667. John 15:5 I am the vine; you are the branches. Whoever abides in me and I in him, he it is that bears much fruit, for apart from me you can do nothing.

    668. Acts 2:42 And they devoted themselves to the apostles' teaching and the fellowship, to the breaking of bread and the prayers.

    669. Colossians 3:16 Let the word of Christ dwell in you richly, teaching and admonishing one another in all wisdom, singing psalms and hymns and spiritual songs, with thankfulness in your hearts to God.

- *We should adhere to congregations that confess and teach the pure Word of God.*

    670. Acts 17:11 Now these Jews [in Berea] were more noble than those in Thessalonica; they received the word with all eagerness, examining the Scriptures daily to see if these things were so.

    671. 2 Corinthians 6:14 Do not be unequally yoked with unbelievers. For what partnership has righteousness with lawlessness? Or what fellowship has light with darkness?

    672. 2 Timothy 4:3-4 For the time is coming when people will not endure sound teaching, but having itching ears they will accumulate for themselves teachers to suit their own passions, and will turn away from listening to the truth and wander off into myths.

- *We should beware of and avoid false teachings and teachers.*

    673. Matthew 7:15-16 Beware of false prophets, who come to you in sheep's clothing but inwardly are ravenous wolves. You will recognize them by their fruits. Are grapes gathered from thorn bushes, or figs from thistles?

    674. Galatians 1:8 But even if we or an angel from heaven should preach to you a gospel contrary to the one we preached to you, let him be accursed.

    675. Romans 16:17-18 I appeal to you, brothers, to watch out for those who cause divisions and create obstacles contrary to the doctrine that you have been taught; avoid them. For such persons do not serve our Lord Christ, but their own appetites, and by smooth talk and flattery they deceive the hearts of the naive.

    676. 2 Corinthians 13:5 Examine yourselves, to see whether you are in the faith. Test yourselves. Or do you not realize this about yourselves, that Jesus Christ is in you?—unless indeed you fail to meet the test!

677. 1 John 4:1 Beloved, do not believe every spirit, but test the spirits to see whether they are from God, for many false prophets have gone out into the world.

- *We should tell others about Jesus, participate in works of service, and support the ministry of the church with prayer and financial gifts.*

    678. John 20:21 Jesus said to them again, "Peace be with you. As the Father has sent me, even so I am sending you."

    679. Acts 8:1, 4 And there arose on that day a great persecution against the church in Jerusalem, and they were all scattered throughout the regions of Judea and Samaria, except the apostles…. Now those who were scattered went about preaching the word.

    680. 1 Peter 2:9 But you are a chosen race, a royal priesthood, a holy nation, a people for his own possession, that you may proclaim the excellencies of him who called you out of darkness into his marvelous light.

    681. 1 Peter 3:15 But in your hearts honor Christ the Lord as holy, always being prepared to make a defense to anyone who asks you for a reason for the hope that is in you; yet do it with gentleness and respect.

    682. Luke 10:2 And he said to them, "The harvest is plentiful, but the laborers are few. Therefore pray earnestly to the Lord of the harvest to send out laborers into his harvest."

    683. Galatians 6:6 Let the one who is taught the word share all good things with the one who teaches.

Read **Acts 2:17-39** where Peter addressed the crowds; **Acts 8:26-35** where Philip witnessed to the eunuch; **Acts 4:23-30** where Christians prayed for the Gospel; and **Philippians 4:16-19** about how they contributed to the support of the ministry.

191. What are some of our responsibilities toward other Christians and church bodies?

- *We should continually pray for all our fellow Christians and work with them wherever possible to alleviate suffering within the world.*

- *We should seek to prevent and heal sinful divisions between Christians and between church bodies that result from such things as political opinions, economic status, race, ethnicity, tribe, caste, and so forth.*

- *We should express the unity of the church by practicing altar and pulpit fellowship with those church bodies with whom we have come to share a common confession of faith based on the Word of God.*

- *When we experience disagreement with other Christians regarding the Word of God, we should not pretend that these divisions are unimportant nor give a false witness of unity by communing together.*

- *We should lament doctrinal disunity among Christian churches and earnestly engage others in conversation with the sincere hope we can be reconciled and again commune together.*

- *We should ask God to heal the divisions that exist within the church today that we might one day express our unity in the faith even as we are united in Christ.*

    684. Ephesians 4:3-6 [Be] eager to maintain the unity of the Spirit in the bond of peace. There is one body and one Spirit—just as you were called to the one hope that belongs to your call—one Lord, one faith, one baptism, one God and Father of all, who is over all and through all and in all.

    685. 1 Corinthians 1:10 I appeal to you, brothers, by the name of our Lord Jesus Christ, that all of you agree, and that there be no divisions among you, but that you be united in the same mind and the same judgment.

686. John 17:17-21 Sanctify them in the truth; your word is truth. As you sent me into the world, so I have sent them into the world. And for their sake I consecrate myself, that they also may be sanctified in truth. I do not ask for these only, but also for those who will believe in me through their word, that they may all be one, just as you, Father, are in me, and I in you, that they also may be in us, so that the world may believe that you have sent me.

687. 1 Corinthians 11:17-18 But in the following instructions I do not commend you, because when you come together it is not for the better but for the worse. For, in the first place, when you come together as a church, I hear that there are divisions among you.

192. Will the Church always exist?

Yes. The Holy Spirit will preserve the Church and keep it with Christ until He returns.

688. Matthew 16:18 And I tell you, you are Peter, and on this rock I will build my church, and the gates of hell shall not prevail against it.

689. Acts 2:41, 47 So those who received his word were baptized, and there were added that day about three thousand souls. And the Lord added to their number day by day those who were being saved.

690. Matthew 28:20 Behold, I am with you always, to the end of the age.

691. John 17:12 While I was with them, I kept them in your name, which you have given me. I have guarded them, and not one of them has been lost except the son of destruction, that the Scripture might be fulfilled.

193. Should I expect the Church's life to be one of continual peace and harmony?

- *No, not in this life. I can expect the Church in the present to be locked in a continual struggle with Satan as he lashes out desperately against Christ's people (Church militant).*

  692. Ephesians 6:12 For we do not wrestle against flesh and blood, but against the rulers, against the authorities, against the cosmic powers over this present darkness, against the spiritual forces of evil in the heavenly places.

  693. 1 Timothy 1:18 This charge I entrust to you, Timothy, my child, in accordance with the prophecies previously made about you, that by them you may wage the good warfare.

  694. 1 Peter 4:12-14 Beloved, do not be surprised at the fiery trial when it comes upon you to test you, as though something strange were happening to you. But rejoice insofar as you share Christ's sufferings, that you may also rejoice and be glad when his glory is revealed. If you are insulted for the name of Christ, you are blessed, because the Spirit of glory and of God rests upon you.

  695. 1 Peter 5:8-9 Be sober-minded; be watchful. Your adversary the devil prowls around like a roaring lion, seeking someone to devour. Resist him, firm in your faith, knowing that the same kinds of suffering are being experienced by your brotherhood throughout the world.

  696. Revelation 12:12 Therefore, rejoice, O heavens and you who dwell in them! But woe to you, O earth and sea, for the devil has come down to you in great wrath, because he knows that his time is short!

- *In the end, yes. I can expect the Church to celebrate the final victory over Satan and the forces of darkness when Christ returns (Church triumphant).*

  697. Isaiah 25:8 He will swallow up death forever; and the LORD God will wipe away tears from all faces, and the reproach of his people he will take away from all the earth, for the LORD has spoken.

  698. Revelation 7:17 For the Lamb in the midst of the throne will be their shepherd, and he will guide them to springs of living water, and God will wipe away every tear from their eyes.

  699. Revelation 21:4 He will wipe away every tear from their eyes, and death shall be no more, neither shall there be mourning, nor crying, nor pain anymore, for the former things have passed away.

Hymn (*LSB* 655) and Prayer: *Holy Father, by Your Spirit You brought me to faith in Your Son and made me a member of His body, the Church. I thank You that You daily and richly forgive my many sins, giving me comfort and peace in this life and a certain hope for the life to come. Give me joy in the promise You made to me in Baptism and a ready heart to hear and keep Your Word; through Jesus Christ my Lord who lives and reigns with You and the Holy Spirit, one God , now and forever. Amen.*

The Third Article (Part 3)

I believe in the Holy Spirit, the holy Christian Church, the communion of saints, the forgiveness of sins, the resurrection of the body, and the life everlasting.

What does this mean?

I believe that I cannot by my own reason or strength believe in Jesus my Lord or come to Him; but the Holy Spirit has called me by the Gospel, enlightened me with His gifts, sanctified and kept me in the true faith.

In the same way He calls, gathers, enlightens, and sanctifies the whole Christian church on earth, and keeps it with Jesus Christ in the one true faith. In this Christian church He daily and richly forgives all my sins and the sins of all believers.

On the Last Day He will raise me and all the dead, and give eternal life to me and all believers in Christ.

This is most certainly true.

The Central Thought

All people yearn for a better future and hope that things in their lives and in the world will improve.

What sort of future do people today hope and long for?

Read **Acts 24:14-21**. For what did Paul claim he was on trial and what was his hope?

✝ *As Christians, we yearn for the resurrection of the body and life eternal in the new heavens and new earth—the time when we will be "perfectly pure and holy people," "free from sin, death, and all evil, in a new, immortal, and glorified body" (LC II, 58).*

How might our hope of the resurrection affect the way we view suffering within this world?

A Closer Reading of the *Small Catechism*

194. What will happen when Jesus returns visibly?

    God will raise me and all the dead.

> **700. Job 19:25-27** For I know that my Redeemer lives, and at the last he will stand upon the earth. And after my skin has been thus destroyed, yet in my flesh I shall see God, whom I shall see for myself, and my eyes shall behold, and not another. My heart faints within me!

> **701. Daniel 12:2** And many of those who sleep in the dust of the earth shall awake, some to everlasting life, and some to shame and everlasting contempt.

> **702. John 5:28-29** Do not marvel at this, for an hour is coming when all who are in the tombs will hear his voice and come out, those who have done good to the resurrection of life, and those who have done evil to the resurrection of judgment.

> **703. 1 Thessalonians 4:16** For the Lord himself will descend from heaven with a cry of command, with the voice of an archangel, and with the sound of the trumpet of God. And the dead in Christ will rise first.

Read **1 Corinthians 15:12-56**.

195. What will my resurrected body be like?

Jesus will raise my body from the earth and transform it into a glorified body for eternal life in the new creation.

> **704. Philippians 3:21** [He] will transform our lowly body to be like his glorious body, by the power that enables him even to subject all things to himself.

> **705. John 5:28-29** Do not marvel at this, for an hour is coming when all who are in the tombs will hear his voice and come out, those who have done good to the resurrection of life, and those who have done evil to the resurrection of judgment.

> **706. 1 Corinthians 15:42-43** So is it with the resurrection of the dead. What is sown is perishable; what is raised is imperishable. It is sown in dishonor; it is raised in glory. It is sown in weakness; it is raised in power.

196. What will happen on the last day to those who have rejected Christ (unbelievers)?

Unbelievers will also rise bodily, but to eternal death, namely, to shame and torment in hell forever.

> **707. Isaiah 66:24** And they shall go out and look on the dead bodies of the men who have rebelled against me. For their worm shall not die, their fire shall not be quenched, and they shall be an abhorrence to all flesh.

> **708. Matthew 10:28** And do not fear those who kill the body but cannot kill the soul. Rather fear him who can destroy both soul and body in hell.

> **709. Matthew 25:41** Then he will say to those on his left, "Depart from me, you cursed, into the eternal fire prepared for the devil and his angels."

> **710. Revelation 1:7** Behold, he is coming with the clouds, and every eye will see him, even those who pierced him, and all tribes of the earth will wail on account of him. Even so. Amen.

Read **Luke 16:19-31** about the rich man and Lazarus.

Connections and Applications

197. Why do people die?

Death is the terrible consequence of sin.

> **711. Romans 5:12** Therefore, just as sin came into the world through one man, and death through sin, and so death spread to all men because all sinned.

> **712. Romans 6:23** For the wages of sin is death, but the free gift of God is eternal life in Christ Jesus our Lord.

198. What happens to me as a Christian when I die?

When I die, the God-given unity of my body and spirit will be broken. I will immediately be in the presence of Christ, in heaven, but my body remains in the grave until the resurrection.

> **713. Philippians 1:23-24** I am hard pressed between the two. My desire is to depart and be with Christ, for that is far better. But to remain in the flesh is more necessary on your account.

> **714. Philippians 3:20** But our citizenship is in heaven, and from it we await a Savior, the Lord Jesus Christ.

> **715. 2 Corinthians 5:8** Yes, we are of good courage, and we would rather be away from the body and at home with the Lord.

716. 2 Timothy 4:18 The Lord will rescue me from every evil deed and bring me safely into his heavenly kingdom. To him be the glory forever and ever. Amen.

717. Revelation 14:13 And I heard a voice from heaven saying, "Write this: Blessed are the dead who die in the Lord from now on." "Blessed indeed," says the Spirit, "that they may rest from their labors, for their deeds follow them!"

718. Luke 23:43 And he said to him, "Truly, I say to you, today you will be with me in Paradise."

719. John 17:24 Father, I desire that they also, whom you have given me, may be with me where I am, to see my glory that you have given me because you loved me before the foundation of the world.

Note: The Bible refers to heaven as both the sky and the dwelling place of God and the holy angels (**1 Kings 8:30**). "Heaven(s) and earth" describes the entire created universe (**Genesis 1:1**). God dwells in heaven (**Genesis 24:7; Deuteronomy 26:15**) far beyond us and our ability to comprehend. Thus, heaven remains a great mystery until we are united with Christ. What we know with confidence is that in heaven God hears our prayers and sees our needs (**1 Kings 8:30-51; Genesis 21:17; Matthew 6:9**) and that He sent His Son from heaven for our salvation (**John 6:38**). Because of Jesus' death, resurrection, and ascension into heaven, He now promises all who trust in Him that death has no power over us and we will be with Him in His heavenly dwelling (**John 14:2-3; Luke 23:43; Ephesians 2:4-7; 2 Timothy 4:18;** and **Hebrews 11:16**).

199. What will happen to me when I am raised from the dead on the Last Day?

I will enjoy being with Christ in His new creation, in body and soul, forever.

720. 1 Corinthians 15:51-52 Behold! I tell you a mystery. We shall not all sleep, but we shall all be changed, in a moment, in the twinkling of an eye, at the last trumpet. For the trumpet will sound, and the dead will be raised imperishable, and we shall be changed.

721. Matthew 25:34 Then the King will say to those on his right, "Come, you who are blessed by my Father, inherit the kingdom prepared for you from the foundation of the world."

722. Psalm 16:11 You make known to me the path of life; in your presence there is fullness of joy; at your right hand are pleasures forevermore.

723. Romans 8:18-21 For I consider that the sufferings of this present time are not worth comparing with the glory that is to be revealed to us. For the creation waits with eager longing for the revealing of the sons of God. For the creation was subjected to futility, not willingly, but because of him who subjected it, in hope that the creation itself will be set free from its bondage to corruption and obtain the freedom of the glory of the children of God.

200. What will happen to this world after we Christians are raised from the dead?

The present creation, like our own bodies, will be set free from its bondage to corruption and a new heaven and a new earth will come forth.

724. Romans 8:19-25 For the creation waits with eager longing for the revealing of the sons of God. For the creation was subjected to futility, not willingly, but because of him who subjected it, in hope that the creation itself will be set free from its bondage to corruption and obtain the freedom of the glory of the children of God. For we know that the whole creation has been groaning together in the pains of childbirth until now. And not only the creation, but we ourselves, who have the firstfruits of the Spirit, groan inwardly as we wait eagerly for adoption as sons, the redemption of our bodies. For in this hope we were saved. Now hope that is seen is not hope. For who hopes for what he sees? But if we hope for what we do not see, we wait for it with patience.

725. James 1:18 Of his own will he brought us forth by the word of truth, that we should be a kind of firstfruits of his creatures.

726. Revelation 21:5 And he who was seated on the throne said, "Behold, I am making all things new."

201. What will the new creation be like?

The new creation is described in ways that are both familiar and mysteriously unfamiliar. The Bible describes a "new heaven and a new earth" in terms much like creation was before the fall, but entirely new and also different in certain ways.

> **727. 2 Peter 3:13** But according to his promise we are waiting for new heavens and a new earth in which righteousness dwells.

> **728. Isaiah 11:6**-7 The wolf shall dwell with the lamb, and the leopard shall lie down with the young goat, and the calf and the lion and the fattened calf together; and a little child shall lead them. The cow and the bear shall graze; their young shall lie down together; and the lion shall eat straw like the ox.

> **729. Isaiah 65:17-18** For behold, I create new heavens and a new earth, and the former things shall not be remembered or come into mind. But be glad and rejoice forever in that which I create; for behold, I create Jerusalem to be a joy, and her people to be a gladness.

> **730. Revelation 21:1-5** Then I saw a new heaven and a new earth, for the first heaven and the first earth had passed away, and the sea was no more. And I saw the holy city, new Jerusalem, coming down out of heaven from God, prepared as a bride adorned for her husband. And I heard a loud voice from the throne saying, "Behold, the dwelling place of God is with man. He will dwell with them, and they will be his people, and God himself will be with them as their God. He will wipe away every tear from their eyes, and death shall be no more, neither shall there be mourning, nor crying, nor pain anymore, for the former things have passed away." And he who was seated on the throne said, "Behold, I am making all things new."

> **731. 1 Corinthians 15:51-53** Behold! I tell you a mystery. We shall not all sleep, but we shall all be changed, in a moment, in the twinkling of an eye, at the last trumpet. For the trumpet will sound, and the dead will be raised imperishable, and we shall be changed. For this perishable body must put on the imperishable, and this mortal body must put on immortality.

> **732. Revelation 21:1** Then I saw a new heaven and a new earth, for the first heaven and the first earth had passed away, and the sea was no more.

> **733. Revelation 22:5** And night will be no more. They will need no light of lamp or sun, for the Lord God will be their light, and they will reign forever and ever.

> **734. 1 Corinthians 15:24** Then comes the end, when he delivers the kingdom to God the Father after destroying every rule and every authority and power.

> **735. Matthew 22:30** For in the resurrection they neither marry nor are given in marriage, but are like angels in heaven.

> **736. Isaiah 60:19-20** The sun shall be no more your light by day, nor for brightness shall the moon give you light; but the LORD will be your everlasting light, and your God will be your glory. Your sun shall no more go down, nor your moon withdraw itself; for the LORD will be your everlasting light, and your days of mourning shall be ended.

> **737. Revelation 22:3** No longer will there be anything accursed, but the throne of God and of the Lamb will be in it, and his servants will worship him.

Read **2 Peter 3:5-13** where Peter compares the end-time cleansing of the creation by fire with the cleansing of the earth by the Flood in Noah's day.

202. Do we know when all this will take place?

- *No, we do not know when the last day will come.*

> **738. 1 Thessalonians 5:2** For you yourselves are fully aware that the day of the Lord will come like a thief in the night.

739. Matthew 24:44 Therefore you also must be ready, for the Son of Man is coming at an hour you do not expect.

- *Although we do not know when the last day will come, we know that we are currently living in the last days of the world and should be watchful for Christ's coming.*

740. Mark 13:3-8 And as he sat on the Mount of Olives opposite the temple, Peter and James and John and Andrew asked him privately, "Tell us, when will these things be, and what will be the sign when all these things are about to be accomplished?" And Jesus began to say to them, "See that no one leads you astray. Many will come in my name, saying, 'I am he!' and they will lead many astray. And when you hear of wars and rumors of wars, do not be alarmed. This must take place, but the end is not yet. For nation will rise against nation, and kingdom against kingdom. There will be earthquakes in various places; there will be famines. These are but the beginning of the birth pains."

741. Mark 13:35-37 Therefore stay awake—for you do not know when the master of the house will come, in the evening, or at midnight, or when the rooster crows, or in the morning—lest he come suddenly and find you asleep. And what I say to you I say to all: Stay awake.

742. Romans 8:22-25 For we know that the whole creation has been groaning together in the pains of childbirth until now. And not only the creation, but we ourselves, who have the firstfruits of the Spirit, groan inwardly as we wait eagerly for adoption as sons, the redemption of our bodies. For in this hope we were saved. Now hope that is seen is not hope. For who hopes for what he sees? But if we hope for what we do not see, we wait for it with patience.

743. Revelation 22:20 He who testifies to these things says, "Surely I am coming soon." Amen. Come, Lord Jesus!

203. What will happen on the last day?

On this great and glorious day when Christ returns, all these things will take place:

- *Jesus will visibly appear in glory with His angels (**Matthew 25:31**);*

- *the kingdoms of this world will give way to the everlasting reign of Christ and human history will come to an end (**Revelation 21:23-24**);*

- *the dead will be raised, the bodies of all believers (those who are alive and those who are raised from the grave) will be glorified (**1 Corinthians 15:51-52**);*

- *Christ will judge all people (**Matthew 25:31-46**);*

- *Satan will be vanquished and banished forever (**Revelation 20:10**);*

- *the current creation will be cleansed by fire and the heavens and earth will be made new again (**2 Peter 3:7-13**);*

- *we will be reunited with all those who have died in faith (**Revelation 7:9**);*

- *there will be a great feast with unending rejoicing (**Revelation 19:6-9**);*

- *and God will dwell with us forever (**Revelation 21:3**).*

204. What are some false teachings about the end of time and life everlasting?

- ***Millennialism*** *typically teaches a literal 1000 year visible reign of Christ on earth before the final judgment, not recognizing that the Scriptures often use numbers symbolically. Lutherans and most Christian churches understand the 1000 year reign of Christ in **Revelation 20:4-6** as a symbolic reference to Christ's reign over His church on earth from His ascension until the last day (**1 Corinthians 15:25**).*

- ***Rapture*** *teaching claims that the 1000 year reign follows a secret return of Jesus when believers are "caught up in the air" and removed from the earth. This turns the simple, comforting hope of*

Christ's second coming (*1 Thessalonians 4:13-18*) into complicated stages (contrary to *1 Thessalonians 5:1-3; Hebrews 9:27-28; and John 5:28-29*); denies that believers will suffer Satan's tribulations (contrary to *Matthew 24:9 and Acts 14:22*); and claims that those who reject Christ will have a second chance to achieve salvation during an earthly reign (contrary to *Luke 16:27-31 and Revelation 20:11-15*).

- **Reincarnation**: *Some philosophers and other religions believe that when people die they are reborn in other bodies or in a series of other bodies. The doctrine of reincarnation is contrary to the biblical promise of the resurrection of our bodies at the return of Christ (see **John 5:28-29; John 11:24; 1 Corinthians 15:50-53; Hebrews 9:27**).*

Hymn (*LSB* 548) and Prayer: *Holy Spirit, Lord and Giver of Life, You have brought me to Christ and by His Gospel, You promise me the final victory over sin, death, and the devil. Keep me firm and confident in the knowledge that on the Last Day, You will raise all the dead, and give eternal life to me and all believers in Christ, my Lord in whose name I pray. Amen.*

The Doctrine of the Trinity

205. What does the word Trinity mean?

It means three in one. The Church has used the word "Trinity" to maintain the Bible's witness that the Father, Son, and Spirit are three distinct persons and yet are one God. This is the greatest mystery of the Christian faith.

> **744. Matthew 28:19** Go therefore and make disciples of all nations, baptizing them in the name of the Father and of the Son and of the Holy Spirit.

> **745. 2 Corinthians 13:14** The grace of the Lord Jesus Christ and the love of God and the fellowship of the Holy Spirit be with you all.

206. What distinguishes the Father, Son, and Spirit from each other?

- *In their relationship to us, they are distinguished by their works for us. The Scriptures ordinarily speak of the Father as creating us, the Son redeeming us, and the Holy Spirit sanctifying us.*

> **746. Galatians 4:4-6** But when the fullness of time had come, God sent forth his Son, born of woman, born under the law, to redeem those who were under the law, so that we might receive adoption as sons. And because you are sons, God has sent the Spirit of his Son into our hearts, crying, "Abba! Father!"

- *In their relationship to each other, they are distinguished by their interactions with each other. The Father begets the Son from eternity; the Son is begotten of the Father from eternity; the Holy Spirit from eternity proceeds from the Father and the Son.*

> **747. John 3:16** For God so loved the world, that he gave his only Son, that whoever believes in him should not perish but have eternal life.

> **748. John 15:26** But when the Helper comes, whom I will send to you from the Father, the Spirit of truth, who proceeds from the Father, he will bear witness about me.

207. What unites the Father, Son, and Holy Spirit as one God?

- *In their relationship to us, the three persons find their unity in the Father as both the source and goal of their work. Out of love the Father sends the Son and together they send the Holy Spirit. The Holy Spirit brings us to Christ, who in turn shows us the Father's love.*

> **749. Galatians 4:4-6** But when the fullness of time had come, God sent forth his Son, born of woman, born under the law, to redeem those who were under the law, so that we might receive adoption as sons. And because you are sons, God has sent the Spirit of his Son into our hearts, crying, "Abba! Father!"

Read **Ephesians 1:1-13** (note who is the subject of all the verbs).

Note: This pattern of talking about the Trinity is reflected in our prayer life. Normally, we pray to the Father, in Jesus' name, *and* by the power of the Holy Spirit.

- *In their relationship to each other, the three persons find their unity as one divine being called God. The Father, Son, and Spirit are alike Almighty, alike creator, alike redeemer.*

> **750. John 8:58** Jesus said to them, "Truly, truly, I say to you, before Abraham was, I am."

Note: For this reason, we can pray to any of the three persons of the Trinity.

The Attributes of the Triune God

208. What are some of God's attributes?

- *God is good (kind, desiring our welfare).*

  751. Psalm 118:1 Oh give thanks to the LORD, for he is good; for his steadfast love endures forever!

  752. Psalm 145:9 The LORD is good to all, and his mercy is over all that he has made.

- *God is merciful (full of compassion).*

  753. Titus 3:5 He saved us, not because of works done by us in righteousness, but according to his own mercy, by the washing of regeneration and renewal of the Holy Spirit.

  754. Jeremiah 3:12 Return, faithless Israel, declares the LORD. I will not look on you in anger, for I am merciful, declares the LORD; I will not be angry forever.

- *God is gracious (showing undeserved kindness).*

  755. Exodus 34:6-7 The LORD passed before him and proclaimed, "The LORD, the LORD, a God merciful and gracious, slow to anger, and abounding in steadfast love and faithfulness, keeping steadfast love for thousands, forgiving iniquity and transgression and sin, but who will by no means clear the guilty, visiting the iniquity of the fathers on the children and the children's children, to the third and the fourth generation.

- *God is faithful (keeping His promises).*

  756. 2 Timothy 2:13 If we are faithless, he remains faithful—for he cannot deny himself.

- *God is spirit (a personal being without a body).*

  757. John 4:24 God is spirit, and those who worship him must worship in spirit and truth.

- *God is eternal (without beginning and end).*

  758. 1 Timothy 1:17 To the King of the ages, immortal, invisible, the only God, be honor and glory forever and ever. Amen.

  759. Psalm 90:1-2 LORD, you have been our dwelling place in all generations. Before the mountains were brought forth, or ever you had formed the earth and the world, from everlasting to everlasting you are God.

- *God is immutable (His nature, being, and promises do not change).*

  760. Exodus 3:14 God said to Moses, "I AM WHO I AM." And he said, "Say this to the people of Israel, 'I AM has sent me to you.'"

  761. Malachi 3:6 For I the LORD do not change; therefore you, O children of Jacob, are not consumed.

Read **Psalm 102:27** and **James 1:17**.

- *God is almighty, all-powerful (omnipotent).*

  762. Matthew 19:26 But Jesus looked at them and said, "With man this is impossible, but with God all things are possible."

Read **Genesis 17:1**.

- *God is all-knowing (omniscient).*

  763. Psalm 139:1-4 O LORD, you have searched me and known me! You know when I sit down and when I rise up; you discern my thoughts from afar. You search out my path and my lying down and are acquainted with all my ways. Even before a word is on my tongue, behold, O LORD, you know it altogether.

Read **John 21:17**.

- *God is present everywhere (omnipresent).*

    764. Jeremiah 23:24 "Can a man hide himself in secret places so that I cannot see him?" declares the LORD. "Do I not fill heaven and earth?" declares the LORD.

    765. Acts 17:27 They should seek God, and perhaps feel their way toward him and find him. Yet he is actually not far from each one of us.

- *God is holy (sinless and hating sin).*

    766. Leviticus 19:2 Speak to all the congregation of the people of Israel and say to them, You shall be holy, for I the LORD your God am holy.

    767. Psalm 5:4-5 For you are not a God who delights in wickedness; evil may not dwell with you. The boastful shall not stand before your eyes; you hate all evildoers.

    768. Isaiah 6:3 Holy, holy, holy is the LORD God of hosts; the whole earth is full of his glory!

- *God is just (fair and impartial).*

    769. Deuteronomy 32:4 The Rock, his work is perfect, for all his ways are justice. A God of faithfulness and without iniquity, just and upright is he.

- *God is love.*

    770. 1 John 4:8 Anyone who does not love does not know God, because God is love.

THE LORD'S PRAYER

Our Father who art in heaven,
Hallowed be Thy name,
Thy kingdom come,
Thy will be done on earth as it is in heaven;
Give us this day our daily bread;
and forgive us our trespasses as we forgive those who trespass against us;
and lead us not into temptation,
But deliver us from evil.
For Thine is the kingdom and the power and the glory
forever and ever.
Amen.

209. Why does the Lord's Prayer come after the Creed in the catechism?

The Ten Commandments reveal how God created us to live with Him and others. The Creed shows us all that God has done that we might be His children and live according to His will. In the Lord's Prayer we now pray for both God's will to be done and His gifts to be received in the face of all dangers.

210. What is the Lord's Prayer?

It is the prayer that Jesus taught His followers. Many Christians refer to it as the "Our Father," based upon its opening words.

211. How did we get the Lord's Prayer?

Jesus' disciples asked Him for instruction on how to pray.

> **771. Luke 11: 1-4** Now Jesus was praying in a certain place, and when he finished, one of his disciples said to him, "Lord, teach us to pray, as John taught his disciples." And he said to them, "When you pray, say: "Father, hallowed be your name. Your kingdom come. Give us each day our daily bread, and forgive us our sins, for we ourselves forgive everyone who is indebted to us. And lead us not into temptation."

> **772. Matthew 6:7-13** "And when you pray, do not heap up empty phrases as the Gentiles do, for they think that they will be heard for their many words. Do not be like them, for your Father knows what you need before you ask him. Pray then like this: Our Father in heaven, hallowed be your name. Your kingdom come, your will be done, on earth as it is in heaven. Give us this day our daily bread, and forgive us our debts, as we also have forgiven our debtors. And lead us not into temptation, but deliver us from evil.)

Note: The Lord's Prayer that we pray today is based on the prayer recorded in Matthew 6. The ending, "for Thine is the kingdom, the power, and the glory forever and ever," is not in the oldest manuscripts of the Bible. These words were included early in church history as a response of praise at the conclusion of the prayer.

212. What kind of a prayer is the Lord's Prayer?

It is a prayer that contains seven petitions or requests to God. Other prayers, such as many psalms, take a variety of other forms (see question 266).

213. What does Jesus teach us to pray for in these petitions?

The Lord's Prayer teaches us to seek all that we need from God. In the first three requests we pray for things pertaining to God. In the last four requests we pray for our needs, both physical and spiritual.

214. How has the Lord's Prayer been used?

The Lord's Prayer has a privileged place within the Christian church because it is the one prayer that Jesus himself gave us. Thus it is not only regularly used in worship services, but serves as a model or template for our own prayers.

The Lord's Prayer

Our Father who art in heaven.
Our Father in heaven.

What does this mean?

With these words, God tenderly invites us to believe that He is our true Father and that we are His true children, so that with all boldness and confidence we may ask Him as dear children ask their dear father.

The Central Thought

"I'll give prayer a chance. What could it hurt?" Sometimes people seek help from God as a last resort or as an act of desperation.

What does praying on the outside chance that it might work or only as a last resort say about someone's view of God?

Read **Luke 15:11-32** about the parable of the lost son. How is God portrayed here?

✝ *As Christians, we confess that God welcomes us with open arms so that we can always approach Him in complete confidence as our dear Father on account of Christ, our Brother.*

Say a prayer in which you thank God for the invitation and encouragement to pray.

A Closer Reading of the *Small Catechism*

215. How does Jesus invite us to pray?

    He invites us to call upon God as "our Father."

    773. Matthew 6:9 Pray then like this: "Our Father in heaven."

216. How is it possible that we can dare to call God Father?

    Because in Christ, we have been adopted as God's children.

    774. Galatians 3:26 In Christ Jesus you are all sons of God, through faith.

    775. Galatians 4:4-6 But when the fullness of time had come, God sent forth his Son, born of woman, born under the law, to redeem those who were under the law, so that we might receive adoption as sons. And because you are sons, God has sent the Spirit of his Son into our hearts, crying, "Abba! Father!"

    776. Romans 8:15-16 For you did not receive the spirit of slavery to fall back into fear, but you have received the Spirit of adoption as sons, by whom we cry, "Abba! Father!" The Spirit himself bears witness with our spirit that we are children of God.

    777. 2 Corinthians 6:18 I will be a father to you, and you will be my sons and daughters, says the Lord Almighty.

    778. 1 John 3:1 See what kind of love the Father has given to us, that we should be called children of God; and so we are. The reason why the world does not know us is that it did not know him.

217. How does calling upon God as "our Father" shape our prayers?

- *We pray with boldness and confidence knowing that God is our "true Father" (that is, loving/beloved father) who wishes to help us.*

    779. John 14:13-14   Whatever you ask in my name, this I will do, that the Father may be glorified in the Son. If you ask me anything in my name, I will do it.

    780. John 15:7   If you abide in me, and my words abide in you, ask whatever you wish, and it will be done for you.

    781. Ephesians 3:11-15   This was according to the eternal purpose that he has realized in Christ Jesus our Lord, in whom we have boldness and access with confidence through our faith in him. So I ask you not to lose heart over what I am suffering for you, which is your glory. For this reason I bow my knees before the Father, from whom every family in heaven and on earth is named.

    782. Hebrews 4:16   Let us then with confidence draw near to the throne of grace, that we may receive mercy and find grace to help in time of need.

- *We pray with and for all Christians for we are all children of our Father in heaven.*

    783. Ephesians 4:6   [There is] one God and Father of all, who is over all and through all and in all.

    784. Galatians 3:26   For in Christ Jesus you are all sons of God, through faith.

218. Why do we call Him our Father who is "in heaven"?

We are not calling upon an earthly father, but a father who is Lord over all creation.

   785. Psalm 124:8   Our help is in the name of the LORD, who made heaven and earth.

   786. Luke 1:37   For nothing will be impossible with God.

   787. Acts 17:24   The God who made the world and everything in it, being Lord of heaven and earth, does not live in temples made by man.

Connections and Applications

219. To whom do we address our prayers?

We pray only to the one true God, the Father, Son, and Holy Spirit (and not to idols, ancestors, saints, angels, or anything else that God has created).

   788. Matthew 4:9-10   And he said to him, "All these I will give you, if you will fall down and worship me." Then Jesus said to him, "Be gone, Satan! For it is written, "'You shall worship the Lord your God and him only shall you serve.'"

   789. Revelation 22:8-9   I, John, am the one who heard and saw these things. And when I heard and saw them, I fell down to worship at the feet of the angel who showed them to me, but he said to me, "You must not do that! I am a fellow servant with you and your brothers the prophets, and with those who keep the words of this book. Worship God."

220. How does the New Testament teach us to address our prayers?

The New Testament typically speaks of prayer being

- *addressed to the Father;*

    790. Matthew 6:9   Pray then like this: "Our Father in heaven."

    791. 1 Peter 1:17   If you call on him as Father who judges impartially according to each one's deeds, conduct yourselves with fear throughout the time of your exile.

    792. Ephesians 3:14-17   For this reason I bow my knees before the Father, from whom every family in heaven and on earth is named, that according to the riches of his glory he may grant you to be strengthened with power through his Spirit in your inner being, so that Christ may dwell in your hearts through faith—that you [may be] rooted and grounded in love.

- *prayed in Jesus' name, that is, through faith in Christ in accordance with His will;*

    793. John 14:14 If you ask me anything in my name, I will do it.

    794. John 15:16 You did not choose me, but I chose you and appointed you that you should go and bear fruit and that your fruit should abide, so that whatever you ask the Father in my name, he may give it to you.

    795. John 16:23 Truly, truly, I say to you, whatever you ask of the Father in my name, he will give it to you.

- *enabled by the power of the Holy Spirit.*

    796. Romans 8:26 Likewise the Spirit helps us in our weakness. For we do not know what to pray for as we ought, but the Spirit himself intercedes for us with groanings too deep for words.

    797. Jude 20 But you, beloved, build yourselves up in your most holy faith and praying in the Holy Spirit.

    798. Ephesians 6:18 [Pray] at all times in the Spirit, with all prayer and supplication.

    Read **Acts 4:23-31.** Notice the requests that are made and the role played by the Holy Spirit.

221. Can we also pray to Jesus and the Holy Spirit?

    Yes. Christians pray to Jesus and the Holy Spirit, for they are one God with the Father.

    799. 1 Corinthians 1:2 To the church of God that is in Corinth, to those sanctified in Christ Jesus, called to be saints together with all those who in every place call upon the name of our Lord Jesus Christ.

    800. Acts 7:59-60 And as they were stoning Stephen, he called out, "Lord Jesus, receive my spirit." And falling to his knees he cried out with a loud voice, "Lord, do not hold this sin against them."

    801. 2 Corinthians 12:7-9 So to keep me from becoming conceited because of the surpassing greatness of the revelations,1 a thorn was given me in the flesh, a messenger of Satan to harass me, to keep me from becoming conceited. Three times I pleaded with the Lord about this, that it should leave me. But he said to me, "My grace is sufficient for you, for my power is made perfect in weakness." Therefore I will boast all the more gladly of my weaknesses, so that the power of Christ may rest upon me.

    802. Revelation 22:20 He who testifies to these things says, "Surely I am coming soon." Amen. Come, Lord Jesus!

    803. Acts 1:24 And they prayed and said, "You, Lord, who know the hearts of all, show which one of these two you have chosen."

    804. 1 John 5:13-15 I write these things to you who believe in the name of the Son of God that you may know that you have eternal life. And this is the confidence that we have toward him, that if we ask anything according to his will he hears us. And if we know that he hears us in whatever we ask, we know that we have the requests that we have asked of him.

Hymn (*LSB* 766, v. 1) and Prayer: *Heavenly Father, Your words give us boldness and confidence to acknowledge You as our true Father and ourselves as Your true children. May Your Holy Spirit lead us to trust in Your fatherly goodness, call upon Your name in every need, and glorify You as the author and giver of every good and perfect gift; through Your Son, Jesus Christ, our Lord. Amen.*

First Petition

Hallowed be Thy name.
Hallowed be Your name.

What does this mean?

God's name is certainly holy in itself, but we pray in this petition that it may be kept holy among us also.

How is God's name kept holy?

God's name is kept holy when the Word of God is taught in its truth and purity, and we, as the children of God, also lead holy lives according to it. Help us to do this, dear Father in heaven! But anyone who teaches or lives contrary to God's Word profanes the name of God among us. Protect us from this, heavenly Father!

The Central Thought

We share our name with people so that they will know us and relate to us appropriately.

How can the words and actions of others affect our good name?

Read **Malachi 1:6-14**. How is God's name being profaned or dishonored?

✝ *As Christians, we pray that God's name—His identity and presence—may be our dearest treasure in our speech and behavior.*

How can I speak or live so as to honor God as my Father?

A Closer Reading of the *Small Catechism*

222. What is the connection between this petition and the Second Commandment?

They both deal with the name of God and our use of it. The commandment requires that we do not misuse His name (see question 30). Here we pray that we may use it properly.

> **805. Exodus 20:7** You shall not take the name of the LORD your God in vain, for the LORD will not hold him guiltless who takes his name in vain.

223. What is meant by "God's name"?

God and His name cannot be separated. It encompasses who He is, what He does, and His very presence among us.

> **806. Isaiah 42:8** I am the LORD; that is my name; my glory I give to no other, nor my praise to carved idols.

> **807. Psalm 9:1-2** I will give thanks to the LORD with my whole heart; I will recount all of your wonderful deeds. I will be glad and exult in you; I will sing praise to your name, O Most High.

> **808. Numbers 6:22-27** [The blessing that God commanded to be spoken over His people repeats His name, the LORD, three times.] "Speak to Aaron and his sons, saying, Thus you shall bless the people of Israel: you shall say to them, 'The LORD bless you and keep you; the LORD make his face to shine

upon you and be gracious to you; the LORD lift up his countenance upon you and give you peace.' So shall they put my name upon the people of Israel, and I will bless them."

809. Exodus 20:24 In every place where I cause my name to be remembered I will come to you and bless you.

810. Matthew 18:20 For where two or three are gathered in my name, there am I among them.

224. What are we asking when we pray that God's name be kept holy?

We pray that God our Father would help us to keep His name holy by our

- *speaking truthfully about His Word;*

  811. Jeremiah 23:28 Let him who has my word speak my word faithfully.

  812. John 17:17 Sanctify them in the truth; your word is truth.

- *living according to His Word.*

  813. Matthew 5:16 Let your light shine before others, so that they may see your good works and give glory to your Father who is in heaven.

  814. Ephesians 4:1 I therefore, a prisoner for the Lord, urge you to walk in a manner worthy of the calling to which you have been called.

Read **Luke 19:1-9** about Zacchaeus, who resolved to live the Christian life after coming to faith.

225. How is God's name profaned?

Our Father's name is profaned, that is, dishonored

- *when anyone teaches something as His Word that is in fact not His Word;*

  815. Jeremiah 23:31 Behold, I am against the prophets, declares the LORD, who use their tongues and declare, "declares the LORD."

- *when anyone lives contrary to His will as expressed in His Word.*

  816. Romans 2:23-24 You who boast in the law dishonor God by breaking the law. For, as it is written, "The name of God is blasphemed among the Gentiles because of you."

Connections and Applications

226. How should we deal with those who dishonor God's name?

- *We should gently admonish those who naively misuse God's name in daily speech or in teaching.*

  817. Colossians 3:16 Let the word of Christ dwell in you richly, teaching and admonishing one another in all wisdom, singing psalms and hymns and spiritual songs, with thankfulness in your hearts to God.

  818. Galatians 6:1 Brothers, if anyone is caught in any transgression, you who are spiritual should restore him in a spirit of gentleness. Keep watch on yourself, lest you too be tempted.

  819. 2 Timothy 2:23-25 Have nothing to do with foolish, ignorant controversies; you know that they breed quarrels. And the Lord's servant must not be quarrelsome but kind to everyone, able to teach, patiently enduring evil, correcting his opponents with gentleness. God may perhaps grant them repentance leading to a knowledge of the truth.

- *We should firmly rebuke those who persist in their errors and refuse to repent.*

  820. Titus 1:9 He must hold firm to the trustworthy word as taught, so that he may be able to give instruction in sound doctrine and also to rebuke those who contradict it.

  821. Titus 3:10 As for a person who stirs up division, after warning him once and then twice, have nothing more to do with him.

Hymn (*LSB* 766, v. 2) and Prayer: *Holy Father, Your name is holy in itself. We pray that through the words which we speak about You and the lives we live as those marked by Your sacred name in Baptism, we may never profane Your name but honor it in all that we say and do; through Jesus Christ, our Lord. Amen.*

The Central Thought

Every kingdom or nation on earth is continually plagued with problems.

If God has ushered in His kingdom through the life, death and resurrection of Christ, why do we still see so many problems in the world today?

Read **John 18:33-40**. How did Pilate misunderstand Jesus as a king and the nature of His kingdom?

✝ *As Christians, we believe and confess that Christ's present (but hidden) reign as king is being extended by the Spirit through the Gospel. It will be fully revealed when Christ returns in glory.*

Since we know that Christ will return to bring an end to the devil's present work of unbelief, sin, and death, how should we live today?

A Closer Reading of the *Small Catechism*

227. What is the kingdom of God for which Jesus teaches us to pray?

It is the gracious rule and reign of God that

- *was promised in the Old Testament;*

    822. Exodus 15:18 The LORD will reign forever and ever.

    823. 2 Samuel 7:12, 16 [God made this promise to David:] "When your days are fulfilled and you lie down with your fathers, I will raise up your offspring after you, who shall come from your body, and I will establish his kingdom. . . . And your house and your kingdom shall be made sure forever before me. Your throne shall be established forever.

    824. Isaiah 9:7 Of the increase of his government and of peace there will be no end, on the throne of David and over his kingdom, to establish it and to uphold it with justice and with righteousness from this time forth and forevermore. The zeal of the LORD of hosts will do this.

- *was ushered in by Jesus' incarnation, public ministry, death and resurrection;*

825. **Mark 1:15** [Jesus said,] "The time is fulfilled, and the kingdom of God is at hand; repent and believe in the gospel."

826. **Colossians 1:13-14** He has delivered us from the domain of darkness and transferred us to the kingdom of his beloved Son, in whom we have redemption, the forgiveness of sins.

- *comes to us here and now by His Spirit through the Word;*

827. **Luke 17:20-21** Being asked by the Pharisees when the kingdom of God would come, he answered them, "The kingdom of God is not coming with signs to be observed, nor will they say, 'Look, here it is!' or 'There!' for behold, the kingdom of God is in the midst of you.'"

828. **John 3:5** Jesus answered, "Truly, truly, I say to you, unless one is born of water and the Spirit, he cannot enter the kingdom of God."

829. **Romans 14:17** The kingdom of God is not a matter of eating and drinking but of righteousness and peace and joy in the Holy Spirit.

830. **Colossians 3:16** Let the word of Christ dwell in you richly, teaching and admonishing one another in all wisdom, singing psalms and hymns and spiritual songs, with thankfulness in your hearts to God.

- *will be brought into its fullness when Christ restores all things upon His return in glory.*

831. **Daniel 7:13-14** I saw in the night visions, and behold, with the clouds of heaven there came one like a son of man, and he came to the Ancient of Days and was presented before him. And to him was given dominion and glory and a kingdom, that all peoples, nations, and languages should serve him; his dominion is an everlasting dominion, which shall not pass away, and his kingdom one that shall not be destroyed.

832. **Matthew 25:34** Then the King will say to those on his right, "Come, you who are blessed by my Father, inherit the kingdom prepared for you from the foundation of the world."

833. **Revelation 11:15** Then the seventh angel blew his trumpet, and there were loud voices in heaven, saying, "The kingdom of the world has become the kingdom of our Lord and of his Christ, and he shall reign forever and ever."

Read **Revelation 21:5** and **Revelation 22:1-5** where we hear that God is "making all things new." The throne of God and the Lamb will be in the middle of the heavenly city. The fullness of the kingdom will be perfect righteousness, peace, and joy according to **Isaiah 11:1-9**.

228. What does it mean that the kingdom of God comes without our prayer?

God's gracious rule and reign does not depend on our prayers or efforts, yet Jesus teaches us to seek God's kingdom and pray for it.

834. **Luke 12:31-32** Seek his kingdom and these things will be added to you. Fear not, little flock, for it is the Father's good pleasure to give you the kingdom.

229. What do we ask and seek from our Father in this petition?

We ask that the kingdom of God would come among us. And so we pray that

- *God would give us His Spirit so that we may believe His Word and live "under Him in His kingdom and serve Him in everlasting righteousness, innocence, and blessedness";*

835. **Isaiah 55:11** [My word] shall not return to me empty, but it shall accomplish that which I purpose, and shall succeed in the thing for which I sent it.

836. **2 Thessalonians 3:1** Finally, brothers, pray for us, that the word of the Lord may speed ahead and be honored, as happened among you.

837. **1 Peter 2:12** Keep your conduct among the Gentiles honorable, so that when they speak against you as evildoers, they may see your good deeds and glorify God on the day of visitation.

- *God's Word would be proclaimed throughout the world—also by us—that His Spirit might bring others under His gracious reign;*

> **838. Acts 4:29** And now, Lord, look upon their threats and grant to your servants to continue to speak your word with all boldness.

> **839. Matthew 9:38** Pray earnestly to the Lord of the harvest to send out laborers into his harvest.

- *Jesus would return soon and fully manifest His rule.*

> **840. Philippians 3:20** But our citizenship is in heaven, and from it we await a Savior, the Lord Jesus Christ.

> **841. Revelation 22:20** He who testifies to these things says, "Surely I am coming soon." Amen. Come, Lord Jesus!

230. What are the benefits of living under God's gracious rule?

Christ has risen from the dead and ascended to the Father's right hand. From there "He sanctifies those who believe in Him, by sending the Holy Spirit into their hearts to rule, comfort, and make them alive" (AC 3).

> **842. Colossians 1:13-14** He has delivered us from the domain of darkness and transferred us to the kingdom of his beloved Son, in whom we have redemption, the forgiveness of sins.

> **843. 2 Timothy 4:18** The Lord will rescue me from every evil deed and bring me safely into his heavenly kingdom. To him be glory for ever and ever. Amen.

> **844. 1 Corinthians 15:58** Therefore, my beloved brothers, be steadfast, immovable, always abounding in the work of the Lord, knowing that in the Lord your labor is not in vain.

> **845. 1 Peter 1:18** You were ransomed from the futile ways inherited from your forefathers.

> **846. Colossians 3:15** Let the peace of Christ rule in your hearts, to which indeed you were called in one body. And be thankful.

> **847. Acts 26:18** The Lord Jesus appointed Paul as a servant and witness to the Gentiles "to open their eyes, so that they may turn from darkness to light and from the power of Satan to God, that they may receive the forgiveness of sins and a place among those who are sanctified by faith in me."

Read **Matthew 5.** In the Beatitudes Jesus encourages us by showing how His kingdom upends all earthly kingdoms and expectations.

Read **Ephesians 4.** St. Paul describes the new life in which we no longer walk "in the futility" of a mind that does not know our Lord and King.

Connections and Applications

231. Does God rule only over believers?

No. God rules as the creator over all people and the entire world in order to maintain and sustain His creation (kingdom of power). God's rule over Christians is a gracious and saving rule (kingdom of grace) that looks forward to the resurrection of the body and the restoration of God's entire creation when Christ returns (kingdom of glory).

> **848. Psalm 103:19** The Lord has established his throne in heaven, and his kingdom rules over all.

232. How does God rule as king over His creation?

God rules over His creation by

- *His goodness in providing for the life and well-being of all creatures;*

849. Acts 14:16-17 In past generations he allowed all the nations to walk in their own ways. Yet he did not leave himself without witness, for he did good by giving you rains from heaven and fruitful seasons, satisfying your hearts with food and gladness.

- *His power as he restrains evil from overwhelming His creation and holds everyone accountable to Him as their creator.*

850. Hebrews 1:3 He is the radiance of the glory of God and the exact imprint of his nature, and he upholds the universe by the word of his power.

Read **Romans 13:1-7** about God ruling through earthly authorities to restrain evil and encourage good.

Hymn (*LSB* 766, v. 3) and Prayer: *Father in heaven, give us Your Holy Spirit so that we believe Your holy Word and live as members of Your gracious kingdom here in time and finally by Your mercy be brought to live as partakers of Your everlasting reign; through Jesus Christ, our Lord. Amen.*

The Third Petition

Thy will be done on earth as it is in heaven.
Your will be done on earth as it is in heaven.

What does this mean?

The good and gracious will of God is done even without our prayer, but we pray in this petition that it may be done among us also.

How is God's will done?

God's will is done when He breaks and hinders every evil plan and purpose of the devil, the world, and our sinful nature, which do not want us to hallow God's name or let His kingdom come; and when He strengthens and keeps us firm in His Word and faith until we die. This is His good and gracious will.

The Central Thought

Christians have always encountered obstacles when bringing the Gospel to the world.

What obstacles do you see in the world today that hinder the spread of the Gospel or keep people from knowing Jesus?

Read **Matthew 26:36-56**. What obstacles did Jesus encounter on His journey to the cross?

✝ *As Christians, we pray here that God would not allow any obstacle to stand in the way of His gracious will, namely, that His word and kingdom be extended.*

What things in my life threaten to pull me away from the Word of God?

A Closer Reading of the *Small Catechism*

233. What is the will of God?

> *God's will is that all people come to know Him as their Father and live under the rule of His Son. This petition is closely related to the petitions that His name be hallowed and His kingdom come.*

>> **851. Ezekiel 18:23** Have I any pleasure in the death of the wicked, declares the Lord GOD, and not rather that he should turn from his way and live?

>> **852. John 6:40** For this is the will of my Father, that everyone who looks on the Son and believes in him should have eternal life, and I will raise him up on the last day.

>> **853. 1 Timothy 2:4** [God] desires all people to be saved and to come to the knowledge of the truth.

>> **854. 1 Thessalonians 4:3** For this is the will of God, your sanctification.

234. What is the specific focus of our prayer in this petition?

It focuses on God's will to prevent Satan, the world, and our sinful flesh from taking God's name and faith from us.

855. 1 Peter 5:8 Be sober-minded; be watchful. Your adversary the devil prowls around like a roaring lion, seeking someone to devour.

856. 1 John 2:15-17 Do not love the world or the things in the world. If anyone loves the world, the love of the Father is not in him. For all that is in the world—the desires of the flesh and the desires of the eyes and pride of life—is not from the Father but is from the world. And the world is passing away along with its desires, but whoever does the will of God abides forever.

857. Romans 7:18 For I know that nothing good dwells in me, that is, in my flesh. For I have the desire to do what is right, but not the ability to carry it out.

Read **Genesis 3:1-7** and see how the devil tempted humanity to sin; **Luke 22:54-62,** how Peter's fear of Jesus' enemies brought about Peter's fall; and **Joshua 7:18-22,** how Achan's sinful nature led him to steal.

235. How does God do this?

- *God restrains Satan (breaks and hinders every evil plan and purpose).*

858. Psalm 23:4-5 Even though I walk through the valley of the shadow of death, I will fear no evil, for you are with me; your rod and your staff, they comfort me. You prepare a table before me in the presence of my enemies; you anoint my head with oil; my cup overflows.

859. 1 Peter 1:5 By God's power [you] are being guarded through faith for a salvation ready to be revealed in the last time

860. 2 Thessalonians 3:3 The Lord is faithful. He will establish you and guard you against the evil one.

- *God strengthens us with His Word so that we can endure the sufferings that will come.*

861. Romans 8:28 We know that for those who love God all things work together for good, for those who are called according to his purpose.

862. 2 Corinthians 12:9 My grace is sufficient for you, for my power is made perfect in weakness.

863. 2 Timothy 1:12 I know whom I have believed, and I am convinced that he is able to guard until that Day what has been entrusted to me.

864. 1 Peter 2:20-21 But if when you do good and suffer for it you endure, this is a gracious thing in the sight of God. For to this you have been called, because Christ also suffered for you, leaving you an example, so that you might follow in his steps.

Note: "As [God's] name must be hallowed and His kingdom come, whether we pray or not, so also His will must be done and succeed. This is true even though the devil with all His followers raise a great riot, are angry and rage against it, and try to exterminate the Gospel completely. But for our own sakes we must pray that, even against their fury, His will be done without hindrance among us also. We pray so that they may not be able to accomplish anything and that we may remain firm against all violence and persecution and submit to God's will" (LC III, 68).

Read **Genesis 50:15-21** and see how God hindered the evil will of Joseph's brothers and kept him faithful; **Job 1:1-2:6,** how God would not let the devil destroy Job; and **Acts 9:1-19,** how, in accordance with God's will, Paul is converted.

236. When will Satan's defeat be complete?

- *Christ has already defeated Satan by means of His life, death, and resurrection.*

865. 1 John 3:8 Whoever makes a practice of sinning is of the devil, for the devil has been sinning from the beginning. The reason the Son of God appeared was to destroy the works of the devil.

- God has promised that Satan will be banished forever and, with that, death will be put to death, and our sinful nature stripped away.

  866. **Romans 16:20** The God of peace will soon crush Satan under your feet. The grace of our Lord Jesus Christ be with you.

  867. **1 John 3:2** Beloved, we are God's children now, and what we will be has not yet appeared; but we know that when he appears we shall be like him, because we shall see him as he is.

  868. **1 Corinthians 15:50-53** I tell you this, brothers: flesh and blood cannot inherit the kingdom of God, nor does the perishable inherit the imperishable. Behold! I tell you a mystery. We shall not all sleep, but we shall all be changed, in a moment, in the twinkling of an eye, at the last trumpet. For the trumpet will sound, and the dead will be raised imperishable, and we shall be changed. For this perishable body must put on the imperishable, and this mortal body must put on immortality.

  869. **Revelation 20:10** And the devil who had deceived them was thrown into the lake of fire and sulfur where the beast and the false prophet were, and they will be tormented day and night forever and ever.

Connections and Applications

237. What is God's will for my life?

God has made known that He wants me

- *to become and remain His child through faith in Jesus;*

- *to live as His adopted child according to His Word and bear witness to Christ;*

- *to resist the devil and all that would prevent these things.*

238. Should I be anxious about discerning God's precise will in my daily decisions?

God has given clear commands about many matters of daily life (Ten Commandments). However, God also leaves many other daily decisions up to us (what to eat, where to go to school, what kind of car to purchase, etc). And so we need not worry about trying to discern God's precise will when making these kinds of decisions for we also know that we live under His fatherly care.

239. How can I make decisions as a Christian about everyday matters?

- *I can pray for God's wisdom in choosing the best course of action.*

- *I can continue learning from God's Word about the type of person he wants me to be.*

- *I can consider my specific callings in life (see Table of Duties), my abilities and interests, the needs of those around me, and the opportunities with which I am presented.*

- *I can seek the counsel and wisdom of others.*

- *I pray for God's blessing upon my decisions.*

Hymn (*LSB* 766, v. 4) and Prayer: *Merciful Father, ruler of all things in heaven and on earth, we acknowledge that Your good and gracious will is done without our prayer. We pray that You would defeat all that opposes Your will: the devil, the world, and our own sinful nature. In Your mercy we implore You to strengthen and keep us firm in Your Word and faith all the days of our lives and bring us at last the inheritance which You have prepared for us in Christ Jesus, who lives and reigns with You and the Holy Spirit, one God, now and forever. Amen.*

Fourth Petition

Give us this day our daily bread.
Give us today our daily bread.

What does this mean?

God certainly gives daily bread to everyone without our prayers, even to all evil people, but we pray in this petition that God would lead us to realize this and to receive our daily bread with thanksgiving.

What is meant by daily bread?

Daily bread includes everything that has to do with the support and needs of the body, such as food, drink, clothing, shoes, house, home, land, animals, money, goods, a devout husband or wife, devout children, devout workers, devout and faithful rulers, good government, good weather, peace, health, self-control, good reputation, good friends, faithful neighbors, and the like.

The Central Thought

Take away our "daily bread," namely, the air we breathe, the water we drink, the food we eat, the homes that shelter us, the government that protects us, and we die.

Since these things are so important, why do we take them for granted and not express gratitude for them?

Read **Exodus 16:1-21.** What is challenging to the Israelites about the way God provides?

✝ *As Christians, we pray that we might be grateful for everything (however ordinary) that God provides each day for our bodily life.*

What habits and practices can help me to better recognize how God sustains my life each day?

A Closer Reading of the *Small Catechism*

240. What is the focus of this petition?

> *It focuses on recognizing God as the giver of all good things and giving thanks for all His gifts of creation that sustain our bodily life (in other words, we pray for all the gifts mentioned in the first article of the creed).*

241. Why does God provide for the earthly needs of everyone, even apart from prayer?

> *As our loving creator, God looks after His entire creation and provides for both Christians and non-Christians, for people and animals.*

> > **870. Matthew 5:45** He makes his sun rise on the evil and on the good, and sends rain on the just and on the unjust.

> > **871. Acts 14:16-17** In past generations he allowed all the nations to walk in their own ways. Yet he did not leave himself without witness, for he did good by giving you rains from heaven and fruitful seasons, satisfying your hearts with food and gladness.

872. Job 38:39-41 Can you hunt the prey for the lion, or satisfy the appetite of the young lions, when they crouch in their dens or lie in wait in their thicket? Who provides for the raven its prey, when its young ones cry to God for help, and wander about for lack of food?

873. Psalm 145:15-16 The eyes of all look to you, and you give them their food in due season. You open your hand and satisfy the desire of every living thing.

242. What do we mean by "daily bread"?

Bread is a biblical way of summarizing all that we need to sustain our lives on earth.

874. Isaiah 55:2 Why do you spend your money for that which is not bread, and your labor for that which does not satisfy? Listen diligently to me, and eat what is good, and delight yourselves in rich food.

Note: "This petition includes everything that belongs to our entire life in the world" (LC III, 73).

243. Why do we specify "daily" bread in this petition?

"Daily" highlights how every moment and every day of our lives depend upon God's provision.

875. Acts 17:28 In Him we live and move and have our being.

876. James 4:15 You ought to say, "If the Lord wills, we will live and do this or that."

877. Psalm 118:24 This is the day that the LORD has made; let us rejoice and be glad in it.

878. Psalm 104:27-29 These all look to you, to give them their food in due season. When you give it to them, they gather it up; when you open your hand, they are filled with good things. When you hide your face, they are dismayed; when you take away their breath, they die and return to their dust.

244. For what then do we pray in this petition?

We pray that, in humility,

- *we would look to God for what we need each day so that we not worry about the future;*

879. Matthew 6:26 Look at the birds of the air: they neither sow nor reap nor gather into barns, and yet your heavenly Father feeds them. Are you not of more value than they?

880. Matthew 6:34 Therefore do not be anxious about tomorrow, for tomorrow will be anxious for itself. Sufficient for the day is its own trouble.

881. 1 Peter 5:6-7 Humble yourselves…casting all your anxieties on him, because he cares for you.

882. Exodus 16:17-21 The people Israel…gathered [manna], some more, some less. But when they measured it with an omer, whoever gathered much had nothing left over, and whoever gathered little had no lack. Each of them gathered as much as he could eat. And Moses said to them, "Let no one leave any of it over till the morning." But they did not listen to Moses. Some left part of it till the morning, and it bred worms and stank. And Moses was angry with them. Morning by morning they gathered it, each as much as he could eat; but when the sun grew hot, it melted.

- *we would receive all our physical blessings with thanksgiving;*

883. Psalm 106:1 Give thanks to the LORD, for he is good; his steadfast love endures forever.

884. Ephesians 5:19-20 Singing and making melody to the Lord with your heart, giving thanks always and for everything to God the Father in the name of our Lord Jesus Christ.

885. 1 Timothy 4:4-5 Everything created by God is good, and nothing is to be rejected if it is received with thanksgiving, for it is made holy by the word of God and prayer.

Read **Mark 10:46-52** about Jesus healing blind Bartimaeus and **Luke 17:11-19** about the 10 lepers.

- *we would find contentment with what we have received.*

886. 1 Timothy 6:8 If we have food and clothing, with these we will be content.

887. John 6:12 When they had eaten their fill, he told his disciples, "Gather up the leftover fragments, that nothing may be lost."

888. Proverbs 30:8-9 Give me neither poverty nor riches; feed me with the food that is needful for me, lest I be full and deny you and say, "Who is the LORD?" or lest I be poor and steal and profane the name of my God.

Read **Luke 12:15-21** about the parable of the rich fool.

Connections and Applications

245. How does God provide our daily bread?

God ordinarily provides for our daily bread through means.

- *He makes the earth fruitful with all that we need.*

    889. Psalm 104:14 You cause the grass to grow for the livestock and plants for man to cultivate, that he may bring forth food from the earth.

    890. Psalm 145:15-16 The eyes of all look to you, and you give them their food in due season. You open your hand; you satisfy the desire of every living thing.

- *He blesses us with the ability to work and thus enjoy the fruitfulness of the earth.*

    891. 2 Thessalonians 3:10-12 Even when we were with you, we would give you this command: If anyone is not willing to work, let him not eat. For we hear that some among you walk in idleness, not busy at work, but busybodies. Now such persons we command and encourage in the Lord Jesus Christ to do their work quietly and to earn their own living.

- *He blesses us with earthly authorities and structures (a stable government and economy) that provide the setting in which we can work and receive our daily bread.*

    892. 1 Timothy 2:1-2 First of all, then, I urge that supplications, prayers, intercessions, and thanksgivings be made for all people, for kings and all who are in high positions, that we may lead a peaceful and quiet life, godly and dignified in every way.

246. Does God give me daily bread only for my own needs?

No. God wants us to share with others in need and to include them in our prayers.

    893. 1 Timothy 5:8 If anyone does not provide for his relatives, and especially for members of his household, he has denied the faith and is worse than an unbeliever.

    894. Hebrews 13:16 Do not neglect to do good and to share what you have, for such sacrifices are pleasing to God.

    895. 1 John 3:17-18 If anyone has the world's goods and sees his brother in need, yet closes his heart against him, how does God's love abide in him? Little children, let us not love in word or talk but in deed and in truth.

247. If God provides for everyone in these ways, why do some lack daily bread?

Famine, scarcity, and need are the result of a fallen creation. Human sin, such as greed, callousness, and laziness, often contribute to these problems. Also, in a sinful world unjust or incompetent governmental systems may result in or contribute to the lack of daily bread.

"There is, indeed, the greatest need to pray for earthly authority and government. By them, most of all, God preserves for us our daily bread" (LC III, 74).

Hymn (*LSB* 766, v. 5) and Prayer: *Gracious Father, You open Your hand and satisfy the desires of every living creature. Teach us to acknowledge You as the Lord who provides for all of our needs in body and soul and so give thanks to You for all of Your bountiful gifts; through Jesus Christ, our Lord. Amen.*

Fifth Petition

And forgive us our trespasses as we forgive those who trespass against us.

And forgive us our sins as we forgive those who sin against us.

What does this mean?

We pray in this petition that our Father in heaven would not look at our sins, or deny our prayer because of them. We are neither worthy of the things for which we pray, nor have we deserved them, but we ask that He would give them all to us by grace, for we daily sin much and surely deserve nothing but punishment. So we too will sincerely forgive and gladly do good to those who sin against us.

The Central Thought

People cannot live in peace with each other for long unless they forgive each other.

How do both the failure to forgive and the failure to receive forgiveness burden us?

Read **Luke 7:36-50**. Reflect on how the woman is freed from the burden of her sin but the Pharisee is not.

✝ *As Christians, we pray that for Christ's sake we may know the joy and peace of being forgiven and of forgiving others.*

Are there people in my life with whom I am not at peace because I have not forgiven them?

A Closer Reading of the *Small Catechism*

248. What do we ask for in this petition?

We ask that our Father in heaven would graciously forgive our sins for Christ's sake.

896. Psalm 51:1-2 Have mercy on me, O God, according to your steadfast love; according to Your abundant mercy blot out my transgressions. Wash me thoroughly from my iniquity and cleanse me from my sin!

897. Psalm 130:3-4 If You, O Lord, should mark iniquities, O Lord, who could stand? But with you there is forgiveness, that you may be feared.

898. Luke 18:13 God, be merciful to me, a sinner!

249. Why do we need to pray for God's forgiveness?

- *We sin every day and deserve nothing but God's displeasure.*

  899. Proverbs 28:13 Whoever conceals his transgressions will not prosper, but he who confesses and forsakes them will obtain mercy.

  900. Psalm 19:12 Who can discern his errors? Declare me innocent from hidden faults.

  901. Genesis 32:10 I am not worthy of the least of all the deeds of steadfast love and all the faithfulness that you have shown to your servant.

- *We pray for God's forgiveness because without it, we cannot pray to God for anything and expect Him graciously to hear and to answer.*

902. Isaiah 1:15 When you spread out your hands, I will hide my eyes from you; even though you make many prayers, I will not listen; your hands are full of blood.

903. Isaiah 59:2 Your iniquities have made a separation between you and your God, and your sins have hidden his face from you so that he does not hear.

904. Proverbs 28:13 Whoever conceals his transgressions will not prosper, but he who confesses and forsakes them will obtain mercy.

905. Ephesians 6:16-18a In all circumstances take up the shield of faith, with which you can extinguish all the flaming darts of the evil one; and take the helmet of salvation, and the sword of the Spirit, which is the word of God, praying at all times in the Spirit, with all prayer and supplication.

- *Forgiveness frees us by giving us peace with God.*

    906. Psalm 32:1-5 Blessed is the one whose transgression is forgiven, whose sin is covered. Blessed is the man against whom the LORD counts no iniquity, and in whose spirit there is no deceit. For when I kept silent, my bones wasted away through my groaning all day long. For day and night your hand was heavy upon me; my strength was dried up as by the heat of summer. I acknowledged my sin to you, and I did not cover my iniquity; I said, "I will confess my transgressions to the LORD," and you forgave the iniquity of my sin.

Note: "If God does not forgive constantly, we are lost…For where the heart is not in a right relationship with God, or cannot take such confidence, it will not dare to pray anymore. Such a confident and joyful heart can spring from nothing else than the certain knowledge of the forgiveness of sins" (LC III, 91-92).

250. Why is forgiveness important for my own Christian walk?

- *My need for God's forgiveness reminds me that I am no better than anyone else.*

    907. Psalm 130:3-4 If you, O LORD, should mark iniquities, O LORD, who could stand? But with you there is forgiveness, that you may be feared.

    908. Romans 3:23-24 For all have sinned and fall short of the glory of God, and are justified by his grace as a gift, through the redemption that is in Christ Jesus.

    909. 1 Timothy 1:15 The saying is trustworthy and deserving of full acceptance, that Christ Jesus came into the world to save sinners, of whom I am the foremost.

    910. 1 John 1:8-10 If we say we have no sin, we deceive ourselves, and the truth is not in us. If we confess our sins, he is faithful and just to forgive us our sins and to cleanse us from all unrighteousness. If we say we have not sinned, we make him a liar, and his word is not in us.

- *God's forgiveness enables me to forgive others thus freeing me from anger and resentment toward them.*

    911. Matthew 6:14-15 For if you forgive others their trespasses, your heavenly Father will also forgive you, but if you do not forgive others their trespasses, neither will your Father forgive your trespasses.

    912. Matthew 18:21-22 Then Peter came up and said to him, "Lord, how often will my brother sin against me, and I forgive him? As many as seven times?" Jesus said to him, "I do not say to you seven times, but seventy-seven times.

    913. Ephesians 4:32 Be kind to one another, tenderhearted, forgiving one another, as God in Christ forgave you.

Read **Genesis 50:15-21** about how Joseph forgave his brothers and **Matthew 18:23-35** about an unmerciful servant.

Note: "Just as we daily sin much against God, and yet He forgives everything through grace, so we, too, must ever forgive our neighbor who does us injury, violence, and wrong, shows malice toward us, and so on. If, therefore, you do not forgive, then do not think that God forgives you" (LC III, 94-95).

251. Does our forgiveness from God depend upon our ability to forgive others?

No. It may appear that Jesus makes our being forgiven dependent upon our forgiving others when He says, "forgive us...as we forgive others." Regarding this, the Scriptures teach two complementary truths. First, God has forgiven the sins of the world solely for Christ's sake; thus I cannot earn forgiveness by forgiving others. Second, if we stubbornly refuse to forgive others we reject God's forgiveness for them and for us.

> **914. Romans 5:2** Through him we have also obtained access by faith into this grace in which we stand, and we rejoice in hope of the glory of God.

> **915. Romans 5:10** For if while we were enemies we were reconciled to God by the death of his Son, much more, now that we are reconciled, shall we be saved by his life.

> **916. Colossians 3:13** Bearing with one another and, if one has a complaint against another, forgiving each other; as the Lord has forgiven you, so you also must forgive.

> **917. Matthew 6:15** But if you do not forgive others their trespasses, neither will your Father forgive your trespasses.

> **918. Matthew 18:35** So also my heavenly Father will do to every one of you, if you do not forgive your brother from your heart.

Note: The forgiveness you receive "is not because of your forgiving. For God forgives freely and without condition, out of pure grace, because he has so promised, as the Gospel teaches" (LC III, 96). See LC sections 93-98 for a fuller explanation of how our forgiveness can be a sign of God's greater mercy and forgiveness.

Connections and Applications

252. Does forgiveness mean that I must "forgive and forget"?

Forgiveness does not mean having no memory of past wrongs. But we ask our Father in heaven to free us from the anger and resentment that may accompany those memories. We relinquish them into His merciful hands and trust Him for healing over time.

> **919. 1 Corinthians 13:5** [Love] does not dishonor others, it is not self-seeking, it is not easily angered, it keeps no record of wrongs. (NIV)

Hymn (*LSB* 766, v. 6) and Prayer: *Most merciful Father, our sins make us unworthy to ask anything of You. For the sake of Your dear Son, do not condemn us for our sins, but hear our cries for mercy and forgive us our trespasses. Enlivened by Your forgiveness we, too, pledge to sincerely forgive and gladly do good to those who sin against us; through Jesus Christ, our Lord. Amen.*

Sixth Petition

And lead us not into temptation.

Lead us not into temptation.

What does this mean?

God tempts no one. We pray in this petition that God would guard and keep us so that the devil, the world, and our sinful nature may not deceive us or mislead us into false belief, despair, and other great shame and vice. Although we are attacked by these things, we pray that we may finally overcome them and win the victory.

The Central Thought

Many gradually drift away from the Christian faith until their faith withers and dies.

How do you think it happens that people drift away from Christ without realizing it?

Read **Mark 4:1-20**. What are the various dangers to faith mentioned in the parable of the sower?

✝ *As Christians, we pray that our Father would keep us strong in His Word since our faith is under constant threat.*

What do you see in your life that could lure you away from Jesus?

A Closer Reading of the *Small Catechism*

[handwritten: FOR 10/27]

253. What is the focus of this particular petition? — *[handwritten: Give out assignments]*

It focuses on the constant attempts of our spiritual enemies to lure us away from God and into the captivity of sin, and ultimately into unbelief and despair.

> **920. 1 Peter 5:8-9** Be sober-minded; be watchful. Your adversary the devil prowls around like a roaring lion, seeking someone to devour. Resist him, firm in your faith, knowing that the same kinds of suffering are being experienced by your brotherhood throughout the world.

> **921. James 1:13-14** Let no one say when he is tempted, "I am being tempted by God," for God cannot be tempted with evil, and he himself tempts no one. But each person is tempted when he is lured and enticed by his own desire.

> **922. 2 Timothy 3:1-4** But understand this, that in the last days there will come times of difficulty. For people will be lovers of self, lovers of money, proud, arrogant, abusive, disobedient to their parents, ungrateful, unholy, heartless, unappeasable, slanderous, without self-control, brutal, not loving good, treacherous, reckless, swollen with conceit, lovers of pleasure rather than lovers of God,

Read **Genesis 3** about how the devil tempted Eve to doubt and disobey God; **John 13:27** and **Matthew 27:4-5**, how the devil tempted Judas to betray Christ; and to despair. Read also **Luke 22:54-60** about how among enemies of Christ, Peter denied his Savior; and **2 Samuel 12:9** about how David's sinful nature led him to commit adultery and murder.

254. What do we ask God to do for us when we pray this petition?

We pray that

- *our faith in and love for Jesus would not grow cold with unbelief;*

923. Matthew 24:9-14 Then they will deliver you up to tribulation and put you to death, and you will be hated by all nations for my name's sake. And then many will fall away and betray one another and hate one another. And many false prophets will arise and lead many astray. And because lawlessness will be increased, the love of many will grow cold. But the one who endures to the end will be saved. And this gospel of the kingdom will be proclaimed throughout the whole world as a testimony to all nations, and then the end will come.

924. Mark 9:24 Immediately the father of the child cried out and said, "I believe; help my unbelief!"

925. Hebrews 6:4-6 For it is impossible, in the case of those who have once been enlightened, who have tasted the heavenly gift, and have shared in the Holy Spirit, and have tasted the goodness of the word of God and the powers of the age to come, and then have fallen away, to restore them again to repentance, since they are crucifying once again the Son of God to their own harm and holding him up to contempt.

- *we would stay alert and to be on guard against threats to our faith;*

926. 1 Corinthians 10:12-13 Therefore let anyone who thinks that he stands take heed lest he fall .No temptation has overtaken you that is not common to man. God is faithful, and he will not let you be tempted beyond your ability, but with the temptation he will also provide the way of escape, that you may be able to endure it.

927. Mark 14:38 Watch and pray that you may not enter into temptation. The spirit indeed is willing, but the flesh is weak.

- *our Father would guard us against all sins that come from the devil, the world, and our sinful flesh.*

928. Galatians 5:19-21 Now the works of the flesh are evident: sexual immorality, impurity, sensuality, idolatry, sorcery, enmity, strife, jealousy, fits of anger, rivalries, dissensions, divisions, envy, drunkenness, orgies, and things like these. I warn you, as I warned you before, that those who do such things will not inherit the kingdom of God.

929. Revelation 3:10 Because you have kept my word about patient endurance, I will keep you from the hour of trial that is coming on the whole world, to try those who dwell on the earth.

930. Proverbs 1:10 My son, if sinners entice you, do not consent.

Read **Genesis 39:1-20** and note how Joseph withstands the temptation of Potiphar's wife.

255. How does God help us to resist those threats?

He provides us with the Word of Christ, the Holy Spirit, and the gift of prayer as our armor and weapons.

931. Ephesians 6:11, 17-18 Put on the whole armor of God, that you may be able to stand against the schemes of the devil…and take the helmet of salvation, and the sword of the Spirit, which is the word of God, praying at all times in the Spirit, with all prayer and supplication.

932. Romans 13:14 But put on the Lord Jesus Christ, and make no provision for the flesh, to gratify its desires.

933. 1 Corinthians 10:13 No temptation has overtaken you that is not common to man. God is faithful, and he will not let you be tempted beyond your ability, but with the temptation he will also provide the way of escape, that you may be able to endure it.

934. 2 Corinthians 4:7-12 But we have this treasure in jars of clay, to show that the surpassing power belongs to God and not to us. We are afflicted in every way, but not crushed; perplexed, but not driven to despair; persecuted, but not forsaken; struck down, but not destroyed; always carrying in the body the death of Jesus, so that the life of Jesus may also be manifested in our bodies. For we who live are always being given over to death for Jesus' sake, so that the life of Jesus also may be manifested in our mortal flesh. So death is at work in us, but life in you.

935. 2 Timothy 4:18 The Lord will rescue me from every evil deed and bring me safely into his heavenly kingdom. To him be the glory forever and ever. Amen.

936. Luke 22:31-32 Simon, Simon, behold, Satan demanded to have you, that he might sift you like wheat, but I have prayed for you that your faith may not fail.

Read **Matthew 4:1-11** and note how Jesus repelled Satan with the Word of God.

Note: "There is no help or comfort except to run here, take hold of the Lord's Prayer, and speak to God from the heart like this: 'Dear Father, You have asked me to pray. Don't let me fall because of temptations'" (LC III, 110).

Connections and Applications

256. Does God ever tempt us?

God does not tempt us to sin. However, He does at times test our faith in order to bring us closer to Himself and make our faith more resilient.

937. James 1:13 Let no one say when he is tempted, "I am being tempted by God," for God cannot be tempted with evil, and he himself tempts no one.

938. John 6:5-6 Lifting up his eyes, then, and seeing that a large crowd was coming toward him, Jesus said to Philip, "Where are we to buy bread, so that these people may eat?" He said this to test him, for he himself knew what he would do.

939. James 1:2-3 Count it all joy, my brothers, when you meet trials of various kinds, for you know that the testing of your faith produces steadfastness.

Read **Genesis 22:1-19** about how the Lord tested Abraham by commanding him to sacrifice Isaac; also **Judges 2:22** God tested Israel to see if they would walk in the way of the Lord; and **Matthew 15:21-28** about how Jesus tested the faith of the Canaanite woman.

Hymn (*LSB* 766, v. 7) and Prayer: *Heavenly Father, guard and keep us from the assaults of the devil, the deception of the world, and the desires of our sinful nature. Protect us that we may not be deceived or misled by lies about You, be overcome by despair of Your mercy, or be seduced into a way of life that leads only to death. Shield us by Your grace and strengthen us by Your Word and Spirit that we may withstand every attack and finally win the victory; through Jesus Christ, our Lord.*

Seventh Petition

But deliver us from evil.

But deliver us from evil.

What does this mean?

We pray in this petition, in summary, that our Father in heaven would rescue us from every evil of body and soul, possessions and reputation, and finally, when our last hour comes, give us a blessed end, and graciously take us from this valley of sorrow to Himself in heaven.

The Central Thought

Every century has been filled with its own evils—diseases, mass killings, tortures, and horrible abuses inflicted upon human beings.

What do people identify as the various causes of evil in our world?

Read **Genesis 3:1-19**. What does this account of Adam and Eve say about why there is evil in this world?

✝ *As Christians, we pray that God would rescue us from the evil one both now and forever.*

What evils do I see in the world for which I need to pray, "Lord, deliver us!"?

A Closer Reading of the *Small Catechism*

257. How does the seventh petition relate to the previous petitions?

   It serves as a summary of the previous six petitions in which we ask our Father in heaven to rescue us from all evil (including the evil one, namely, Satan).

   940. Psalm 121:7-8 The LORD will keep you from all evil; he will keep your life. The LORD will keep your going out and your coming in from this time forth and forevermore.

   941. 2 Thessalonians 3:3 But the Lord is faithful. He will establish you and guard you against the evil one.

258. What do we ask God our Father to do for us here?

   We ask Him to

   - *help us endure the troubles that befall us and keep us faithful until death;*

     942. Acts 14:22 Through many tribulations we must enter the kingdom of God.

     943. Psalm 91:9-10 Because you have made the LORD your dwelling place—the Most High, who is my refuge—no evil shall be allowed to befall you, no plague come near your tent.

     944. Proverbs 3:11-12 My son, do not despise the LORD's discipline or be weary of his reproof, for the LORD reproves him whom he loves, as a father the son in whom he delights.

   Read **Daniel 3** about the three men in the fiery furnace and **Daniel 6** about Daniel in the lions' den.

   - *free us from this present evil age in which sin, death, and Satan rule.*

     945. Luke 2:29-32 Lord, now you are letting your servant depart in peace, according to your word; for my eyes have seen your salvation that you have prepared in the presence of all peoples, a light for revelation to the Gentiles, and for glory to your people Israel.

946. Galatians 1:4-5 [Christ] gave himself for our sins to deliver us from the present evil age, according to the will of our God and Father, to whom be the glory forever and ever. Amen.

947. 2 Timothy 4:18 The Lord will rescue me from every evil deed and bring me safely into his heavenly kingdom. To him be the glory forever and ever. Amen.

948. Revelation 14:13 Blessed are the dead who die in the Lord.

949. Revelation 21:4 He will wipe away every tear from their eyes, and death shall be no more, neither shall there be mourning, nor crying, nor pain anymore, for the former things have passed away.

Connections and Applications

259. What kind of a being is Satan?

He is God's enemy, the evil one, who was originally a holy angel, but led a rebellion against God and remains opposed to God and all that is good.

950. Isaiah 14:12-15 How you are fallen from heaven, O Day Star, son of Dawn! How you are cut down to the ground, you who laid the nations low! You said in your heart, I will ascend to heaven; above the stars of God I will set my throne on high; I will sit on the mount of assembly in the far reaches of the north; I will ascend above the heights of the clouds; I will make myself like the Most High. But you are brought down to Sheol, to the far reaches of the pit.

951. Matthew 13:38-39 The field is the world, and the good seed is the sons of the kingdom. The weeds are the sons of the evil one, and the enemy who sowed them is the devil. The harvest is the close of the age, and the reapers are angels.

952. John 17:15 I do not ask that you take them out of the world, but that you keep them from the evil one.

953. 2 Thessalonians 3:3 But the Lord is faithful. He will establish you and guard you against the evil one.

954. 2 Corinthians 11:14 Even Satan disguises himself as an angel of light.

955. 1 Peter 5:8 Be sober-minded; be watchful. Your adversary the devil prowls around like a roaring lion, seeking someone to devour.

956. 1 John 5:18 We know that everyone who has been born of God does not keep on sinning, but he who was born of God protects him, and the evil one does not touch him.

957. Revelation 12:9 And the great dragon was thrown down, that ancient serpent, who is called the devil and Satan, the deceiver of the whole world—he was thrown down to the earth, and his angels were thrown down with him.

260. Why does Satan concern himself with us?

In arrogance, rage, and spite, Satan sought to claim God's good creation as his own kingdom. His goal is to deceive and destroy the human race. To that end, he seduced Adam and Eve (along with all their descendants) into captivity and made them his allies, subject to God's condemnation.

958. John 8:44 You are of your father the devil, and your will is to do your father's desires. He was a murderer from the beginning, and does not stand in the truth, because there is no truth in him. When he lies, he speaks out of his own character, for he is a liar and the father of lies.

959. Genesis 3:1 Now the serpent was more crafty than any other beast of the field that the LORD God had made.

960. Ephesians 2:1-2 And you were dead in the trespasses and sins in which you once walked, following the course of this world, following the prince of the power of the air, the spirit that is now at work in the sons of disobedience.

961. Matthew 4:8-10 Again, the devil took him to a very high mountain and showed him all the kingdoms of the world and their glory. And he said to him, "All these I will give you, if you will fall down and worship me." Then Jesus said to him, "Be gone, Satan!"

Read **Ezekiel 28:11-19**, which connects God's judgment against the King of Tyre's arrogant claims with Satan's creation as an angel and his arrogant rebellion and sin. See also question 112.

261. Where do we find our hope in the battle against Satan?

We find our hope and refuge in the Lord Jesus Christ whose Word frees us from Satan's tyranny.

962. Psalm 46:1-3 God is our refuge and strength, a very present help in trouble. Therefore we will not fear though the earth gives way, though the mountains be moved into the heart of the sea, though its waters roar and foam, though the mountains tremble at its swelling.

963. Colossians 1:11-14 May you be strengthened with all power, according to his glorious might, for all endurance and patience with joy, giving thanks to the Father, who has qualified you to share in the inheritance of the saints in light. He has delivered us from the domain of darkness and transferred us to the kingdom of his beloved Son, in whom we have redemption, the forgiveness of sins.

Note: We sing about our gracious Father's power over evil in "A Mighty Fortress" (*LSB* 656, v.4):

Though devils all the world should fill, All eager to devour us,
We tremble not, we fear no ill; They shall not overpow'r us.
This world's prince may still Scowl fierce as he will,
He can harm us none. He's judged, the deed is done;
One little word can fell him.

Hymn (*LSB* 766, v. 8) and Prayer: *Father in heaven, look on our neediness with the eyes of Your mercy and compassion. Rescue us from everything that would cause harm and destruction to us both physically and spiritually. Keep us in the true faith and finally bring us through the disappointments and sorrows of this life to live with You forever; through Jesus Christ, our Lord. Amen.*

> ## Conclusion
>
> **For Thine is the kingdom and the power and the glory forever and ever. Amen.**
>
> *For the kingdom, the power, and the glory are Yours now and forever. Amen.*
>
> *What does this mean?*
>
> This means that I should be certain that these petitions are pleasing to our Father in heaven, and are heard by Him; for He Himself has commanded us to pray in this way and has promised to hear us. Amen, amen, which means "yes, yes, it shall be so."

262. Why did the early church add these words at the end of the Lord's Prayer?

They regarded it as a joyful acclamation that our Father is able to do all that we ask in these petitions.

964. 1 Chronicles 29:11 Yours, O LORD, is the greatness and the power and the glory and the victory and the majesty, for all that is in the heavens and in the earth is yours. Yours is the kingdom, O LORD, and you are exalted as head above all.

God our Father alone

- *is the king who bestows every good gift;*

965. James 1:17 Every good gift and every perfect gift is from above, coming down from the Father of lights with whom there is no variation or shadow due to change.

966. Psalm 103:2-3 Bless the LORD, O my soul, and forget not all his benefits, who forgives all your iniquity, who heals all your diseases.

- *has the power to grant our petitions;*

967. Psalm 33:6 By the word of the LORD were the heavens made, and by the breath of his mouth all their host.

968. Ephesians 3:20-21 To him who is able to do far more abundantly than all that we ask or think, according to the power at work within us, to him be glory in the church and in Christ Jesus throughout all generations, forever and ever. Amen.

- *is exalted as the one true God.*

969. Psalm 113:4-5 The LORD is high above all nations, and his glory above the heavens! Who is like the LORD our God, who is seated on high?

970. 1 Timothy 1:17 To the King of the ages, immortal, invisible, the only God be honor and glory forever and ever. Amen.

263. Why do we end the Lord's Prayer with the word amen?

Amen is an Old Testament word that means "so shall it be." It emphasizes that God will hear prayers, which He has commanded, and answer our prayers, just as He has promised.

971. Psalm 50:15 Call upon me in the day of trouble; I will deliver you, and you shall glorify me.

972. Proverbs 15:8 The sacrifice of the wicked is an abomination to the LORD, but the prayer of the upright is acceptable to him.

973. Proverbs 15:29 The LORD is far from the wicked but he hears the prayer of the righteous.

> Hymn (*LSB* 766, v. 9) and Prayer: *Our Father in heaven, grant us certainty to pray according to Your command and in the confidence that You have promised to hear us; through Jesus Christ, our Lord. Amen.*

264. What is prayer?

Prayer is a conversation with God that is initiated by Him.

> **974. Psalm 27:8** You have said, "Seek my face." My heart says to you, "Your face, LORD, do I seek."

265. How does God initiate this conversation?

God first comes and speaks to us through His Word thus inviting us to respond. In His Word, God

- *commands us to approach Him in prayer to show how earnestly He wants to help us;*

   > **975. Psalm 105:1** O give thanks to the LORD, call upon his name.

   > **976. 1 Thessalonians 5:17-18** Pray without ceasing, give thanks in all circumstances; for this is the will of God in Christ Jesus for you.

- *promises to hear our prayers so that we can approach Him in confidence;*

   > **977. Matthew 21:22** And whatever you ask in prayer, you will receive, if you have faith.

   > **978. John 16:24** Until now you have asked nothing in my name. Ask, and you will receive, that your joy may be full.

   > **979. James 1:6-7** Let him ask in faith, with no doubting, for the one who doubts is like a wave of the sea that is driven and tossed by the wind. For that person must not suppose that he will receive anything from the Lord.

- *gives us the very words that we can use in prayer.*

   > **980. Matthew 6:9** Pray then like this: "Our Father in heaven."

Note: The book of Psalms, often called "the prayer book of the Bible," is filled with prayers that our Father gives us to use. Jesus often prayed in the words of psalms (**Matthew 27:46 [Psalm 22:1]; Luke 23:46 [Psalm 31:5]; Matthew 21:16 [Psalm 8:2]; Matthew 22:44 [Psalm 110:1]; John 10 [Psalm 23, Psalm 95]**) and Christians have followed His example in worship and personal prayer ever since.

266. What kinds of prayer do we find in the Bible?

Prayers in the Bible take the form of

- *confession in which we acknowledge our sins to God;*

- *request in which we seek God's help;*

- *intercession in which we pray for others;*

- *thanksgiving in which we express our gratitude to God for His gifts;*

- *lamentation or complaint in which we express our plight to God;*

- *praise or adoration in which we extol the wonderful deeds and qualities of God.*

267. What do all these forms of prayer have in common?

In each case, prayer acknowledges that we receive life and all good gifts from God.

268. How does God answer prayer?

God our Father hears the prayers of His children and answers in His own way and in His own time.

   > **981. Isaiah 65:24** Before they call I will answer; while they are yet speaking I will hear.

   > **982. 2 Corinthians 12:8-9** Three times I pleaded with the Lord about this, that it should leave me. But he said to me, "My grace is sufficient for you, for my power is made perfect in weakness." Therefore I will boast all the more gladly of my weaknesses, so that the power of Christ may rest upon me.

These passages encourage us to pray in faith and confidence: **Matthew 8:5-13** where Jesus healed a centurion's servant; **Matthew 9:1-8** where Jesus healed a paralytic; **Exodus 3:7-10** about how the Lord planned to rescue Israel from Egypt; and **Luke 18:1**-8 where Jesus tells the parable of the persistent widow.

269. For whom should we pray?

We should pray for ourselves and for all other people, even for our enemies.

    983. 1 Timothy 2:1-2 I urge that supplications, prayers, intercessions, and thanksgivings be made for all people, for kings and all who are in high positions, that we may lead a peaceful and quiet life, godly and dignified in every way.

    984. Matthew 5:44 Pray for those who persecute you.

    Read **Luke 18:13** about the tax collector who prayed for himself; **Genesis 18:23-32** about how Abraham prayed for Sodom; **Matthew 15:22-28** about the Canaanite woman who prayed for her daughter; **Luke 23:34** about how Jesus prayed for His enemies; and **Acts 7:60** about Stephen praying for his enemies.

270. Where should we pray?

We should pray everywhere—when we are alone, with our families, and in church.

    985. 1 Timothy 2:8 I desire then that in every place the men should pray, lifting holy hands without anger or quarreling.

    986. Matthew 6:6 But when you pray, go into your room and shut the door and pray to your Father who is in secret. And your Father who sees in secret will reward you.

    987. Luke 5:16 [Jesus] would withdraw to desolate places and pray.

    988. Acts 12:5 Peter was kept in prison, but earnest prayer for him was made to God by the church.

271. How often should we pray?

Our Father encourages us to pray regularly and frequently—even constantly, and especially in time of trouble. The Holy Spirit turns even our sighs and groans into prayers.

    989. Psalm 65:8 You make the going out of the morning and the evening to shout for joy.

    990. Psalm 119:164 Seven times a day I praise you for your righteous rules.

    991. Luke 18:1 [Jesus] told them a parable to the effect that they ought always to pray and not lose heart.

    992. Romans 8:26 Likewise the Spirit helps us in our weakness. For we do not know what to pray for as we ought, but the Spirit himself intercedes for us with groanings too deep for words.

    993. 1 Thessalonians 5:17-18 Pray without ceasing, give thanks in all circumstances; for this is the will of God in Christ Jesus for you.

    994. Psalm 50:15 Call upon me in the day of trouble; I will deliver you, and you shall glorify me.

Read **Acts 2:46-3:1** and note how the early Christians kept the customary hours of prayer.

Note: See Martin Luther's suggestions in this catechism for daily morning, evening, and mealtime prayers and also these comments about prayer: "You can not find a Christian who is not always praying, as little as a living person is without a pulse, which never rests, but beats continuously, though the person may be sleeping or is occupied otherwise, so that he is not aware of its beating." (*Luther's Works*, vol. 24).

272. Do my prayers need to be in a polished form or in a set pattern of words?

As dear children of our heavenly Father, we pray through faith in Christ even if our words are simple and unadorned. As members of Christ's Church, we also have access to a rich treasury of prayers in the Scriptures, liturgy, and devotional writings.

The Nature of Baptism

First

What is Baptism? Baptism is not just plain water, but it is the water included in God's command and combined with God's word.

Which is that word of God? Christ our Lord says in the last chapter of Matthew: "Therefore go and make disciples of all nations, baptizing them in the name of the Father and of the Son and of the Holy Spirit." **[Matthew 28:19]**

The Central Thought

Baptism is from God (LC 4, 6) since our Lord Jesus instituted Baptism (**Matthew 28:19**), joining water to God's Word and His triune name. This is how God makes us His dear children and disciples.

What does it mean to have a last name (family name)? When God places His name on us in Baptism, what does that mean?

Read **Matthew 3:13-17**. How are all three persons of the Trinity present and active in Jesus' Baptism? How does His Baptism help us to understand the work of the Father, Son, and Holy Spirit in our Baptism?

✝ *As Christians, we are God's baptized people! We are His adopted children together with all believers, and we live and die in the confidence that He has redeemed us and we are His.*

How do people answer the question, "Who am I?" How does Baptism help me answer that question?

A Closer Reading of the *Small Catechism*

273. What does the word "baptize" mean?

"Baptize" simply means to wash with water, whether by immersing, pouring, or sprinkling. Christian Baptism refers to washing with water in the name of the Father, Son, and Holy Spirit according to the institution of Christ.

> **995. Mark 7:4** And when they come from the marketplace they do not eat unless they wash [literally "baptize"]. And there are many other traditions that they observe, such as the washing [literally "baptizing"] of cups and pots and copper vessels and dining couches.

274. What is different about the water of baptism?

The water in itself is not different or holier than any other water, but because "God's Word and commandment are added to it," it is a "divine water" (LC IV:14).

> **996. Ephesians 5:25-26** Christ loved the church and gave himself up for her, that he might sanctify her, having cleansed her by the washing of water with the word."

275. Who instituted Holy Baptism?

Our Lord Jesus Christ, after His death and resurrection, commanded His church to baptize all nations.

> **997. Matthew 28:19-20** Go therefore and make disciples of all nations, baptizing them in the name of the Father and of the Son and of the Holy Spirit, teaching them to observe all that I have commanded you. And behold, I am with you always, to the end of the age.

276. What does it mean to baptize "in the name of the Father and of the Son and of the Holy Spirit"?

"To be baptized in God's name is to be baptized not by human beings but by God Himself. Although it is performed by human hands, it is nevertheless truly God's own act" (LC IV:10). In Baptism, God puts His saving name on us and is truly present to bless us with all His gifts as His children and heirs.

> **998. Numbers 6:23-27** Thus you shall bless the people of Israel: you shall say to them, "The LORD bless you and keep you; the LORD make his face to shine upon you and be gracious to you; the LORD lift up his countenance upon you and give you peace. So shall they put my name upon the people of Israel, and I will bless them."
>
> **999. Exodus 20:24** In every place where I cause my name to be remembered I will come to you and bless you.

Read **1 Kings 8:27-30** and **9:3.** Where is the LORD placing his name and for what purpose?

277. Who is to baptize?

Normally pastors, Christ's called ministers, are to baptize, but in an emergency when no pastor is available, any Christian should baptize.

> **1000. 1 Corinthians 4:1** This is how one should regard us, as servants of Christ and stewards of the mysteries of God.

Note: For a short form of Baptism in cases of emergency (that is, when death is imminent), see *LSB* 1023.

278. To whom does Jesus refer when He says that "all nations" are to be baptized?

"All nations," refers to all people outside of the Church regardless of age, sex, ethnicity, etc.

Connections and Applications

279. Why should babies be baptized?

- *Babies are included in the words "all nations"(Matthew 28:19);*

  > **1001. Acts 2:38-39** And Peter said to them, "Repent and be baptized, every one of you, in the name of Jesus Christ for the forgiveness of your sins, and you will receive the gift of the Holy Spirit. For the promise is for you and for your children and for all who are far off, everyone whom the Lord our God calls to himself."

  Read **Acts 16:13-15, 25-34; 1 Corinthians 1:16.** The apostles baptized whole households, which likely included children.

- *Babies are sinners who need what Baptism promises, the forgiveness of sins and the gift of the Holy Spirit;*

  > **1002. Psalm 51:5** Behold, I was brought forth in iniquity, and in sin did my mother conceive me.
  >
  > **1003. Romans 5:12, 18-19** Therefore, just as sin came into the world through one man, and death through sin, and so death spread to all men because all sinned…Therefore as one trespass led to condemnation for all men, so one act of righteousness leads to justification and life for all men. For as by the one man's disobedience the many were made sinners, so by the one man's obedience the many will be made righteous.
  >
  > **1004. John 3:5-6** "Truly, truly, I say to you, unless one is born of water and the Spirit, he cannot enter the kingdom of God. That which is born of the flesh is flesh and that which is born of the Spirit is spirit."

- *The Holy Spirit is able to work faith in babies;*

  > **1005. Matthew 18:6** Whoever causes one of these little ones who believe in me to sin, it would be better for him to have a great millstone fastened around his neck and to be drowned in the depth of the sea.

1006. Psalm 22:9-10 Yet you are he who took me from the womb; you made me trust you at my mother's breasts. On you was I cast from my birth, and from my mother's womb you have been my God.

Read **Luke 1:13-17, 39-45**. When was John the Baptist filled with the Holy Spirit?

- *Jesus invites children, including infants, to come to come and be blessed by Him.*

   1007. Luke 18:15-17 Now they were bringing even infants to him that he might touch them. And when the disciples saw it, they rebuked them. But Jesus called them to him, saying, 'Let the children come to me, and do not hinder them, for to such belongs the kingdom of God. Truly, I say to you, whoever does not receive the kingdom of God like a child shall not enter it."

Note: Faith is not to be confused with intellectual ability. Those who argue for "believer's baptism" and reject the baptism of infants (or those with severe mental handicaps) often wrongly maintain that (1) infants are not guilty of (accountable for) sin or able to commit sinful acts; (2) faith is a human decision that infants cannot make; and (3) Baptism is primarily our promise to God rather than God's promise to us. None of these views is based on Scripture.

280. What is the connection between Baptism and teaching?

- *Baptism and teaching are inseparably connected by Jesus (**Matthew 28:19-20**).*

- *Those who are able to receive instruction are normally baptized after being taught the main articles of the Christian faith.*

   Read **Acts 2:38-41; Acts 8:26-39;** and **Acts16:25-33**.

- *Infants and young children should be brought to Baptism as soon as possible, then instructed in the Christian faith as they are able to receive instruction.*

   Read **Luke 18:15-17** (verse 1007); **Mark 10:13-15**; and **2 Corinthians 6:2**.

281. Why does the church encourage sponsors at Baptism?

Sponsors are to confess the faith expressed in the Apostles' Creed and taught in the Small Catechism, witness the Baptism of those they sponsor (whenever possible), pray for them, support them in their ongoing instruction and nurture in the Christian faith, and encourage them toward faithful reception of the Lord's Supper. They are also to be examples to them of the life of faith and love for the neighbor (see LSB 269).

282. Are all "baptisms" to be recognized as valid?

When Christ's words and command are doubted, changed or ignored, such a "baptism"cannot be recognized as Christ's work. No other names or titles are to be substituted for the name and words which Christ gives us (the Father, Son and Holy Spirit). The "baptisms" of groups that do not confess faith in the Triune God also cannot be recognized as Christian Baptism, no matter what words they use in baptizing. In Christian churches where Baptism is administered according to Christ's institution (using water and His words "in the name of the Father and of the Son and of the Holy Spirit"), there Christ fulfills His promise. Such Baptisms are to be recognized.

Hymn (*LSB* 590) and Prayer: *Gracious Father, thank You for the gift of Baptism which Your Son has established by His Word and promise. Teach us to treasure all that Jesus has done for us in His cross and resurrection. Give us confidence that through our Baptism we bear Your holy name and so are Your holy children for time and eternity; through the same, Jesus Christ, our Lord. Amen.*

The Blessings of Baptism

Second

What benefits does Baptism give? It works the forgiveness of sins, rescues from death and the devil, and gives eternal salvation to all who believe this, as the words and promises of God declare.

Which are these words and promises of God? Christ our Lord says in the last chapter of Mark: "Whoever believes and is baptized will be saved, but whoever does not believe will be condemned." **[Mark 16:16]**

The Central Thought

Baptism is far more than a human religious ceremony. Baptism "is not a work that we do but it is a treasure that God gives us and faith grasps" (LC IV, 37).

What is the "treasure" that God promises to give to us in Baptism?

Read **Acts 2:22-41**. What does Peter's Pentecost sermon tell us about Jesus and about the blessings of Baptism?

✝ *As Christians, we confess that "I am baptized! God promises that because I have been washed with water, He has forgiven and saved me. I can trust His promises."*

God promises that wonderful gifts come in Baptism—God's Spirit, His forgiveness and acceptance today, and resurrection and eternal life forever (**Acts 2:38-39** and **Galatians 5:5**).

A Closer Reading of the *Small Catechism*

283. What great things does God do through Baptism?

- *God works forgiveness of sins.*

    1008. Acts 2:38 And Peter said to them, "Repent and be baptized every one of you in the name of Jesus Christ for the forgiveness of your sins, and you will receive the gift of the Holy Spirit."

    1009. Acts 22:16 [Ananias said to Paul:] "And now why do you wait? Rise and be baptized and wash away your sins, calling on his name."

- *God rescues from death and the devil.*

    1010. Romans 6:3-5 Do you not know that all of us who have been baptized into Christ Jesus were baptized into his death? We were buried therefore with him by baptism into death, in order that, just as Christ was raised from the dead by the glory of the Father, we too might walk in newness of life. For if we have been united with him in a death like his, we shall certainly be united with him in a resurrection like his.

    1011. Colossians 1:13-14 He has delivered us from the domain of darkness and transferred us to the kingdom of his beloved Son, in whom we have redemption, the forgiveness of sins.

    1012. Colossians 2:11-12 In him also you were circumcised with a circumcision made without hands, by putting off the body of the flesh, by the circumcision of Christ, having been buried with him in baptism, in which you were also raised with him through faith in the powerful working of God, who raised him from the dead.

- *God gives eternal salvation.*

1013. 1 Peter 3:21 Baptism, which corresponds to [Noah's flood], now saves you, not as a removal of dirt from the body but as an appeal to God for a good conscience, through the resurrection of Jesus Christ.

1014. Titus 3:5-7 He saved us, not because of works done by us in righteousness, but according to his own mercy, by the washing of regeneration and renewal of the Holy Spirit, whom he poured out on us richly through Jesus Christ our Savior, so that being justified by his grace we might become heirs according to the hope of eternal life.

Read **Mark 16:16** and note how this is consistent with the teaching of Jesus and the entire Bible even though this verse does not appear in the oldest New Testament manuscripts.

Connections and Applications

284. If Christ has already won full forgiveness and salvation for us why do we need Baptism?

*Christ has indeed atoned for the sins of the whole world (**1 John 2:2**), reconciling the world to Himself (**2 Corinthians 5:18-19**). Through Baptism He gives to us personally the forgiveness of sins that He acquired for all of humanity. As such, Baptism is a means of grace.*

1015. 1 Corinthians 6:11 But you were washed, you were sanctified, you were justified in the name of the Lord Jesus Christ and by the Spirit of our God.

Read **Titus 3:5-7** (verse 1014).

285. To whom does Baptism give these blessings?

Baptism gives these blessings to all who believe God's saving promises. Faith does not make Baptism what it is, but it is through faith alone that we receive Baptism's blessings.

1016. Acts 2:39 For the promise is for you and for your children and for all who are far off, everyone whom the Lord our God calls to himself.

Read **Acts 16:25-34.** Faith and Baptism are put together in the account of the jailer and his family.

286. Where are the blessings of Baptism received?

In Baptism we are adopted as children of God and are incorporated into the body of Christ where we continue to receive all that our Lord has promised to His holy people.

1017. 1 Corinthians 12:12-13 For just as the body is one and has many members, and all the members of the body, though many, are one body, so it is with Christ. For in one Spirit we were all baptized into one body—Jews or Greeks, slaves or free—and all were made to drink of one Spirit.

1018. Ephesians 2:19-22 So then you are no longer strangers and aliens, but you are fellow citizens with the saints and members of the household of God built on the foundation of the apostles and prophets, Christ Jesus himself being the cornerstone, in whom the whole structure, being joined together, grows into a holy temple in the Lord. In him you also are being built together into a dwelling place for God by the Spirit.

Read **Acts 2:41-47,** where we see how the newly baptized believers were included in church life in teaching, fellowship, "the breaking of bread" and prayer.

287. Is it possible for an unbaptized person to be saved?

*Yes. Only unbelief condemns. Before the institution of Baptism, Old Testament believers were saved through faith in the promise of Christ. Those who believe the Gospel and yet die before Baptism are not condemned, because they "have been born again, not of perishable seed but of imperishable, through the living and abiding word of God" (**1 Peter 1:23**). However, faith does not despise what the Lord promises and gives in Baptism. The unbaptized should not delay in receiving Baptism.*

Read **Luke 23:39-43**. Although Christ had not yet instituted Baptism, the thief on the cross was saved through the word of Christ; and **Luke 7:28-30.** The Pharisees and experts in the Law, in unbelief, rejected John's baptism.

288. Is it possible for a baptized person to fall from faith and be eternally lost?

Yes. It is true that God's promises in Baptism stand even if we do not believe them. However, all who reject God's promises to them and die in unbelief have abandoned Baptism and do not receive what God has promised. They will be lost.

> **1019. 1 Corinthians 10:1-5, 12** For I do not want you to be unaware brothers, that our fathers were all under the cloud, and all passed through the sea, and all were baptized into Moses in the cloud and in the sea, and all ate the same spiritual food, and all drank the same spiritual drink. For they drank from the spiritual Rock that followed them, and the Rock was Christ. Nevertheless, with most of them God was not pleased, for they were overthrown in the wilderness...Therefore let anyone who thinks that he stands take heed lest he fall.

> **1020. Luke 8:13** And the ones on the rock are those who, when they hear the word, receive it with joy. But these have no root; they believe for a while, and in time of testing fall away.

> **1021. 1 Timothy 4:1** Now the Spirit expressly says that in later times some will depart from the faith by devoting themselves to deceitful spirits and teachings of demons.

289. How does Baptism help me in my life and death?

*Baptism is God's work, and what He does is sure and certain. In times of doubt, temptation, failure, and especially in the face of death, we have God's own pledge and promise in Baptism that He has forgiven our sins and delivered us from death, hell and the devil. We can boldly say "I am baptized into Christ" and be certain that the comforting words of **Romans 8:1** are true: "There is therefore now no condemnation for those who are in Christ Jesus."*

Hymn (*LSB* 601) and Prayer: *Lord Jesus Christ, You have forgiven our sins by Your blood, rescued us from Satan, and won for us eternal life and salvation in Your resurrection. As You bestow these gifts on us in Baptism, grant that in life and death we may always cling to our Baptism, trusting in Your promises, and finally be brought into Your heavenly kingdom. Amen.*

The Power of Baptism

Third

How can water do such great things? Certainly not just the water, but the word of God in and with the water does these things, along with the faith which trusts this word of God in the water. For without God's word the water is plain water and no Baptism. But with the word of God it is a Baptism, that is, a life-giving water, rich in grace, and a washing of the new birth in the Holy Spirit, as St. Paul says in Titus chapter three:

"He saved us through the washing of rebirth and renewal by the Holy Spirit, whom He poured out on us generously through Christ, our Savior, so that, having been justified by His grace, we might become heirs having the hope of eternal life. This is a trustworthy saying." **[Titus 3:5-8]**

The Central Thought

Did you choose to be born? When the Bible calls Baptism a "birth," how does that help you understand that your relationship to God is not something you choose for yourself but a gift that He gives?

God's Spirit, Word, and name make Baptism more than water. It is a "washing of new birth" (LC IV: 27), in which our heavenly Father adopts us and gives the inheritance of eternal life through faith in His Son.

Read **John 3:1-15**. Why are Jesus' words confusing for Nicodemus? What does it mean to be "born again" (that is, born from above)? According to verses 3 and 5, what does the new birth give?

✝ *As Christians, we can say, "I am baptized—I am washed—I am God's own child and an heir of heaven. My confidence in these great gifts is based entirely on God's Word and promises."*

I have so many faults and problems that I might lose hope. But "God does not lie" and His "Word cannot deceive" (LC IV, 57). He has washed me clean. I can trust Him. He will help me in every trouble.

A Closer Reading of the *Small Catechism*

290. We only see water in Baptism. How does water work the forgiveness of sins, rescue from death and the devil, and give eternal salvation?

    Our Lord's institution of Baptism puts these blessings into baptismal water and faith receives them. In the Old Testament, God's words promised healing for Naaman in the water of the Jordan. When Naaman believed God's word and washed in the Jordan, he was cleansed of his leprosy (2 Kings 5:1-15). Now, in the New Testament, God joins His word to the water so that it is the instrument of God's saving work.

    Read **Ephesians 5:25-26; Gal 3:26-27; Colossians 2:11-15;** and **Acts 22:16.**

291. Why is Baptism called "the washing of rebirth and renewal of the Holy Spirit" (**Titus 3:5-8**)?

    The Holy Spirit works in and through Baptism to create faith in Christ Jesus, adopting us as children of the Father and making us new creatures in Christ who now live not according to the flesh but by the Spirit.

    1022. Titus 3:5-8 He saved us, not because of works done by us in righteousness, but according to his own mercy, by the washing of regeneration and renewal of the Holy Spirit, whom he poured out on us richly through Jesus Christ our Savior, so that being justified by his grace we might become heirs according to the hope of eternal life. The saying is trustworthy, and I want you to insist on these things, so that those who have believed in God may be careful to devote themselves to good works. These things are excellent and profitable for people.

1023. 2 Corinthians 5:17 Therefore, if anyone is in Christ, he is a new creation. The old has passed away; behold, the new has come.

Read **Romans 8:11-17**, noting its emphasis on life according to the Spirit and not the flesh (our sinful nature).

Connections and Applications

292. Is a Christian's faith in Baptism or in Jesus?

This is a false alternative. The Christian's faith is in Jesus and in Baptism, for Jesus has put His Word of promise in the water. Faith takes hold of Christ where He has promised to be for us. To trust in Baptism is to trust in Christ who saves us through the washing He has joined to His Word. As Luther explains, it is "certainly not just the water, but the Word of God in and with the water [that] does these things, along with the faith which trusts this Word of God in the water."

1024. 1 Peter 3:21 Baptism, which corresponds to this [Noah's flood], now saves you, not as a removal of dirt from the body but as an appeal to God for a good conscience, through the resurrection of Jesus Christ.

Note: At the time of the Reformation there were several false understandings of Baptism. On the one hand, there was the Roman Catholic teaching that Baptism worked simply by the performance of the rite apart from faith. On the other hand, there were those (Luther calls them "new spirits) who wrongly taught that Baptism was an empty ceremony with no power to bestow the salvation promised by God's Word. These false teachings are also present today so (as expressed in the answer above) it is important to emphasize both the power of Baptism to create faith and the need to receive Baptism in faith (See LC IV, 28-29).

293. Are we to seek a 'baptism with the Holy Spirit' in addition to Holy Baptism?

No, the Holy Spirit works through the one Baptism instituted by Christ.

- *There is only "one Baptism for the remission of sins" (Nicene Creed).*

  1025. Ephesians 4:5 One Lord, one faith, one baptism.

  1026. 1 Corinthians 12:13 For in one Spirit we were all baptized into one body.

Note:The "instruction about baptisms" (**Hebrews 6:2**) does not mean that there are several Christian baptisms, but that the one Baptism must be clearly distinguished from the many religious washings that were common in the ancient world (see **Mark 7:4**).

- *Christian Baptism is not a water-only or a Spirit-only baptism, but a Baptism of water **and** the Holy Spirit.*

  1027. John 3:5 Jesus answered, "Truly, truly, I say to you, unless one is born of water and the Spirit, he cannot enter the kingdom of God."

  1028. Titus 3:5 He saved us, not because of works done by us in righteousness, but according to his own mercy, by the washing of regeneration and renewal of the Holy Spirit.

  1029. 1 Corinthians 6:11 And such were some of you. But you were washed, you were sanctified, you were justified in the name of the Lord Jesus Christ and by the Spirit of our God.

Note: **Matthew 3:11**and **Acts 1:4-5** speak of John baptizing with water and Jesus baptizing with the Spirit. The difference here is not between a "water Baptism" versus a "Spirit baptism." John's baptism gave the forgiveness of sins but was in anticipation of Jesus' saving work and the Baptism Christ would institute, which is received until the end of the age. Christ's Baptism is with water *and* the Holy Spirit, whom He poured out after His resurrection (see **John 7:39** and **Acts 2**).

- *The special signs granted by the Holy Spirit were not another "baptism," but they testified to the truth and power of the apostles' preaching.*

1030. Acts 2:42-43 And they devoted themselves to the apostles' teaching and the fellowship, to the breaking of bread and the prayers. And awe came upon every soul, and many wonders and signs were being done through the apostles.

1031. 2 Corinthians 12:12-13 The signs of a true apostle were performed among you with utmost patience, with signs and wonders and mighty works. For in what were you less favored than the rest of the churches, except that I myself did not burden you? Forgive me this wrong!

Hymn (*LSB* 406) and Prayer: *O God, our Father, You have saved us through the washing of rebirth and renewal which You have poured out on us in our Baptism into Your Son. We thank You for this life-giving water, rich in grace by Your trustworthy promise. Give us faith always to trust Your Word in the water, that justified by grace, we remain heirs of eternal life; through the same Jesus Christ, Your Son, our Lord. Amen.*

What Baptism Indicates

Fourth

What does such baptizing with water indicate? It indicates that the Old Adam in us should by daily contrition and repentance be drowned and die with all sins and evil desires, and that a new man should emerge and arise to live before God in righteousness and purity forever.

Where is this written? St. Paul writes in Romans chapter six: "We were therefore buried with Him through baptism into death in order that, just as Christ was raised from the dead through the glory of the Father, we too may live a new life." **[Romans 6:4]**

The Central Thought

How do people today try to "make themselves new?"

Baptism embraces our entire lives as believers. It means death to all our selfishness and sin, and that God is making new people out of us.

Read **Romans 6:1-11**. What happened to us in Baptism? What are the implications for our lives?

☩ *As Christians, we confess "I am baptized—and now I have a daily battle, confessing my sins and drowning them, and also living the new life according to God's goodness and love."*

Baptism sets the rhythm for our daily lives as Christians. How do we drown our sins and evil desires? What kind of new person ("new man") is God making out of me?

A Closer Reading of the *Small Catechism*

294. What is the old Adam?

   The old Adam (sometimes called the "old man" or the "old self") refers to us as fallen creatures. We have inherited a complete and total corruption of our created nature from Adam, which results in unbelief and rebellion against the creator.

   1032. Ephesians 4:22 Put off your old self, which belongs to your former manner of life and is corrupt through deceitful desires.

295. What is the new man?

   The new man refers to us as restored creatures of God in Christ. We have been united with Christ by the washing of rebirth, which results in new Spirit-created attitudes, desires, and actions.

   1033. 2 Corinthians 5:17 Therefore, if anyone is in Christ, he is a new creation. The old has passed away; behold, the new has come.

296. How do the old Adam and the new man interact?

   They are engaged in an ongoing life and death struggle with each other.

   1034. Galatians 5:17 For the desires of the flesh are against the Spirit, and the desires of the Spirit are against the flesh, for these are opposed to each other, to keep you from doing the things you want to do.

297. How does Baptism picture what the Christian's daily life should look like?

In the waters of Baptism we have been buried and raised with Christ. Therefore we should continually resist every impulse of the old Adam until he is drowned once and for all when we die. At the same time we should continually give free reign to the new man until he rises in final victory on the last day.

> **1035.** **Romans 6:3-4** Do you not know that all of us who have been baptized into Christ Jesus were baptized into his death? We were buried therefore with him by baptism into death, in order that, just as Christ was raised from the dead by the glory of the Father, we too might walk in newness of life.

> **1036.** **Ephesians 4:24** Put on the new self, created after the likeness of God in true righteousness and holiness.

> **1037.** **Galatians 2:20** I have been crucified with Christ. It is no longer I who live, but Christ who lives in me. And the life I now live in the flesh I live by faith in the Son of God, who loved me and gave himself for me.

> Read **Colossians 3:1-10.**

Connections and Applications

298. What words do we use to remember our Baptism?

*We remember our Baptism with the words "in the name of the Father and of the Son and of the Holy Spirit" (**Matthew 28:19**)—the Trinitarian invocation. When these words are used in the Divine Service or in our prayers (for example, Luther's morning and evening prayers), we recall and confess before heaven, earth, and hell all that God has given us in our Baptism: "victory over death and the devil, forgiveness of sins, God's grace, the entire Christ, and the Holy Spirit with His gifts" (LC, IV 41).*

Note: The Trinitarian Invocation may be accompanied by the sign of the cross, made at our Baptism upon our foreheads and hearts to mark us as "redeemed by Christ the crucified."

299. How do we rightly use our Baptism?

We rightly use our Baptism when we live in repentance and faith in the Triune God who has made us His beloved children. "In this way one sees what a great, excellent thing Baptism is. It delivers us from the devil's jaws and makes us God's own. It suppresses and takes away sin and daily strengthens the new man. It is working and always continues working until we pass from this estate of misery to eternal glory" (LC IV, 83)

Hymn (*LSB* 596) and Prayer: *Heavenly Father, You have forgiven our sins, rescued us from death and the devil, and given us eternal life by Baptism into the death and resurrection of Your beloved Son. Strengthen our faith so that we daily put to death all sins and evil desires and, trusting Your sure promises, are raised to live before You in righteousness and purity. Finally bring us to the fulfillment of our Baptism in the resurrection of the body to life everlasting; through your Son, Jesus Christ, our Lord. Amen.*

The Office of the Keys

What is the Office of the Keys? The Office of the Keys is that special authority which Christ has given to His Church on earth to forgive the sins of repentant sinners, but to withhold forgiveness from the unrepentant as long as they do not repent.

Where is this written? This is what St. John the Evangelist writes in chapter twenty: The Lord Jesus breathed on His disciples and said, "Receive the Holy Spirit. If you forgive anyone his sins they are forgiven; if you do not forgive them, they are not forgiven." **(John 20:22-23)**

What do you believe according to these words? I believe that when the called ministers of Christ deal with us by His divine command, in particular when they exclude openly unrepentant sinners from the Christian congregation and absolve those who repent of their sins and want to do better, this is just as valid and certain even in heaven, as if Christ our dear Lord dealt with us Himself.

The Central Thought

By His death on the cross, Christ accomplished salvation, providing forgiveness of sins for the entire world. Unless His good news is made known to me, it would not benefit me.

How do I know my sins are forgiven before God in heaven?

Read **John 20:19-23**. How does Jesus make known His forgiveness?

✝ *As Christians, we confess that Jesus sends His servants to proclaim the good news, forgiving the sins of all who repent and withholding forgiveness from those who insist on remaining in their sin.*

What comfort does forgiveness through a pastor give me when I am tempted to doubt my identity as God's child?

A Closer Reading of the *Small Catechism*

300. What special authority has Christ given to His Church on earth?

   Christ has given His Church the authority to forgive the sins of all who repent and to withhold His forgiveness from those who will not repent.

   1038. Matthew 18:18 Truly, I say to you, whatever you bind on earth shall be bound in heaven; and whatever you loose on earth shall be loosed in heaven.

   1039. John 20:22-23 And when he had said this, he breathed on them and said to them, "Receive the Holy Spirit. If you forgive the sins of any, they are forgiven them; if you withhold forgiveness from any, is it withheld."

301. What is the authority or power of the keys?

   It is twofold: One key is called the releasing key as it absolves from sin and opens heaven. The other is called the binding key as it retains sins and closes heaven to those who are impenitent.

1040. Matthew 16:19 I will give you the keys of the kingdom of heaven, and whatever you bind on earth shall be bound in heaven, and whatever you loose on earth shall be loosed in heaven.

302. Why is the office of the keys called *the special authority* which Christ has given to His Church?

Because outside of the Christian Church, where there is no Gospel, there is also no forgiveness of sins.

"Everything, therefore, in the Christian Church is ordered toward this goal: we shall daily receive in the Christian Church nothing but the forgiveness of sin through the Word and signs, to comfort and encourage our consciences as long as we live here" (LC II, 55).

1041. Ephesians 2:11-12 Therefore remember that at one time you Gentiles in the flesh, called "the uncircumcision" by what is called the circumcision, which is made in the flesh by hands— remember, that you were at that time separated from Christ, alienated from the commonwealth of Israel and strangers to the covenants of promise, having no hope and without God in the world.

1042. John 14:6 Jesus said to him, "I am the way, and the truth, and the life. No one comes to the Father except through me."

303. Who are to be forgiven?

All those who repent and ask for forgiveness of their sins are to be absolved.

1043. Acts 3:19 Repent therefore, and turn back, that yours sins may be blotted out.

1044. Psalm 32:5 I acknowledged my sin to you and I did not cover my iniquity; I said I will confess my transgressions to the LORD, and you forgave the iniquity of my sin.

304. Who are not to be forgiven?

Those who do not repent and believe in Jesus Christ are not to be forgiven as long as they continue in their impenitence.

1045. Matthew 18:17 If he refuses to listen to them, tell it to the church. And if he refuses to listen even to the church, let him be to you as a Gentile and a tax collector.

305. Who receives the forgiveness given in absolution?

All sinners who are sorry for their sins (contrition) and trust in Christ as their Savior (faith).

1046. Psalm 32:5 I acknowledged my sin to you and I did not cover my iniquity; "I said I will confess my transgressions to the LORD," and you forgave the iniquity of my sin.

1047. Mark 1:15 The time is fulfilled, and the kingdom of God is at hand, repent and believe in the gospel.

Read about Zacchaeus the repentant tax collector in **Luke 19:1-10**.

306. How is the Office of the Keys related to the proclamation of the Gospel?

*The Office of the Keys is a special, God-given way of applying the Gospel to the individual. "God is superabundantly generous in His grace: First, through the spoken Word, by which the forgiveness of sins is preached to the whole world (**Luke 24:45-47**). This is the particular office of the Gospel. Second, through Baptism. Third, through the holy Sacrament of the Altar. Fourth, through the Power of the Keys. Also through the mutual conversation and consolation of the brethren, 'Where two or three are gathered' (**Matthew 18:20**) and other such verses (especially **Romans 1:12**)." (SA IV).*

1048. Matthew 18:20 For where two or three are gathered in my name, there am I among them.

1049. Matthew 28:18-20 And Jesus came and said to them, "All authority in heaven and on earth has been given to me. Go therefore and make disciples of all nations, baptizing them in the name of the Father and of the Son and of the Holy Spirit, teaching them to observe all that I have commanded you. And behold, I am with you always, to the end of the age."

1050. 1 Peter 2:9 But you are a chosen race, a royal priesthood, a holy nation, a people for his own possession, that you may proclaim the excellencies of him who called you out of darkness into his marvelous light.

Connections and Applications

307. What is excommunication?

"Excommunication is also pronounced against the openly wicked and the haters of the Sacraments" (Ap XI).

Excommunication is the exercise of the binding key. In it the church announces to impenitent sinners that their sins are not forgiven before God and that they are excluded from the Lord's Supper and every other privilege of fellowship in the Christian church except hearing God's Word.

1051. Matthew 18:15-18 If your brother sins against you, go and tell him his fault, between you and him alone. If he listens to you, you have gained your brother. But if he does not listen, take one or two others along with you, that every charge may be established by the evidence of two or three witnesses. If he refuses to listen to them, tell it to the church. And if he refuses to listen even to the church, let him be to you as a Gentile a tax collector. Truly, I say to you, whatever you bind on earth shall be bound in heaven, and whatever you loose on earth shall be loosed in heaven.

308. What is the purpose of excommunication?

Excommunication is enacted to show a person who refuses to repent the seriousness of his or her sin and ultimately to rescue such persons from eternal condemnation and win them back to Christ. Thus they are always welcomed and encouraged to hear God's Word.

1052. 1 Corinthians 5:4-5 When you are assembled in the name of the Lord Jesus and my spirit is present, with the power of our Lord Jesus, you are to deliver this man to Satan for the destruction of the flesh, so that his spirit may be saved in the day of the Lord.

1053. 1 Corinthians 5:13 God judges those outside. "Purge the evil person from among you."

1054. Galatians 6:1-2 Brothers, if anyone is caught in any transgression, you who are spiritual should restore him in a spirit of gentleness. Keep watch on yourself, lest you too be tempted. Bear one another's burdens and so fulfill the law of Christ.

309. What is the responsibility of a congregation toward an excommunicated sinner who repents?

The congregation joyfully forgives all who repent and receives them back into the fellowship of Christ's altar.

1055. 2 Corinthians 2:7-8 So you should rather turn to forgive and comfort him, or he may be overwhelmed by excessive sorrow. So I beg you to reaffirm your love for him.

1056. Luke 15:7 Just so, I tell you, there will be more joy in heaven over one sinner who repents than over ninety-nine righteous persons who need no repentance.

310. How does the church publicly exercise the Office of the Keys?

Christ has instituted the pastoral office through which the Office of the Keys is exercised publicly, that is, on behalf of the Church. The Christian congregation, acting in accordance with the will of Christ, calls qualified men to serve as His ministers, forgiving and retaining sins according to His command.

1057. Ephesians 4:11 And he gave the apostles, the prophets the evangelists, the shepherds and teachers

1058. Acts 20:28 Pay careful attention to yourselves and to all the flock, in which the Holy Spirit has made you overseers, to care for the church of God, which he obtained with his own blood.

1059. 1 Corinthians 4:1 This is how one should regard us, as servants of Christ and stewards of the mysteries of God.

311. May every Christian, without a call, presume to exercise the Office of the Keys publicly?

No. While the Office of the Keys is given to the whole Church, only those who are called as pastors are given the responsibility to exercise it publicly, that is, on behalf of the Church.

"Our churches teach that no one should publicly teach in the Church, or administer the Sacraments, without a rightly ordered call" (AC XIV).

> **1060. Romans 10:15** And how are they to preach unless they are sent? As it is written, How beautiful are the feet of those who preach the good news!
>
> **1061. 1 Corinthians 12:29** Are all apostles? Are all prophets? Are all teachers?
>
> **1062. James 3:1** Not many of you should become teachers, my brothers; for you know that we who teach will be judges with greater strictness.

312. May only pastors then forgive sins?

No. All Christians are given the word of Christ's forgiveness to proclaim in their daily vocations.

> **1063. 1 Peter 2:9-10** But you are a chosen race, a royal priesthood, a holy nation, a people for his own possession, that you may proclaim the excellencies of him who called you out of darkness into his marvelous light. Once you were not a people, but now you are God's people; once you had not received mercy, but now you have received mercy.
>
> **1064. Colossians 3:12-13** Put on then, as God's chosen ones, holy and beloved, compassionate hearts, kindness, humility, meekness, and patience, bearing with one another and, if one has a complaint against another, forgiving each other, as the Lord has forgiveness you, so you also must forgive.
>
> **1065. Luke 11:4** And forgive us our sins, for we ourselves forgive everyone who is indebted to us.

313. Who should be considered for the office of pastor?

Congregations are to call men who are spiritually qualified in life and doctrine to serve as pastors.

> **1066. 1 Timothy 3:1-2** The saying is trustworthy: If anyone aspires to the office of overseer he desires a noble task. Therefore an overseer must be above reproach, the husband of one wife, sober-minded, self-controlled, respectable, hospitable, able to teach.
>
> **1067. Titus 1:5-9** This is why I left you in Crete, so that you might put what remained into order, and appoint elders in every town as I directed you—if anyone is above reproach, the husband of one wife, and his children are believers and not open to the charge of debauchery or insubordination. For an overseer, as God's steward, must be above reproach. He must not be arrogant or quick tempered or a drunkard or violent or greedy for gain, but hospitable, a lover of good, self-controlled, upright, holy, and disciplined. He must hold firm to the trustworthy word as taught so that he may be able to give instruction in sound doctrine and also to rebuke those who contradict it.

314. May women serve in the pastoral office?

All Christians, both men and women, are redeemed and gifted for service in Christ's Church but each according to God's ordering of life in His creation. God's Word prohibits women from serving in the pastoral office.

> **1068. 1 Corinthians 14:33-36** For God is not a God of confusion but of peace. As in all the churches of the saints, the women should keep silent in the churches. For they are not permitted to speak, but should be in submission, as the Law also says. If there is anything they desire to learn, let them ask their husbands at home. For it is shameful for a woman to speak in church. Or was it from you that the word of God came? Or are you the only ones it has reached?
>
> **1069. 1 Timothy 2:11-14** Let a woman learn quietly with all submissiveness. I do not permit a woman to teach or to exercise authority over a man; rather, she is to remain quiet. For Adam was formed first, then Eve; and Adam was not deceived, but the woman was deceived and became a transgressor.

Hymn (*LSB* 614) and Prayer: *Heavenly Father, You delivered Your Son for our offenses and raised Him for our justification. Grant that we may also trust in the word of forgiveness which You have given Your pastors to proclaim, that clinging to Your good and gracious promises, we might be brought to eternal life; through Jesus Christ our Lord. Amen.*

Confession

What is confession? Confession has two parts. First that we confess our sins, and second, that we receive absolution, that is forgiveness, from the pastor as from God Himself, not doubting, but firmly believing that by it our sins are forgiven before God in heaven.

What sins should we confess? Before God we should plead guilty of all sins, even those we are not aware of, as we do in the Lord's Prayer; but before the pastor we should confess only those sins which we know and feel in our hearts.

Which are these? Consider your place in life according to the Ten Commandments: Are you a father, mother, son, daughter, husband, wife, or worker? Have you been disobedient, unfaithful, or lazy? Have you been hot-tempered, rude, or quarrelsome? Have you hurt someone by your words or deeds? Have you stolen, been negligent, wasted anything, or done any harm?

The Central Thought

What are some ways in which people attempt to deal with sin and its consequences in their lives?

The Christian life is one of repentance as we look at our daily responsibilities and wrongdoings. But we do not despair because of the assurance of forgiveness for Jesus' sake that God gives through His servants.

Read **2 Samuel 11:1-12:15.** How does David attempt to deal with the sin of adultery? How is David brought to confess his sins? What does the absolution spoken by Nathan do?

✝ *As Christians, when we confess our sins we acknowledge the truth that we have failed to fear, love, and trust in God above all things. Christ's absolution "declares me free of my sin through His Word placed in the mouth of a man" (LC V, 15).*

How does life change when I recognize that every day is a day for repentance?

A Closer Reading of the *Small Catechism*

"When I urge you to go to confession, I am simply urging you to be a Christian" (LC, Brief Exhortation 32).

315. What is the first part of confession?

> *First, we confess, that is, acknowledge our sins. In confession we admit that our sins have offended God and are deserving of His eternal punishment.*

> **1070. Psalm 32:3, 5** For when I kept silent, my bones wasted away through my groaning all day long...I acknowledged my sin to you, and I did not cover my iniquity; I said, "I will confess my transgressions to the LORD," and you forgave the iniquity of my sin.

> **1071. Psalm 51:1-4** Have mercy on me, O God, according to your steadfast love; according to your abundant mercy blot out my transgressions. Wash me thoroughly from my iniquity, and cleanse me from my sin! For I know my transgressions, and my sin is ever before me. Against you, you only, have I sinned and done what is evil in your sight, so that you may be justified in your words and blameless in your judgment.

316. What sins should we confess before God?

In our prayers before God both public and personal, when we say forgive us our trespasses as Jesus teaches us, we are confessing all of our sins, known and unknown, intended and unitended. In praying this petition, the Christian is reminded that all of our life is one of repentance.

> **1072. 1 John 1:8-9** If we say we have no sin, we deceive ourselves, and the truth is not in us. If we confess our sins, he is faithful and just to forgive us our sins and to cleanse us from all unrighteousness.

> **1073. Psalm 19:12** Who can discern his errors? Declare me innocent from hidden faults.

Note: "If only sins that can be named are forgiven, consciences could never find peace. For many sins cannot be seen or remembered" (AC XXV, 9).

Read Jeremiah 17:9 and Luke 15:11-32.

317. What sins should we confess before our neighbor?

We should confess to our neighbors our sins against them. We recognize the harm our sin has done to our neighbors and we seek their forgiveness and reconciliation.

> **1074. James 5:16** Therefore, confess your sins to one another and pray for one another, that you may be healed. The prayer of a righteous person has great power as it is working.

> **1075. Matthew 5:23-24** If you are offering your gift at the altar and there remember that your brother has something against you, leave your gift there before the altar and go. First go and be reconciled to your brother, and then come and offer your gift.

Read Genesis 50:15-21; Colossians 3:12-15; Philippians 4:2; and Luke 19:1-10.

318. What sins should we confess to our pastor?

When we are deeply troubled by our sin and its consequences in our lives, we have the opportunity to go to our pastor for individual confession and absolution.

> **1076. 2 Samuel 12:13** David said to Nathan, "I have sinned against the LORD. " And Nathan said to David, "The LORD also has put away your sin; you shall not die."

> **1077. Proverbs 28:13** Whoever conceals his transgressions will not prosper, but he who confesses and forsakes them will obtain mercy.

> **1078. Psalm 38:18** I confess my iniquity; I am sorry for my sin.

Note: Individual confession before the pastor is not a biblical requirement to receive the gift of forgiveness. However, it is a precious gift which should not be despised or neglected for here a troubled sinner is given the opportunity to hear the absolution personally.

319. What is the second part of confession before the pastor?

After we have confessed our sins the word of Christ's absolution is spoken by our pastor. By it our sins are fully and completely forgiven before God.

> **1079. 2 Corinthians 5:18** All this is from God, who through Christ reconciled us to himself and gave us the ministry of reconciliation.

> **1080. Colossians 1:13-14** He has delivered us from the domain of darkness and transferred us to the kingdom of his beloved Son, in whom we have redemption, the forgiveness of sins.

Connections and Applications

320. How should we regard the absolution spoken by the pastor?

"Our people are taught that they should highly prize the Absolution as being God's voice and pronounced by God's command" (AC XXV, 3).

When the pastor absolves us—that is, says "I forgive you all your sins"—he speaks with Christ's authority and on His behalf. Therefore we can firmly believe that God Himself has completely forgiven our sins.

> **1081. John 20:23** If you forgive the sins of any, they are forgiven them; if you withhold forgiveness from any, it is withheld.

> **1082. Luke 10:16** The one who hears you hears me, and the one who rejects you rejects me, and the one who rejects me rejects him who sent me.

> **1083. Matthew 18:18** Truly, I say to you, whatever you bind on earth shall be bound in heaven, and whatever you loose on earth shall be loosed in heaven.

321. Can I be sure that my private confession to the pastor will remain confidential?

Yes, in the rite of ordination the pastor promises before God never to divulge the sins that have been confessed to him, for God has removed these sins.

> **1084. Psalm 103:12** As far as the east is from the west, so far does he remove our transgressions from us.

Note: See the "Rite of Ordination" in the *LSB Agenda.*

322. What is the benefit of individual confession and absolution?

In individual confession, the Christian has a safe place to name his or her sins so that they are no longer carried alone. Here the word of absolution is spoken specifically to the person confessing his or her sins. There can be no mistaking to whom these words of Jesus are addressed: "I forgive you all your sins."

On the basis of this word of forgiveness, the pastor is there to give counsel and help in the struggle against temptation and enslavement to sin. In this way, the use of confession and absolution equips the Christian to stand firm against "false belief, despair, and other great shame and vice" (Sixth Petition).

> **1085. Matthew 9:2** And behold, some people brought to him a paralytic, lying on a bed. And when Jesus saw their faith, he said to the paralytic, take heart, my son; your sins are forgiven.

> **1086. 2 Samuel 12:13** David said to Nathan, "I have sinned against the Lord." And Nathan said to David, "The Lord also has put away your sin; you shall not die."

> **1087. Psalm 32:2** Blessed is the man against whom the Lord counts no iniquity, and in whose spirit there is no deceit.

> **1088. Psalm 130:3-4** If you, O Lord, should mark iniquities, O Lord, who could stand? But with you there is forgiveness, that you may be feared.

Read **Luke 7:36-50** about the forgiveness Jesus gives to a repentant woman.

323. How do I prepare for confession?

Consider how the Ten Commandments act as a mirror showing us where we have sinned in our various places in life. How have you as a husband, wife, mother, father, daughter, son, teacher, student, employer, employee, etc. failed to fear, love, and trust in God and love your neighbor.

> **1089. 2 Corinthians 13:5** Examine yourselves, to see whether you are in the faith. Test yourselves. Or do you not realize this about yourselves, that Jesus Christ is in you?—unless indeed you fail to meet the test!

Note: "If there is a heart that feels its sin and desires consolation, it has here a sure refuge when it hears in God's Word that through a man God looses and absolves him from his sins" (LC, Brief Exhortation 14).In preparing for confession, you may also wish to read and meditate on the penitential psalms (**Psalms 6, 32, 38, 51, 102, 130, 143**).

A Short Form of Confession

[A form of individual confession and absolution based on Luther's order is in *LSB*, pp. 292-293]

The penitent says: Dear Confessor, I ask you please to hear my confession and to pronounce forgiveness in order to fulfill God's will.

I, a poor sinner, plead guilty before God of all sins. In particular I confess before you that as a servant, maid, etc., I, sad to say, serve my master unfaithfully, for in this and that I have not done what I told to do. I have made him angry and caused him to curse. I have been negligent and allowed damage to be done. I have also been offensive in words, and deeds. I have quarreled with my peers. I have grumbled about the lady of the house and cursed her. I am sorry for all of this and I ask for grace. I want to do better.

A master or lady of the house may say: In particular I confess before you that I have not faithfully guided my children, servants, and wife to the glory of God. I have cursed. I have set a bad example by indecent words and deeds. I have hurt my neighbor and spoken evil of him. I have overcharged, sold inferior merchandise, and given less than was paid for.

[*Let the penitent confess whatever else he has done against God's commandments and his own position.*]

If, however, someone does not find himself burdened with these or greater sins, he should not trouble himself or search for or invent other sins, and thereby make confession a torture. Instead, he should mention one or two that he knows: In particular I confess that I have cursed; I have used improper words; I have neglected this or that etc. Let that be enough.

But if you know of none at all (which hardly seems possible), then mention none in particular, but receive the forgiveness upon the general confession which you make to God before the confessor.

Then the confessor shall say: God be merciful to you and strengthen your faith. Amen.

Furthermore: Do you believe that my forgiveness is God's forgiveness?

Yes, dear confessor.

Then let him say: Let it be done for you as you believe. And I, by the command of our Lord Jesus Christ, forgive you your sins in the name of the Father and of the Son and of the Holy Spirit. Amen. Go in peace.

[A confessor will know additional passages with which to comfort and to strengthen the faith of those who have great burdens of conscience or are sorrowful and distressed. This is intended only as a general form of confession.]

Hymn (*LSB* 608) and Prayer: *Lord Jesus Christ, I give You thanks that my sins are forgiven before Your Father in heaven. By the Holy Spirit give me grace to trust in Your promises and so live in the freedom and peace which You have won for me in Your death and resurrection. Amen.*

The Sacrament of the Altar

First

What is the Sacrament of the Altar?

It is the true body and blood of our Lord Jesus Christ under the bread and wine, instituted by Christ Himself for us Christians to eat and to drink.

Where is this written?

The holy Evangelists Matthew, Mark, Luke, and St. Paul write:

> Our Lord Jesus Christ, on the night when He was betrayed, took bread, and when He had given thanks, He broke it and gave it to the disciples and said: "Take, eat; this is My body, which is given for you. This do in remembrance of Me."

> In the same way also He took the cup after supper, and when He had given thanks, He gave it to them, saying, "Drink of it, all of you; this cup is the new treatment in My blood, which is shed for you for the forgiveness of sins. This do as often as you drink it, in remembrance of Me."

The Central Thought

Just before He died, Jesus gave Christians a holy meal to eat and drink—His "true body and blood…in and under the bread and wine" (LC V, 9).

What might people think when they hear Christians say they are eating Christ's body and drinking His blood in the Lord's Supper?

Read **Matthew 26:17-30**. Why did Jesus establish the Lord's Supper? How is this sacrament connected with Jesus' death?

☩ *As Christians, we confess that we receive the very body and blood of Christ—in, with, and under the bread and wine—in our hands and in our mouths. This is a profound wonder and unexplainable mystery.*

Jesus wants to be with me and within me (**John 17:26**). In the Sacrament of the Altar He gives Himself to me and pledges never to leave me or forsake me.

A Closer Reading of the *Small Catechism*

324. Who instituted the Sacrament of the Altar?

Jesus Christ, who is true God and true man, instituted this sacrament.

> **1090. 1 Corinthians 11:23-24** For I received from the Lord what I also delivered to you, that the Lord Jesus on the night when he was betrayed took bread, and when he had given thanks, he broke it, and said, "This is my body which is for you. Do this in remembrance of me."

325. What does Christ give us in this sacrament?

Christ gives us His own true body and blood for the forgiveness of sins.

1091. Matthew 26:26-28 Now as they were eating. Jesus took bread, and after blessing it broke it and gave it to the disciples and said, "Take, eat, this is my body." And he took a cup, and when he had given thanks he gave it to them, saying, "Drink of it, all of you, or this is my blood of the covenant, which is poured out for many for the forgiveness of sins."

326. Why do we take the words "This is my body" and "This is my blood" at face value?

Our Lord's words which establish the Sacrament are to be taken at face value because

- *these words are spoken by Christ our Lord, the Word to whom all authority in heaven and earth is given and through whom the universe came into existence;*

    1092. John 1:1-3 In the beginning was the Word, and the Word was with God, and the Word was God. He was in the beginning with God. He was in the beginning with God. All things were made through him, and without him was not anything made that was made.

    1093. Hebrews 11:3 By faith we understand that the universe was created by the word of God, so that what is seen was not made out of things that are visible.

- *these are testamentary words [a covenant] spoken on the eve of His death, and no person's last will and testament may be changed once that person has died;*

    1094. 1 Corinthians 11:25 In the same way also he took the cup, after supper, saying, "This cup is the new covenant in my blood. Do this, as often as you drink it, in remembrance of me."

    1095. Galatians 3:15 To give a human example, brothers, even with a man-made covenant, no one annuls it or adds to it once it has been ratified.

Read **Hebrews 9:15-22** about the importance of a testamentary covenant that takes effect at the time the one who makes it dies (a last will and testament).

- *These words of Jesus recall God's covenant which He made with Israel in **Exodus 24:1-11.** The blood of the covenant was thrown against the altar and on the people, giving access to God, so that the elders of the people of Israel beheld God and ate and drank in His presence. In the Lord's Supper we receive **Christ**'s true blood of the **new** covenant (or testament) and, in it, the forgiveness of sins and communion with our God;*

    1096. Exodus 24:8 Moses took the blood and threw it on the people and said, "Behold the blood of the covenant that the LORD has made with you in accordance with all these words."

- *God's Word clearly teaches that in the Sacrament the bread and wine are a communion or participation in the body and blood of Christ;*

    1097. 1 Corinthians 10:16 The cup of blessing that we bless, is it not a participation in the blood of Christ? The bread that we break, is it not a participation in the body of Christ?

- *God's Word clearly teaches that those who misuse the Sacrament sin not against bread and wine but against the body and blood of Christ.*

    1098. 1 Corinthians 11:27, 29 Whoever, therefore, eats the bread or drinks the cup of the Lord in an unworthy manner will be guilty concerning the body and blood of the Lord…For anyone who eats and drinks without discerning the body eats and drinks judgment on himself.

327. What are the earthly elements Jesus uses in this Sacrament?

Jesus uses bread and wine.

    1099. Matthew 26:26-27 Now as they were eating, Jesus took bread, and after blessing it broke it and gave it to the disciples, and said, "Take eat, this is my body." And he took a cup, and when he had given thanks he gave it to them, saying, "Drink of it, all of you."

    1100. 1 Corinthians 11:27, 29 Whoever, therefore, eats the bread or drinks the cup of the Lord in an unworthy manner will be guilty concerning the body and blood of the Lord…For anyone who eats and drinks without discerning the body eats and drinks judgment on himself.

Note: The expression "fruit of the vine" (**Luke 22:18**) in the Bible means wine, not merely grape juice. See also **1 Corinthians 11:21**.

328. How then are the bread and wine in the Sacrament the body and blood of Christ?

By the power of Christ's almighty Word, He gives us His true body and blood in, with, and under the consecrated bread and wine. This union of the bread with His body and the wine with His blood is called a sacramental union.

> **1101. 1 Corinthians 10:16** The cup of blessing that we bless, is it not a participation in the blood of Christ? The bread that we break, is it not a participation in the body of Christ?

> Note: The mystery of the presence of Christ's body and blood in the Lord's Supper is often expressed using the words "in, with, and under" the bread and wine. The word "in" reminds us that where the bread and wine is, there is the body and blood of Christ; the word "with" reminds us that with the bread and wine we receive the body and blood of Christ; and the word "under" reminds us that the body and blood of Christ are hidden yet present under bread and wine, since bread and wine still continue to exist.

> **1102. 1 Corinthians 11:26** For as often as you eat this bread and drink the cup, you proclaim the Lord's death until he comes.

329. Do all communicants receive the body and blood in the Sacrament, whether or not they believe?

Yes, because Christ's Word, not our faith, establishes His bodily presence in the Sacrament. However, only those who believe receive it to their blessing.

> **1103. 1 Corinthians 11:27** Whoever, therefore, eats the bread or drinks the cup of the Lord in an unworthy manner will be guilty concerning the body and blood of the Lord.

330. What does Christ command when He says, "This do in remembrance of Me"?

*Christ commands in these words that this Sacrament be administered in His Church until the Last Day. In this Sacrament His saving death is proclaimed and the fruits of His atonement are distributed for the forgiveness of our sins. This is done as bread and wine are consecrated with our Lord's words (the Words of Institution), distributed to the communicants, and eaten and drunk. Jesus' command to do "**this**" includes all these aspects of the Lord's Supper: "In an assembly of Christians bread and wine are taken, consecrated, distributed, received, eaten and drunk, and the Lord's death is shown forth at the same time." (FC SD VIII, 84).*

> **1104. 1 Corinthians 11:26** For as often as you eat this bread and drink the cup, you proclaim the Lord's death until he comes.

Connections and Applications

331. Why is this sacrament called the "Sacrament of the Altar"?

*We speak of the "Sacrament of the Altar" because an altar is a place of sacrifice. Jesus sacrificed His body and blood on the cross for the sins of the whole world. The table from which the fruits of Jesus' sacrifice are distributed in the church is called the altar. At the altar we are not repeatedly **offering** Jesus' body and blood but **receiving** His body and blood as the once and for all sacrifice for the forgiveness of our sins.*

> **1105. Hebrews 10:12** But when Christ had offered for all time a single sacrifice for sins, he sat down at the right hand of God, waiting from that time until his enemies should be made a footstool for his feet.

Note: Jesus gave the Lord's Supper while eating the Passover with His disciples. His selection of the Passover for the first Lord's Supper connects it with Israel's history, showing that now God's redemptive purpose in Israel is fulfilled. The blood of the new covenant or "testament" replaces the Old Testament covenant's blood sacrifices (**Matthew 26:28; Jeremiah 31:31; 1 Corinthians 11:25**) since Jesus' sacrifice on Golgotha is the complete sacrifice for the sins of all people (**Hebrews 10:12-14**).

332. Why are Jesus' words always spoken over the bread and the wine by the pastor?

Without Jesus' words there would be no sacrament for it is by the power of His Word that He gives us His body and blood. "In the administration of the Holy Supper the words of institution are to be publicly spoken or sung before the congregation distinctly and clearly. They should in no way be left out" (FC SD VII, 79).

> **1106. 1 Corinthians 10:16** The cup of blessing that we bless, is it not a participation in the blood of Christ? The bread that we break, is it not a participation in the body of Christ?

> **1107. Luke 21:33** Heaven and earth will pass away, but my words will not pass away.

333. Are communicants to receive both the body and the blood of Christ in the Sacrament?

Yes, all communicants should receive both the consecrated bread and cup, since Christ said "Take and eat; this is My body...Drink from it, all of you."

> **1108. Matthew 26:26-27** Now as they were eating, Jesus took bread, and after blessing it broke it and gave it to the disciples, and said, "Take eat, this is my body." And he took a cup, and when he had given thanks he gave it to them, saying, "Drink of it, all of you."

334. How often are we to receive the Sacrament?

*Christ has not specified a particular timetable but invites us to come often to this Sacrament on account of the gifts He bestows here and our own great need. In the New Testament, the Sacrament was a regular and major feature of congregational worship, not an occasional extra (**Acts 2:42; Acts 20:7; 1 Corinthians 11:20, 33**). In Reformation times our church celebrated the Sacrament "every Lord's Day and on other festivals" (Ap XXIV, 1).*

335. Do the bread and wine merely symbolize the body and blood of Christ?

*No. Although this is the teaching of many Protestant churches, Jesus' own words clearly identify the bread as His body and the wine as His blood. We take Jesus' words—"This **is** my body...my blood"—at face value. (See question 326.)*

> **1109. 1 Corinthians 11:24-25** And when he had given thanks, he broke it, and said, "This is my body which is for you. Do this in remembrance of me." In the same way also he took the cup, after supper, saying, "This is the new covenant [testament] in my blood. Do this, as often as you drink it, in remembrance of me."

336. Do Christ's body and blood in the Sacrament replace the bread and the wine, so that the bread and wine only appear to be there?

No. This is the Roman Catholic theory of transubstantiation. The Scriptures, however, testify that the bread and wine remain in the Sacrament. Communicants eat and drink both bread and wine and the Lord's true body and blood in the Lord's Supper.

> **1110. 1 Corinthians 11:26** For as often as you eat this bread and drink the cup, you proclaim the Lord's death until he comes.

337. Are the body and blood of Christ in the Sacrament sacrificed again to God for the sins of the living and the dead?

No. The body and blood of Christ in the Sacrament are the complete sacrifice offered to God once and for all on the cross and are now distributed to us in the Sacrament together with all the blessings and benefits which this sacrifice has won for us.

> **1111. 1 Corinthians 5:7** Cleanse out the old leaven that you may be a new lump, as you really are unleavened. For Christ, our Passover lamb, has been sacrificed.

> **1112. Hebrews 10:14** For by a single offering he has perfected for all time those who are being sanctified.

> **1113. Hebrews 10:17-18** He adds, "I will remember their sins and their lawless deeds no more." Where there is forgiveness of these, there is no longer any offering for sin.

Hymn (*LSB* 617) and Prayer: *Lord Jesus Christ, on the night of Your betrayal You established the Supper of Your body and blood for us Christians to eat and to drink. Give us faith to trust in the words of Your testament and so rightly receive the fruits of Your suffering and death and through Your merit finally be brought to rejoice in the marriage feast of the Lamb where You live and reign with the Father and the Spirit forever. Amen.*

The Benefit of the Sacrament of the Altar

Second

What is the benefit of this eating and drinking?

These words, "Given and shed for you for the forgiveness of sins," show us that in the Sacrament forgiveness of sins, life, and salvation are given us through these words. For where there is forgiveness of sins, there is also life and salvation.

The Central Thought

In the Sacrament we receive a great treasure: the forgiveness of sins. Our Lord's words assure us that this treasure "is passed along and made our very own" when we receive His body and blood (LC V: 28).

Why is forgiveness such a treasure and something we should earnestly desire?

Read **1 Corinthians 11:23-26**. What do we proclaim when we eat Christ's body and drink His blood in the Lord's Supper?

✝ *As Christians, we confess that the forgiveness of sins won by the death of Jesus on the cross is now delivered to us in the body and blood of Christ. This is the most important gift that we can receive.*

This forgiveness sets me free from my sinful past in which death and the tyranny of Satan were my only future. Christ's body and blood give me a new life and a new future every day.

A Closer Reading of the *Small Catechism*

338. What is the benefit promised in the Sacrament?

- *The forgiveness of sins which Christ won when He suffered in His body on the cross and shed His blood to redeem us is now promised in His body and blood given to us to eat and to drink.*

  1114. Hebrews 10:10 And by that will we have been sanctified through the offering of the body of Jesus Christ once for all.

  1115. Colossians 1:22 He has now reconciled [you] in his body of flesh by his death, in order to present you holy and blameless and above reproach before him.

  1116. 1 Peter 2:24 He himself bore our sins in his body on the tree, that we might die to sin and live to righteousness. By his wounds you have been healed.

  1117. Matthew 26:28 This is my blood of the covenant, which is poured out for many for the forgiveness of sins.

  1118. 1 Peter 1:18-19 Knowing that you were ransomed from the futile ways inherited from your forefathers, not with perishable things such as silver or gold, but with the precious blood of Christ, like that of a lamb without blemish or spot.

  1119. 1 John 1:7 The blood of Jesus his Son cleanses us from all sin.

  Read **Leviticus 17:10-14**. It is significant that in the Old Testament God strictly forbids the eating of blood under the penalty of death for "the life of the flesh is in the blood" (v. 11). Yet in establishing the Lord's Supper, the Son of God gives us His blood to drink for the forgiveness of our sin. This is another indication that the Lord who institutes this sacrament is true God. It also demonstrates that in Christ's blood we are forgiven and now share in His life. Also see **Hebrews 9:11-14, 22**.

- *Where sin is forgiven there is life with God now and everlasting salvation.*

1120. John 6:32-33 Jesus said to them, "Truly, truly, I say to you, it was not Moses who gave you the bread from heaven, but my Father gives you the true bread from heaven. For the bread of God is he who comes down from heaven and gives life to the world."

1121. John 6:40 For this is the will of my Father, that everyone who looks on the Son and believes in him should have eternal life, and I will raise him upon the last day.

1122. Hebrews 12:22-24 But you have come to Mount Zion and to the city of the living God, the heavenly Jerusalem, and to innumerable angels in festal gathering, and to the assembly of the firstborn who are enrolled in heaven and to God, the judge of all and to the spirits of the righteous made perfect, and to Jesus the mediator of a new covenant, and to the sprinkled blood that speaks a better word than the blood of Abel.

Note: "Here in the Sacrament you are to receive from the lips of Christ forgiveness of sin. It contains and brings with it God's grace and the Spirit with all His gifts, protection, shelter, and power against death and the devil and all misfortune" (LC V, 70).

- *As Christ gives us victory over sin and Satan in the Sacrament, He strengthens us for new life in Him.*

  1123. Romans 8:10 But if Christ is in you, although the body is dead because of sin, the Spirit is life because of righteousness.

  1124. 1 Peter 2:24 He himself bore our sins in his body on the tree, that we might die to sin and live to righteousness. By his wounds you have been healed.

  1125. 1 John 3:8 The reason the Son of God appeared was to destroy the works of the devil.

Connections and Applications

339. Why should Christians be encouraged to receive the Sacrament frequently?

- *Jesus invites and urges us to come.*

  1126. Matthew 26:26 Take eat, this is my body.

- *We need the comfort and strength of Christ's forgiveness for living our new life while we are assaulted by the devil and struggle with our sinful nature.*

  1127. Matthew 26:28 This is my blood of the covenant which is poured out for many for the forgiveness of sins.

- *We are united with Christ and our fellow believers in this Sacrament.*

  1128. 1 Corinthians 10:17 Because there is one bread, we who are many are one body, for we all partake of the one bread

- *As Christ has given Himself to us so completely with His body and blood, so, too, the Sacrament strengthens us to give ourselves in sacrificial love and service to the neighbor.*

  1129. John 15:12 This is my commandment, that you love one another as I have loved you.

Note: The Sacrament is "a pure, wholesome, comforting remedy that grants salvation and comfort. It will cure you and give you life both in soul and body. For where the soul has recovered, the body also is relieved" (LC V: 68).

Hymn (*LSB* 623) and Prayer: *Lord Jesus Christ, You suffered in Your holy body and shed Your precious blood to redeem Your fallen creatures. Grant us to come often to Your Supper, trusting in Your promise, and so to receive to our everlasting benefit the gifts You give in Your body and blood: the forgiveness of our sins, life with You, and eternal salvation; for You live and reign with the Father and the Holy Spirit, one God now and forever. Amen.*

The Power of the Sacrament

Third

How can bodily eating and drinking do such great things?

Certainly not just eating and drinking do these things, but the words written here: "Given and shed for you for the forgiveness of sins." These words, along with the bodily eating and drinking, are the main thing in the Sacrament. Whoever believes these words has exactly what they say: "forgiveness of sins."

The Central Thought

Jesus' words make eating a morsel of bread and taking a sip of wine a great and gracious feast rather than an empty ceremony.

Why should we take Jesus at His Word?

Read **Mark 4:39-41.** What does this miracle reveal about the power of Jesus' word?

✝ *As Christians, we confess that the words of our Lord Jesus do just what they say. "What Christ's lips say and speak, so it is" (LC V, 14).*

Because these words do what they say, there should be no doubt in my mind that the bread and wine are Jesus' body and blood for my forgiveness.

A Closer Reading of the *Small Catechism*

340. How can bodily eating and drinking give us such great spiritual benefits as forgiveness, life, and salvation?

It is not simply the eating and drinking, but the words of Christ—together with His body and blood under the bread and the wine—that are the means through which forgiveness is bestowed. "Now the only way this treasure is passed along and made our very own is in the words 'Given...and shed for you.' For the words have both truths, that it is Christ's body and blood, and that it is yours as a treasure and gift" (LC V: 29).

Connections and Applications

341. Does everyone who eats and drinks the Sacrament also receive forgiveness of sins, life, and salvation?

No. All who eat and drink in the Sacrament receive Christ's body and blood and so are offered the benefits which He has promised. But it is only through faith in Christ's words that we receive the benefits offered in our Lord's testament.

> **1130. Romans 1:17** For in it the righteousness of God is revealed from faith for faith, as it is written, "The righteous shall live by faith."

> **1131. Luke 1:45** And blessed is she who believed that there would be a fulfillment of what was spoken to her from the Lord.

> **1132. Luke 11:27-28** As he said these things, a woman in the crowd raised here voice and said to him, "Blessed is the womb that bore you, and the breasts at which you nursed!" But he said, "Blessed rather are those who hear the word of God and keep it!"

Note: In the Sacrament Jesus joins bodily eating and drinking to faith in His promise. This connection between bodily action and faith can also be seen in Jesus' healing miracles where there is blessing in touching Jesus or being touched by Him and faith receiving the blessing (see **Matthew 9:20-22; 27-29**).

342. How, then, should we eat and drink the Lord's Supper?

We should eat Christ's body and drink His blood confidently believing that He was delivered for our offenses and raised for our justification. Trusting in His saving work, we receive His body and blood, given to us under the bread and wine, as the guarantee of our forgiveness.

> **1133. Romans 4:23-25** But the words "it was counted to him" were not written for his sake alone, but for ours also. It will be counted to us who believe in him who raised him from the dead Jesus our Lord, who was delivered up for our trespasses and raised for our justification.

> **1134. 1 Corinthians 10:16** The cup of blessing that we bless, is it not a participation in the blood of Christ? The bread that we break, is it not a participation in the body of Christ?

> **1135. 1 Corinthians 11:26** For as often as you eat this bread and drink the cup, you proclaim the Lord's death until he comes.

> Hymn (*LSB* 395, v. 3) and Prayer: *Lord Jesus Christ, You give Your body and blood under bread and wine that we may know with certainty that our sins are forgiven by Your atoning sacrifice on the cross. Grant us so to eat Your body and drink Your blood trusting in Your Word that we may receive what it declares: the forgiveness of sins and so live in You even as You live and reign with the Father and the Holy Spirit, one God, now and forever. Amen.*

How to Receive This Sacrament Worthily

Fourth

Who receives this sacrament worthily?

Fasting and bodily preparation are certainly fine outward training. But that person is truly worthy and well prepared who has faith in these words: "Given and shed for you for the forgiveness of sins."

But anyone who does not believe these words or doubts them is unworthy and unprepared, for the words "for you" require all hearts to believe.

The Central Thought

The essential way to prepare for the Lord's Supper is to believe Jesus' promise that His body and blood are "given and shed **for you** for the forgiveness of sins." "Ponder, then, and include yourself personally in the 'you,' so that He may not speak to you in vain" (LC V, 65).

What are some reasons that people might feel they should not take Communion?

Read **1 Corinthians 11:23-29** The Apostle shows us that the Lord's Supper is not an ordinary meal, but Christ's body and blood. When we "examine" ourselves what do we find?

✝ *As Christians, we confess that we sinners are "worthy" to commune because Jesus welcomes sinners who repent of their sins and believe His promise that He gave His life and shed His blood for their forgiveness.*

How can I prepare for the Lord's Supper so that I receive it as a blessing?

A Closer Reading of the *Small Catechism*

343. Who receives the Sacrament worthily?

We receive it worthily when we have faith in Christ and His words, "Given and shed for you for the forgiveness of sins."

344. Why should we be concerned about receiving the Sacrament worthily?

The Sacrament of the Altar is not our supper, but the Lord's Supper, where He gives us His body and blood for the forgiveness of our sins. To eat and drink the Lord's body and blood without trust in His words, however, is to eat and drink judgment on oneself.

> 1136. **1 Corinthians 11:27-28** Whoever, therefore, eats the bread or drinks the cup of the Lord in an unworthy manner will be guilty concerning the body and blood of the Lord. Let a person examine himself, then, and so eat of the bread and drink of the cup.

345. When are we unworthy and unprepared?

We are unworthy and unprepared when we do not believe Christ's words, or doubt them, since the words "for you" require all hearts to believe.

346. What is "fasting and bodily preparation"?

Fasting is denying oneself food or other pleasures for a particular period of time. Bodily preparation may include proper rest, personal cleanliness, modest and reverent clothing, and the like. In the Scriptures fasting and bodily preparation are often associated with repentance and prayer. These can be outward expressions of reverence and physical ways of drawing our attention to our Lord and His gifts. However, in themselves they do not make us worthy and well prepared to receive the Sacrament.

"Fasting, prayer, and other such things may indeed be outward preparations and discipline...so that the body may keep and bring itself modestly and reverently to receive Christ's body and blood. Yet the body cannot seize and make its own what is given in and with the Sacrament. This is done by the faith in the heart, which discerns this treasure and desires it" (LC V: 37).

> **1137. 1 Timothy 4:8** For while bodily training is of some value, godliness is of value in every way, as it holds promise for the present life and also for the life to come.

Note: In Luther's day the Roman Catholic Church made fasting mandatory before one would be allowed to commune.

Connections and Applications

347. How are we to examine ourselves before receiving the Sacrament?

We are to examine ourselves to see whether

- *we are sorry for our sin;*

  > **1138. Psalm 38:18** I confess my iniquity; I am sorry for my sin.

  > **1139. 2 Corinthians 7:10-11** For godly grief produces a repentance that leads to salvation without regret, whereas worldly grief produces death. For see what earnestness this godly grief has produced in you, but also what eagerness to clear yourselves, what indignation, what fear, what longing, what zeal, what punishment! At every point you have proved yourself innocent in the matter.

- *we believe in our Savior Jesus Christ and in His words in the Sacrament;*

  > **1140. Luke 22:19-20** And he took bread, and when he had given thanks, he broke it and gave it to them, saying, "This is my body, which is given for you. Do this in remembrance of me." And likewise the cup after they had eaten, saying, "This cup that is poured out for you is the new covenant in my blood."

- *we intend, with the help of the Holy Spirit, to live as forgiven sinners resisting the devil, saying no to sinful desires, and walking in the newness of life.*

  > **1141. Ephesians 4:22-24** To put off your old self, which belongs to your former manner of life and is corrupt through deceitful desires, and to be renewed in the spirit of your minds, and to put on the new self, created after the likeness of God in true righteousness and holiness.

  > **1142. Romans 6:11-14** So you also must consider yourselves dead to sin and alive to God in Christ Jesus. Let not sin therefore reign in your mortal body, to make you obey its passions. Do not present your members to sin as instruments for unrighteousness, but present yourselves to God as those who have been brought from death to life, and your members to God as instruments for righteousness. For sin will have no dominion over you, since you are not under law but under grace.

Note: In preparing to come to the Sacrament, Christians may also take advantage of the opportunity for individual confession and absolution with the pastor. For personal reflection prior to coming to the Sacrament, you may use "Christian Questions with Their Answers."

348. May those who are weak or struggling in faith come to the Sacrament?

Yes. The words "for you" show us that Christ instituted this sacrament for weak and struggling sinners like us, to draw us to Himself and to strengthen our faith in Him.

> **1143. Mark 9:24** Immediately the father of the child cried out and said, "I believe, help my unbelief!"

> **1144. John 6:37** All that the Father gives me will come to me, and whoever comes to me I will never cast out.

> **1145. Isaiah 42:3** A bruised reed he will not break, and a faintly burning wick he will not quench; he will faithfully bring forth justice.

Note: "Such people must learn that it is the highest art to know that our Sacrament does not depend on our worthiness... On the contrary, we go exactly because we are poor, miserable people. We go exactly because we are unworthy. This is true unless we are talking about someone who desires no grace and Absolution nor intends to change" (LC V, 61).

349. What should I do if I feel no need for the Sacrament?

*Those who feel no need of the Sacrament should first "put their hand into their shirt to check whether they have flesh and blood" (LC V, 75). Our own flesh wars against God's Spirit (**Galatians 5:19-21**) demonstrating that nothing good dwells in us (**Romans 7:18**) and Satan is constantly on the attack as a liar and murderer (**John 8:44**). If this knowledge does not drive you to the Sacrament, "at least believe the Scriptures. They will not lie to you, and they know your flesh better than you yourself" (LC V, 76).*

> **1146. Galatians 5:19-21** Now the works of the flesh are evident: sexual immorality, impurity, sensuality, idolatry, sorcery, enmity, strife, jealousy, fits of anger, rivalries, dissensions, divisions, envy, drunkenness, orgies, and things like these. I warn you, as I warned you before, that those who do such things will not inherit the kingdom of God.

> **1147. Romans 7:18** For I know that nothing good dwells in me, that is, in my flesh. For I have the desire to do what is right, but not the ability to carry it out.

> **1148. John 8:44** You are of your father the devil, and your will is to do your father's desires. He was a murderer from the beginning, and has nothing to do with the truth, because there is no truth in him. When he lies, he speaks out of his own character, for he is a liar and the father of lies.

350. Who should not be given the Sacrament?

The Sacrament should not be given to

- *those who are not Christian or who are not baptized;*

    Note: The Lord's Supper is for Jesus' disciples who are baptized and instructed in the Christian faith (**Matthew 26:17; Matthew 28:19-20**).

- *those Christians who are unable to examine themselves, such as infants and very young children, people who have not received proper instruction in the Christian faith, or the unconscious;*

    > **1149. 1 Corinthians 11:28** Let a person examine himself, then, and so eat of the bread and drink of the cup.

Note: Luther is cautious about who should receive the Lord's Supper (LC V, 1-2): "Just as we have heard about Holy Baptism, so we must also speak about the other Sacrament, in these same three points: What is it? What are its benefits? and Who is to receive it? And all these points are established through the words by which Christ has instituted this Sacrament. Everyone who desires to be a Christian and go to this Sacrament should know them. For it is not our intention to let people come to the Sacrament and administer it to them if they do not know what they seek or why they come."

- *those Christians of a different confession of faith, since the Lord's Supper is a testimony to our unity in faith and doctrine;*

1150. **Acts 2:42** And they devoted themselves to the apostles' teaching and the fellowship, to the breaking of bread and the prayers.

1151. **1 Corinthians 11:26** For as often as you at eat this bread and drink the cup, you proclaim the Lord's death until he comes.

1152. **1 Corinthians 10:17** Because there is one bread, we who are many are one body, for we all partake of the one bread.

1153. **Romans 16:17** I appeal to you brothers, to watch out for those who cause divisions and create obstacles contrary to the doctrine that you have been taught; avoid them.

Note: The practice of close(d) communion—in our church the terms "close" and "closed" communion have been used synonymously—seeks to guard those who eat and drink in the Lord's Supper from sinning against Christ's body and blood or receiving it to their harm. At the same time this practice professes that those who partake of Christ's body and blood together are united in the same teaching and confession.

- *those who are openly ungodly and unrepentant, living contrary to God's Word;*

    1154. **1 Corinthians 5:11, 13** But now I am writing to you to not associate with anyone who bears the name of brother if he is guilty of sexual immortality or greed, or is an idolater, reviler, drunkard, or swindler—not even to eat with such a one …God judges those outside. "Purge the evil person from among you."

    1155. **1 Corinthians 10:20-21** No, I imply that what pagans sacrifice they offer to demons and not to God. I do not want you to be participants with demons. You cannot drink the cup of the Lord and the cup of demons. You cannot partake of the table of the Lord and the table of demons.

- *those who are unforgiving, refusing to be reconciled with their neighbors.*

    1156. **Matthew 6:15** But if you do not forgive others their trespasses, neither will your Father forgive your trespasses.

Note: In all these instances pastors are "stewards of the mysteries of God" (**1 Corinthians 4:1**) which includes a sacred responsibility for admission to the Lord's Supper. The individual communicant is to examine him or herself, but this does not relieve the pastor of faithful and loving oversight at the Lord's altar which includes the examination of those who would commune. The congregation also has a responsibility for upholding faithful Communion practices. "No one is admitted to the Sacrament without first being examined. The people are also advised about the dignity and use of the Sacrament, about how it brings great consolation to anxious consciences, so that they too may learn to believe God and to expect and ask from Him all that is good" (AC XXIV, 6).

Hymn (*LSB* 618) and Prayer: *Lord Jesus, I have no worthiness of my own to merit the eating and drinking of Your holy body and precious blood. Trusting not in my righteousness but only in Your promise of the forgiveness of sins, I come to Your altar imploring You for mercy that, delivered from Your wrath and condemnation, I might live for You alone, always giving thanks for Your undeserved benefits and finally be brought to praise You forever at the heavenly banquet. Amen.*

351. What is a sacrament?

The Lutheran Church usually speaks of a sacrament as a sacred act

- *instituted by the command of Christ;*

- *in which Christ joins His Word of promise to a visible element,*

- *by which He offers and bestows the forgiveness of sins which He has earned for us by His suffering, death, and resurrection.*

Note: The word sacrament comes to us from the Latin translation of the Bible, where the Greek word mystery is rendered as *sacrament*. Originally this word described the saving truths of the Christian faith, such as the Trinity, Christ's incarnation, redemption, and the Church (see for example **1 Corinthians 4:1; Ephesians 5:32;** and **1 Timothy 3:16**). Later it was narrowed down to our present usage. The sacraments along with God's Word are sometimes called "the means of grace" because through them as through creaturely elements the Triune God delivers His gifts of forgiveness of sins, life, and salvation. We distinguish the sacraments, those rites that are established by God's command and convey His promise of grace, from ceremonies and rites established by human beings. As we have seen, Baptism and the Lord's Supper are not human ceremonies but divinely-instituted rites to which the Lord has attached the promise of His grace.

352. How many sacraments are there?

Actually, the Lutheran Confessions leave the exact numbering of the sacraments open. Holy Baptism and the Lord's Supper are certainly to be regarded as sacraments. Also, although it does not have a "visible element" (like water or bread and wine), Holy Absolution is sometimes (and properly) counted as a "third sacrament" as Luther does in the Large Catechism: "Here you see that Baptism, both in its power and meaning, includes the third Sacrament, which has been called repentance" (LC IV, 74). The Apology of the Augsburg Confession also says "Therefore, Baptism, the Lord's Supper, and Absolution (which is the Sacrament of Repentance) are truly Sacraments. For these rites have God's command and promise of grace, which is peculiar to the New Testament (Ap XIII, 4).

1157. Matthew 28:19 Go therefore and make disciples of all nations, baptizing them in the name of the Father and of the Son and of the Holy Spirit.

1158. Mark 14:22-25 And as they were eating, [Jesus] took bread, and after blessing it broke it and gave it to them, and said, "Take; this is my body." And he took a cup, and when he had given thanks he gave it to them, and they all drank of it. And he said to them, "This is my blood of the covenant, which is poured out for many. Truly, I say to you, I will not drink again of the fruit of the vine until that day when I drink it new in the kingdom of God."

1159. John 20:22-23 And when he had said this, he breathed on them and said to them, "Receive the Holy Spirit. If you forgive the sins of any, they are forgiven them; if you withhold forgiveness from any, it is withheld."

353. Why are we to treasure the sacraments, when water, bread, and wine are such ordinary elements?

God delights to use ordinary things to do extraordinary works. "We always teach that the Sacraments and all outward things that God ordains and institutes should not be considered according to the coarse, outward mask, the way we look at a nutshell. But we respect them because God's Word is included in them" (LC IV, 19).

1160. 1 Corinthians 1:28 God chose what is weak in the world to shame the strong; God chose what is low and despised in the world, even things that are not, to bring to nothing things that are.

Read **2 Kings 5:1-14.** By God's promise plain water from the Jordan had the power to cure Naaman's leprosy.

354. How are the sacraments to be used?

The sacraments are rightly used when we in faith trust the promises offered and given by Christ through them. "They were instituted to awaken and confirm faith in those who use them. Therefore, we must use them in such a way that faith, which believes the promises offered and set forth through the Sacraments is increased" (AC XIII, 3). Faith does not make the sacrament but it is only through faith that we receive the divinely promised benefit of the sacrament.